MW01256667

Food Power Politics

BLACK FOOD JUSTICE

Ashanté Reese and Hanna Garth, editors

Black Food Justice publishes scholarship at the intersection of Black studies and critical food studies. The titles in this series explore how food studies can inform the theorization of Blackness, and how Black thought and liberation can transform meanings of food. The series aims to materially advance the protection, nourishment, and celebration of Black life by articulating new futures for Black food justice scholarship.

A complete list of books published in Black Food Justice is available at https://uncpress.org/series/black-food-justice/.

Food Power Politics

The Food Story of the Mississippi Civil Rights Movement

Bobby J. Smith II

The University of North Carolina Press CHAPEL HILL

© 2023 The University of North Carolina Press
All rights reserved
Set in Merope Basic by Westchester Publishing Services
Manufactured in the United States of America

Library of Congress Cataloging-in-Publication Data
Names: Smith, Bobby J., II, author.
Title: Food power politics : the food story of the Mississippi civil rights movement / Bobby J. Smith II.
Other titles: Black food justice.
Description: Chapel Hill : The University of North Carolina Press, [2023] | Series: Black food justice | Includes bibliographical references and index.
Identifiers: LCCN 2023004225 | ISBN 9781469675060 (cloth ; alk. paper) | ISBN 9781469675077 (pbk. ; alk. paper) | ISBN 9781469675084 (ebook)
Subjects: LCSH: Civil rights movements—Mississippi—History. | Black people—Food—Mississippi—History. | Food—Political spects—Mississippi—History. | Social justice—Mississippi—History.
Classification: LCC E185.93.M6 S64 2023 | DDC 323.1196/07307620904—dc23/eng/20230216
LC record available at https://lccn.loc.gov/2023004225

Cover illustration: Vegetable cooperative in Mississippi, 1968. Photograph by Dr. Doris A. Derby.

Chapter 1 was previously published in a different form as "Food and the Mississippi Civil Rights Movement: Re-reading the 1962–1963 Greenwood Food Blockade," *Food, Culture & Society* 23, no. 3 (2020): 382–98. Portions of chapter 2 were previously published in essay form in "Mississippi's War against the War on Poverty: Food Power, Hunger, and White Supremacy," *Study the South*, the Center for the Study of Southern Culture's online journal, and supported by a Study the South Research Fellowship at the University of Mississippi (July 1, 2019).

For Cheryl, Bobby Sr., Sherry, Kyleigh, and Josiah

Contents

Illustrations

FIGURES

MAPS

Abbreviations in the Text

ASU	Alcorn State University
COFO	Council of Federated Organizations
CORE	Congress of Racial Equality
FSC	Federation of Southern Cooperatives
MCHR	Medical Committee for Human Rights
MFDP	Mississippi Freedom Democratic Party
MFLU	Mississippi Freedom Labor Union
MFIP	Mississippi Food Insecurity Project
NAACP	National Association for the Advancement of Colored People
NBCFC	North Bolivar County Farm Cooperative
NBCGFR	North Bolivar County Good Food Revolution
NCNW	National Council of Negro Women
OEO	Office of Economic Opportunity
SCLC	Southern Christian Leadership Conference
SNAP	Supplemental Nutrition Assistance Program
SNCC	Student Nonviolent Coordinating Committee
TDHC	Tufts-Delta Health Center
USDA	US Department of Agriculture

Food Power Politics

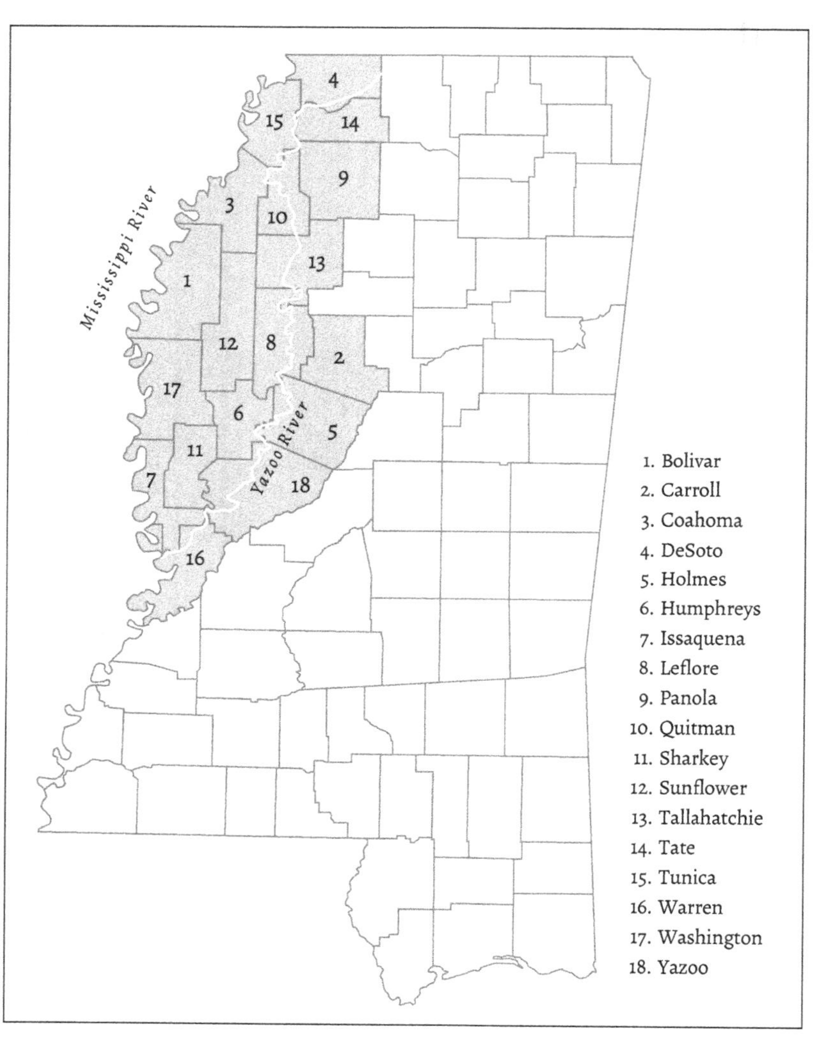

Eighteen counties of the Yazoo–Mississippi Delta region (the Delta).

Introduction

> Food is a weapon that has been used against us,
> but food is also a shield.
>
> —OMAR TATE

Food has been used as a weapon to reinforce racial dominance since the beginning of slavery in America. In their memoirs, Frederick Douglass and Harriet Jacobs recalled how slave masters would withhold food to control enslaved people and starve them into submission.[1] Enslaved people used food as a form of resistance to these tactics by creating and maintaining open and hidden garden plots on plantations in the face of inhumane social conditions.[2] These kinds of practices that used food coercively and in liberatory ways occurred regularly through the Jim Crow era in the South when white political and economic actors controlled access to food as a means to undermine Black life.[3] By the civil rights and Black power movements of the 1960s and 1970s, Black activists in the South and beyond created their own food mechanisms to shield themselves from the weaponization of food that sought to control their food realities. In the Chicago Freedom Movement, for example, the Southern Christian Leadership Conference's (SCLC) "Operation Breadbasket" campaign commissioned a food "inspection team" of Black mothers to evaluate the quality of food in grocery stores in Black neighborhoods to ensure that members of these communities would have affordable and adequate nutritious food to purchase for their families.[4] Throughout the nation, chapters of the Black Panther Party created food distribution initiatives ranging from a free breakfast program for children to community-based free food programs with Black political thought at the center.[5] Black religious communities like the Nation of Islam created farms, bakeries, restaurants, and grocery stores to adhere to their own dietary needs and control every aspect of their food lives.[6]

These previous Black struggles over food in times of racial conflict raise historical and sociological questions about how we define and understand the concept of "power." Who decides the terms by which Black people access food? What conditions shape these terms? How do Black people navigate these terms and conditions? What happens when they decide to reformulate these terms and conditions? These questions challenge us to think about how power shapes historical and contemporary relationships between Black people and food, especially in social, political, and economic struggle. Power is one of the most highly debated concepts in the social sciences—creating a theoretical minefield to navigate in making sense of the concept in the context of food.[7] What is common among these debates, though, is that power can be understood dialectically in social relationships shaped by particular social, political, and economic structures.[8]

Building on this line of thinking about power vis-à-vis food struggles, the language of historians, legal scholars, and political scientists is helpful. They use the term "food power" to describe how food is weaponized and used as a form of control between nations in times of international conflict and war. Food power is exercised when one nation or group withholds food (or the means to access or produce it) from another nation or group to manipulate the outcome of the conflict.[9] For one nation to wield food power over another, it must operate within a hierarchical world system that enables that nation to control the other nation's food supply, thus impacting the other nation's ability to access food. Such macro power dynamics operate beyond a hierarchical world system and trickle down into everyday life, thus shaping micro-power relations between people and surrounding food accessibility. In the context of Black life, specifically, micro-power relations are shaped by questions of domination, that is, as bell hooks argues, a system of politics—struggles for power—that creates and maintains racial hierarchies and structures built on ideologies that white people are superior and Black people are inferior.[10] This is what is meant by power "over" a social actor or group in the social sciences.[11] Food, as a weapon used against Black people in times of social conflict, is designed to exert power over Black people to control them and ensure that Black people remain at the bottom of a racialized social hierarchy.

While the concept of food power is useful for interpreting how food was used as a weapon against Black people, it fails to interpret how they responded to such oppression. I argue that Black people engaged in a process that enabled them to reconfigure and reimagine what it meant to weaponize food through emancipatory terms—what I call "emancipatory food power."[12] This scenario situates power as the capacity or the ability of social actors or groups to shape and control their entire lives. Put differently, this is what is meant by power "to" or "with" people.[13] Emancipatory food power can be situated in how activist Kwame Ture (formerly known as Stokely Carmichael), and Charles V. Hamilton defined power in the context of Black life. In *Black Power*, Ture and Hamilton argued that power is the capacity of Black people to create their own terms by which they define themselves in relation to society.[14] Power in the hands of Black people is also about having these terms recognized by society, which assumes that society will have to be restructured or dismantled altogether to accept these terms. Placing food into this context amplifies the ways in which emancipatory food power shows up in Black life as Black people march toward an emancipatory future where they control when, where, and how they produce, consume, distribute, and access food. Put differently, emancipatory food power mobilizes Black people to fight against domination, as exercised by food power while struggling to emancipate themselves from a racialized social hierarchy and building a movement to control and shape their food realities. As such, the pursuit of emancipatory food power is always relational to food power because the concept of power is dynamic and context dependent. I theorize this relationship as "food power politics"—any set of interactions during times of conflict, whether formal or informal, between social actors who strategically use food in oppressive or emancipatory ways to mitigate the impact of the conflict.

In this book, *Food Power Politics: The Food Story of the Mississippi Civil Rights Movement*, I argue that what I call the food story of the Mississippi civil rights movement in the Yazoo-Mississippi Delta provides a quintessential perspective on understanding food power politics in Black life. Activists, writers, and scholars have hinted at this food story by shedding a crucial light on activist Fannie Lou Hamer's Freedom Farms Cooperative and its impact on the food realities of poor rural Black communities in the region.[15] But Hamer's work is one moment in a larger food story about the movement. The food story I tell spans across at least four moments from the civil rights era to today: the 1962–63 Greenwood Food Blockade, an understudied food stamp campaign ignited by white grocery store owners, the development of the North Bolivar County Farm Cooperative (NBCFC), and the contemporary food justice efforts of a group of rural Black youth in the North Bolivar County Good Food Revolution (NBCGFR). Together these moments—often precluded from our historical memory of the movement—unearth a food story that shows how power struggles over food between Black sharecropping communities and white political and economic opposition to the civil rights movement inform current struggles for food justice in rural Black communities in the Yazoo-Mississippi Delta. The Delta, as the majority Black and rural area is colloquially known, consists of eighteen counties that make up the 200-mile-long, seventy-mile-wide massive agricultural region between Memphis, Tennessee, and Vicksburg, Mississippi. The region is known historically for its fertile soil and occupies a space in the American memory as "the most southern place on earth."[16] This moniker was born out of the Delta's legacy of plantation agriculture and racial conflicts motivated by organized white opposition to Black social movements designed to secure political and economic power for Black people.

During the civil rights movement, Fannie Lou Hamer declared that the Delta was the place where "food is used as a political weapon."[17] It was also the birthplace of both the White Citizens' Council, the southern white supremacist organization, and the concept of "Black Power" as a slogan that ignited the 1960s and 1970s global Black power movement. The White Citizens' Council was created in 1954 by what Clyde Woods described as the Delta's "plantation bloc"—white plantation owners, businessmen, and elected officials. Plantation bloc members descended from generations of white landowners who depended on sharecropping systems to build a cotton plantation empire and solidify the power of white supremacy over the region.[18] Black sharecroppers and their families represented the Black working class, who were the backbone of the region's agricultural economy. The relationship between the plantation bloc and Black sharecroppers in the Delta evolved in to what Saidiya Hartman calls the "afterlife of slavery" and is characterized by two phases of the sharecropping system from the 1800s through the 1960s that perpetuated uneven racialized power relations that trickled down to every aspect of Black life in the region, including the ways in which Black sharecroppers secured food for their families.[19]

In *The Transformation of Plantation Politics*, political scientist Sharon D. Wright Austin observes that the Delta sharecropping system "was instituted supposedly to provide job opportunities, wages, and housing for ex-slaves as a way to keep their labor in the area." The first phase of this sharecropping system was the "heyday" of the system when the plantation bloc "had an unchallenged, invincible domination of local affairs from the 1800s until the early 1960s. . . . Landowners employed black laborers to do backbreaking labor in temperatures that surpassed 100 degrees on many summer days plowing land with mule-drawn planters (and tractors in later years) and chopping cotton."[20] This social domination forced Black sharecroppers to be relegated to a life of impoverishment fabricated by forced dependency on the plantation bloc for housing, economic mobility, and food security. At the same time, Black sharecroppers were consistently denied the right to participate in electoral politics at the state and local levels, despite efforts to be included. In contrast, the second phase of the sharecropping system, which lasted from the 1960s through the 1970s, was characterized by the mechanization and chemicalization of the Delta's agricultural economy that decimated the Delta's Black labor force of sharecroppers. This technological shift in production agriculture replaced Black hands with machines and herbicides, transformed the plantation culture of the region, and clarified a global trend toward large monocropping systems to support a world crop market. Technological changes left Black sharecroppers jobless and even more dependent on antipoverty food programs like the Federal Surplus Commodities Program and, later, the Federal Food Stamp Program. These programs were administered and controlled by the plantation bloc, which used them as a weapon to support its white supremacist agenda for the region. While many jobless Black sharecroppers migrated to the North and other parts of the United States, the strong contingency that stayed behind to build a life on the ruins of a plantation economy was the target of the 1960s Mississippi civil rights movement in the Delta that sought to improve the social, economic, political, and environmental conditions of rural Black life.

It is important to note that across both phases of the Delta sharecropping system, food was an everyday preoccupation for Black sharecroppers. Food was carefully sewn into the fabric of plantation life as sharecroppers needed food to work and depended on the plantation bloc to dictate the conditions by which they could access and secure food. The main site to access food was the plantation commissary, a business enterprise that supplied plantation labor with the supplies to live on the land. This business enterprise was owned by the plantation, and food in the commissary was most often supplied by white grocers and wholesalers who literally fed the labor. In some cases, plantation owners allowed Black sharecroppers to grow fresh vegetables on "truck patches" or "truck gardens" alongside their shacks as well as raise animals for protein. Scholars who have studied the Delta have often overlooked food as a site of power, drawing our attention to a powerful plantation bloc and powerless poor Black sharecroppers. Of course, in the power structure of the Delta, the scales of power always tipped toward proponents of white supremacy in the plantation bloc. It is not that Black sharecroppers did not have power; it is that they envisioned power as *through* people, and the plantation bloc saw power as *over* people. These contrasting versions of power set the stage for a racial conflict that questioned the power of the plantation bloc and empowered Black sharecroppers to work with activists to ignite the Mississippi civil rights movement in the Delta. Indeed, as historian Chris Myers Asch noted, in the Delta, "freedom for which the movement had struggled implied liberation from the fields," linking plantation agriculture to oppression to civil rights.[21]

It is in this backdrop of power relations, embedded in a sharecropping system designed to promote white authority and Black inferiority, that food power politics took center stage in the Mississippi civil rights movement. Yet, the food story of the Mississippi civil rights movement is omitted from mainstream narratives of the movement. There are at least six reasons for this that point to the ways in which food enters civil rights history. The first reason is that food enters civil rights history as a supporting actor in lunch counter scenes from the student sit-in movement that led to the development of the Student Nonviolent Coordinating Committee (SNCC) in 1960.[22] Even though Ella Baker made it clear that lunch counter activism was "concerned with something much bigger than a hamburger," the student sit-in movement still exposed the detrimental impact of racial segregation on the ways in which Black people accessed food in public eating places.[23] The second reason is historiographic: whether narratives are focused on temporal angles that characterize a "long" or "short" movement, told "from the top down" with a focus on campaigns, charismatic leaders, and their organizations, or viewed "from the bottom up" through the lens of communities and everyday local people, food is not a story in and of itself.[24] The third reason is interpretation: while new scholarship has questioned movement origins, ideologies, and actors, the literature still reinforces a civil rights struggle solely characterized by electoral politics, education, and access to public accommodations.[25] The fourth reason is geographic: as millions of Black people migrated in the 1950s and 1960s from the South to the North, the rural to the urban, social scientists followed them, which in effect cast a decades-long shadow over the study of Black people in the context of rural relations in the South where food had always been a central issue, especially in plantation counties.[26] As a result, in the words of historian Valerie Grim, the study of rural Black people is "sufficiently deficient."[27] The fifth reason is structural as it relates to class and gender dynamics in the movement: poor rural Black people and Black women, who often championed Black food efforts, were not recognized or afforded the opportunity to be leaders of the movement and develop the movement's agenda to place their material needs at the center of the struggle for political power.[28] The sixth reason, expanding on the gendered structure of the movement, is that the gendered nature of food reinforced food work as "women's work" that operated as a crucial yet background variable in an equation that placed prominent middle-class Black men in the forefront of movement struggles.[29] Even if men engaged in food work, it was still coded as women's work, rendering such work less visible or erased altogether in narratives and records of the movement.

Food Power Politics breaks the silence surrounding the centrality of food struggles in narratives of the civil rights movement. It shows, as the James

Beard Award–winning Black food writer and anthropologist Jessica B. Harris argues, that "the Civil Rights Movement in the United States in the 1960s was a crucial turning point in the history of African Americans and food."[30] It furnishes a theoretical framework for exploring how food, and control over access to food, mattered to movement politics, demonstrating a much more expansive struggle for civil rights that reached beyond the polling place and schools to include issues of food, agriculture, economic justice, health, and land. This framework provides a vehicle that transports us back in time to recover a food focus that is often diluted or muted in the historical retelling of movements of the civil rights and Black power eras. This food focus uncovers a neglected stage of the civil rights movement that amplifies the overlooked and unacknowledged collaborative food efforts between Black sharecroppers and women who joined arms with local and national activists to get food on their tables in the Delta. Such efforts, including the 1963 Food for Freedom program and the development of the NBCFC in 1967, were part of what civil rights activist Marvin Rich described as a new wave of 1960s civil rights activism that "produc[ed] remarkable results without big headlines."[31] At the same time, *Food Power Politics* documents how white elected officials, landowners, grocery store owners, and merchants opposed Black food efforts, revealing hidden sources of injustice and power that operated against the movement.

By expanding the cast of characters on both sides of the struggle for civil rights in the Delta, this book provides a different angle of Black resistance that illuminates a profound portrait of how food struggles reconfigured the civil rights movement in Mississippi and, by extension, the nation. It also offers a rare glimpse into the inner workings of white opposition that caused a head-on collision between the movement and federal food policy and antipoverty interventions. The inner workings of white opposition have been dormant in the scholarly purview of the movement and appear in and out of the spotlight in stories that center activist responses and strategies. *Food Power Politics* provides a front-row view of the ways in which food was integral to the rubric of white opposition and how Black communities and activists responded. For example, it illuminates how the 1962–63 Greenwood Food Blockade was initiated as well as how white grocers campaigned for the Federal Food Stamp Program that exacerbated food disparities among Black sharecroppers and their communities in the mid- to late 1960s. Such tensions reflect how food power politics were amplified due to the centrality of plantation relations that shaped Black life in the Delta. While the plantation system is usually situated as a backdrop in movement stories, this book brings the system in and out of focus, revealing how past and present Black food realities are shaped by the shadow of the plantation that haunted the movement. The shadow of the plantation reinforced unequal power relations and provided the impetus for Black sharecroppers to envision freedom through civil rights with food at the center. In many respects, food was a canvas that Black sharecroppers and activists collectively used to sketch a path toward emancipatory food power during the civil rights movement in the Delta.

Simultaneously, *Food Power Politics* shows how this line of thinking and strategizing is used today as a model of emancipatory food power in the food justice work of rural Black youth in the NBCGFR in the Delta. Food justice is a social movement that builds the capacity of marginalized communities to use agriculture and food as vehicles to reshape social, cultural, political, economic, and environmental relations between inadequate access to food and larger societal structures of inequality.[32] This movement creates a pathway to food sovereignty that empowers communities to define their own food and agricultural systems as a way to counter food disparities. By exploring the food justice work of the NBCGFR, *Food Power Politics* reveals that the food story of the Mississippi civil rights movement continues in the present, demonstrating that the roots of the contemporary food justice movement lie deep in the history of the Mississippi civil rights movement.

In the last decade, the field of critical food studies has begun to explore some of the historical roots of contemporary struggles for food justice, as seen through the works of Monica White, Ashanté Reese, Joshua Sbicca, Garrett Broad, and Lana Dee Povitz, to name a few.[33] This scholarship places current activist debates within a historical context in which Black communities navigate the persistence of food disparities in their communities. While this research breaks new ground, the majority of these projects are urban-focused—contributing to what social scientist Jesse McEntee describes as the "urban bias" in food justice scholarship that "marginalizes the acute food access problems faced by rural populations."[34] This urban bias has largely ignored how food justice movements emerge in the South and the role of youth in food justice efforts. *Food Power Politics* complements this scholarship and extends it by focusing on how rural Black communities in the South address issues of food disparities through food justice in historical and contemporary contexts and examines how these communities empower Black youth to create solutions.

Located at the intersection of multiple disciplines, including critical food studies, Black studies, history, sociology, agri-food studies, and southern studies, *Food Power Politics* creates a conversation between the study of the civil rights movement and research on the contemporary food justice movement. The lens and language of food power politics can be used to shed light on largely unidentifiable forms of activism surrounding food and that seemingly operated outside of the rubric of civil rights. The theory of food power politics also fills a void in food justice research. At present, a considerable amount of this scholarship concentrates on one side or the other of the debate: either the injustice, the structural mechanisms that exacerbate food insecurity, or justice, the community-based strategies that developed as a response to food insecurity in Black communities. *Food Power Politics* examines the food story of the Mississippi civil rights movement that bridges the gap between these opposing food injustice/justice perspectives. As such, this book offers one food angle of the movement that asks a new set of questions about Black struggles for civil rights and food justice. These questions include the following: How does our understanding of the civil rights episode of the Black freedom struggle shift if food access and activism are the starting points? How do power struggles over food during the civil rights movement help us theorize the past to inform contemporary social movements for food justice and food sovereignty in Black communities? What does this new way of thinking about the movement teach us about the relationships between inadequate access to food, structural inequalities, and social movements in Black life? How does this reframe how we study and understand food, both as an instrument of oppression and as a tool for liberation? In answering these questions, this book offers a way to avoid, as sociologist Charles Payne put it, "our tendency to reduce the [civil rights] movement to a 'civil rights' movement, taking a narrow label more seriously than did the people who participated in the movement."[35]

Drawing on extensive archival materials, including never-before-used primary sources, newspapers, interviews, oral histories, memoirs, participant observation, and scholarship, *Food Power Politics* rejects the tendency to reduce the civil rights movement to a preset list of social struggles. Indeed, this tendency paralyzes our ability to clearly identify critical lessons from the movement that could directly contribute to the production of new knowledge surrounding food justice and food sovereignty movements in Black and other marginalized communities. As one of the most celebrated and studied social movements in American history, the civil rights movement is often used as a litmus test to determine how far the nation has progressed. By emphasizing a civil rights movement through the prism of food power politics, this book helps us see how far the nation has come and identify social, political, and economic blind spots that perpetuate inequalities at the core of social protest and power struggles for food in and beyond Black life. At the same time, the food story of the Mississippi civil rights movement that this book tells can be archived in the arsenal of stories that Black food activists draw on when strategizing about the future as concerns for food security are intensified by social unrest, gentrification, climate change, and the ongoing COVID-19 global pandemic.

Methods

To write this book, I assembled a diverse set of materials to generate the food story of the Mississippi civil rights movement. These materials illuminate the centrality of food power politics in the struggle for civil rights in Mississippi and how rural Black youth navigate such politics today in the Delta. They were retrieved from marginal subparts of archives, sources, and historical narratives that produce competing story lines of the civil rights movement in Mississippi and across the nation. This retrieval process was an interactive, multimethodological approach to thinking about how the food story of the movement challenges and contributes to the widely accepted story lines that have been laid down about the movement. Such story lines have been profoundly shaped by generations of civil rights historiography that draw on extensive archival research and oral histories. To be sure, these story lines are not neutral. They reflect decisions made by the repositories that preserve and scholars who create narratives about the movement. Following anthropologist Michel-Rolph Trouillot, these decisions are instantiations of archival power in the production of narratives about the struggle for civil rights.[36] As such, the ways in which power operates within the production of archives, sources, and narratives of the Mississippi civil rights movement cultivate "silences" surrounding the stories we tell about the movement. Methodologically, I use the silences to recover the crucial role that food played in the Mississippi civil rights movement and question how narratives about the struggle for civil rights blind us from the significance of food in movement politics.

Through the research process that gave birth to *Food Power Politics*, I reckoned with the silences around food in the civil rights movement. This process required a specific reading of archives, sources, and narratives that document the movement. I relied on the framing of archives by Trouillot and the reading of archives suggested by historian Philippa Levine. Trouillot and Levine both interrogate how archival power excludes particular aspects of narratives that don't readily fit in dominant epistemologies of moments in history. Trouillot asserts that "historical narratives are premised on previous understandings, which are themselves premised on the distribution of archival power."[37] Levine suggests that "archive[s] . . . bolster a particular position that might be read at an angle."[38] In thinking with Trouillot and Levine, narratives of the civil rights movement support a particular position that relegates forms of activism such as food activism to the periphery that exists beyond public strategies such as protests, boycotts, and sit-ins. But when read at an "angle," a space is created that sheds light on the power that reveals and conceals the food story of the Mississippi civil rights movement. It is in this space that my research for this book navigated.

I unknowingly started the research process for *Food Power Politics* in the spring of 2016 while taking a graduate seminar course on community organizing and development at Cornell University. At the time, I was an activist in the food justice movement in Ithaca, New York, where I served as an inaugural member of the Tompkins County Food Policy Council and cofounded the Ithaca chapter of Black Lives Matter. These experiences shaped my thinking in the graduate seminar when I first encountered Charles Payne's *I've Got the Light of Freedom*, a groundbreaking book on the Black freedom struggle in the Delta.[39] As I was reading Payne's book, I wondered how the struggle for civil rights in Mississippi could speak directly to the high levels of food insecurity in Black communities where food justice activists were organizing. It wasn't until chapter 5 of Payne's book that I discovered a direct thread between civil rights and food justice in Black communities. In a short passage covering roughly ten pages of chapter 5 in his book of over 400 pages, Payne narrated the story of what activists in SNCC and the Council of Federated Organizations (COFO) described as the 1962–63 Greenwood Food Blockade. Payne's account of this event illustrated how food was used as a weapon of voter suppression and a tool of Black resistance in the Delta town of Greenwood in Leflore County. It also provided me with a starting point to investigate the circumstances and conditions preceding and following the blockade. This initial investigation into the Greenwood Food Blockade laid the foundation for the food story of the Mississippi civil rights movement.

After reading Payne's book, I began my investigation into the Greenwood Food Blockade, which laid the foundation for the food story of the Mississippi civil rights movement. Each step of this investigation illuminated another aspect of this food story, and my initial goal was to construct an alternate version of the blockade to foreground food in the movement and inform contemporary Black struggles for food justice. To do this, I read other movement histories that provided a treatment of the struggle for civil rights in Mississippi. These histories included Howard Zinn's *SNCC: The New Abolitionists*, Clayborne Carson's *In Struggle*, and John Dittmer's *Local People*.[40] While reading through these histories, I soon discovered that the blockade had been documented to a certain extent. But food in and of itself was not fully examined in historical treatments of the blockade, and when discussed, it was seemingly treated as a mere prop in a larger movement narrative.

Moving from scholarly accounts of the blockade to the archives, I started my archival journey in the summer of 2017 at the Mississippi Department of Archives and History (MDAH). Departing from the traditional line of civil rights inquiry and following Trouillot, I repositioned food to the center of materials related to the movement in Mississippi that were readily available in the archives. Put differently, I tracked the appearance of food throughout the materials to capture the circumstances and conditions surrounding the blockade. Tracking food in the materials at MDAH enabled me to approach the archives with questions that had not previously been asked. These questions included: How were Black people's everyday preoccupations with food addressed before and after the blockade? How was food framed and used by proponents and opponents of civil rights in Mississippi? Were there any other groups or activists, apart from SNCC, that responded to the Greenwood blockade? Who else was impacted by the food blockade? What can we learn about the relationship between food and the civil rights movement if we place the event outside of SNCC's history? What lessons can we draw from this event to understand the role of food in the civil rights movement?

With these questions in mind, I combed through more than 100 collections, including papers, memoirs, manuscripts, print media, and organizational records related to the civil rights movement in the state. The specific civil rights archives and related collections at MDAH are categorized along the same lines as the political story of the movement with a strong focus on voting rights activism, integration, and education. This construction of the archives corroborates the historical scholarship on the topic and depends mostly on materials generated by activists and civil rights organizations. This diverse set of holdings includes the papers of Mississippi civil rights icons Aaron Henry, Medgar Evers, Myrlie Beasley Evers, and Fannie Lou Hamer; the historic Tougaloo College Mississippi Civil Rights Collection, which contains documents such as oral histories of activists and personal papers of groups active in the movement; Mississippi print media including the *Greenwood Commonwealth*, *Enterprise Tocsin*, *Jackson Advocate*, and *Jackson Daily News*; and manuscripts on key figures in groups such as the White

Citizens' Council and the Mississippi State Sovereignty Commission that opposed civil rights in Mississippi. I also examined the records of the Mississippi Council on Human Relations, which provided data on issues of food, nutrition, hunger, and poverty during the civil rights era in the wake of the blockade.

Working with these materials, I sketched out the contours of the blockade and supplemented the sources with interviews with activists. Over the course of my time at MDAH, I was connected with six people—through archival staff and local networks—to interview based on their affiliation or participation in the Mississippi civil rights movement. All six were men and ranged in age from sixty-four to ninety-five.[41] The interviews, ranging from sixty to ninety minutes in length, were conducted in person and recorded using a digital audio recorder and then transcribed. I asked broad questions about their role in the movement and direct questions about their own experiences or local struggles around food and the food blockade. When asked about the blockade or their participation in food efforts, specifically, respondents recalled the event but informed me that their civil rights work did not include organizing around food or the creation of food efforts to address the blockade. As one activist told me, "Many of the women and folks in the movement who worked with food in the movement have since died, and they would have been more helpful in terms of your research." This activist's response was representative of how the six male activists whom I interviewed talked about food. For them, food seemed to be something that was beyond the scope of what they did. In many respects, they all characterized food work as largely "women's work," which further illustrates how the gendered nature of food presupposed food onto Black women in the movement. Such food activism practiced by Black women, historian Françoise N. Hamlin argued, "is rendered invisible in many instances because strategies of nurturing are often considered 'natural' or the ordinary activities of women in their communities."[42] Black women's care work in the movement was behind the scenes and took a back seat to the work of the national agenda in local spaces focused on voter registration efforts. As a result, the interviews conducted provided rich data on the social and political conditions that surrounded the blockade, but minimal information on the blockade itself. Such recollections reflected the organization of the archives and the treatment of the blockade and food in civil rights history.

In 2018, I traveled to the University of Mississippi to examine the wealth of primary materials on powerful Mississippi congressmen Senator James Eastland and US Representative Jamie Whitten at the Department of Archives and Special Collections at the J. D. Williams Library. Both Eastland

and Whitten were segregationists and vocal opponents of the civil rights movement. Together, their materials include never-before-used primary sources, notably their personal papers, political writings, and unprocessed collections. Eastland's papers revealed that the senator tracked the circumstances surrounding the Greenwood Food Blockade and how the blockade ended. The Eastland papers also include letters that made up the largely unknown food stamp campaign initiated by the Delta-based Lewis Grocer Company just days after the blockade began. This campaign was championed by white grocers in the Delta who saw the federal food stamp program as a way to increase their profits in poor rural Black communities. Eastland, who coauthored the 1964 federal food stamp bill, supported this campaign and used it as a basis for his views on the legislation. The papers and unprocessed collections of Jamie Whitten, who controlled the US Department of Agriculture's (USDA) budget from the late 1940s through the early 1990s, reveal how he worked in tandem with Eastland to ensure that the white power structure of the Delta maintained political and economic dominance over the region. The maneuverings of Eastland and Whitten are a window through which we can examine their local ties and how those ties played a significant role in the food story of the Mississippi civil rights movement.

In 2019, I conducted research at the University of Illinois at Urbana-Champaign Library, working with SNCC's microfilm collection, and at the Wisconsin Historical Society to study the records of the NBCFC and the society's extensive civil rights collection. The SNCC collection provided important details about the blockade that the MDAH did not provide. The meticulous records kept by SNCC were extremely helpful in generating a narrative of the Greenwood Food Blockade, as were articles in the organization's newspaper, the *Student Voice*. The records of the NBCFC at the Wisconsin Historical Society revealed how poor rural Black actors, who were mostly sharecroppers, women, and their families, organized to place food at the center of the post–1965 civil rights movement. What is interesting about the NBCFC is that the organization was born out of a relationship between Black women activists, including Mrs. L. C. Dorsey, sharecroppers, and staff members at the Tufts-Delta Heath Center (TDHC) in the all-Black Delta town of Mound Bayou in Bolivar County, Mississippi. The TDHC was one of the nation's first rural health-care centers that focused on adequate food and nutrition as a way to remedy poverty-induced hunger, and Dorsey was an employee there before she became the leader of the NBCFC. As the leader of the NBCFC, Dorsey expanded the meaning of civil rights to address food as integral to social and economic conditions. She aligned herself with activists and community members who believed that if Black people had access to food and land, they could escape the visible and invisible hand of white supremacy to achieve freedom and liberation. Because of this relationship, primary data on the cooperative can also be found in archives, including those at Duke University and the University of North Carolina at Chapel Hill, which document the work of the TDHC. Additional data on the origins of the NBCFC can also be found in the September 1970 hearings of the US Senate Select Committee on Nutrition and Human Needs when Dorsey testified about the work of the cooperative alongside NBCFC stakeholders.

In 2020, to construct how the food story of the Mississippi civil rights movement continues today, I traveled to the Delta to learn about a growing food justice movement organized by Black youth in the NBCGFR. Founded in 2017, the NBCGFR is an effort to empower Black youth to address the food realities of poor rural Black communities in the region. It is the central food justice project of the Black-led Delta Fresh Foods Initiative (known regionally as Delta Fresh). Delta Fresh explicitly views the work of the NBCGFR as a continuation of the work that was started by the NBCFC during the civil rights movement. What is even more fascinating is that the NBCGFR farm is located on the same street where the NBCFC operated. Yet, while the NBCGFR's work builds on the past, it looks different. The members of the NBCGFR align themselves with the grammar of Black food struggles to forge a path toward sustainable Black food futures. For them, food justice is just one step toward their ultimate goal of food sovereignty that is aligned with what the National Black Food and Justice Alliance (NBFJA) views as Black food sovereignty, which seeks to "ensure that Black people have not only the right but the ability to control [their] food, through means including but not limited to the means of production & distribution."[43]

I learned about the NBCGFR in the fall of 2018 during my time as an affiliate of the Mississippi Food Insecurity Project (MFIP) at Mississippi State University. For this part of my research process, since no archive existed that could tell the story of the NBCGFR, I created my own archive. I assembled documents from the group's website and public organizational records kept in an online repository by the organization WhyHunger, which funded the NBCGFR in its early years. I also tracked media stories about the organization through local newspapers like the *Bolivar Commercial* and analyzed multimedia created by the NBCGFR. At the time of my research, there was only one published study of the NBCGFR conducted by members of the MFIP and Delta Fresh. The purpose of this study was to understand how community-based participatory research can be used to build community capacity to address issues of food insecurity. Due to a lack of sources that captured the voices of Black youth in the NBCGFR, I conducted interviews with the group and community members. I was able to interview six of the thirteen active members of the NBCGFR, ranging from ages sixteen to twenty.[44] Four of them were female, and the other two were male. Interviews with the youth were conducted at the project's headquarters in Mound Bayou, Mississippi, and lasted from 30 to 120 minutes and were divided into four parts: (1) life stories and experiences, (2) history of the NBCGFR and the area's local food context, (3) personal reflection on the food realities of the region, and (4) open discussion about the use of food as a weapon. I also interviewed the NBCGFR's coordinator of youth leadership development and four other community members whom I met in the area's local food and farming scene, ranging in ages from twenty-four to ninety-two.[45] Four of them were women, and one was male. These interviews provided a snapshot of the wider community context that was critical to understanding the ways in which the food story of the Mississippi civil rights movement continues in the present-day food justice movement led by the NBCGFR. I used sources from the USDA, congressional research service, state agencies in Mississippi, and community-based organizations that provide data on agricultural, social, economic, and health issues related to food in the Delta to reconstruct and understand the context of the interviews.

Together, these archives and sources were critical to my ability to generate the food story of the Mississippi civil rights movement and its legacy today. Throughout this entire research process, I consulted memoirs of Mississippi civil rights activists, historical narratives of the movement, Black newspapers, and digital repositories controlled by activists, such as the Veterans of the Civil Rights Movement website, which houses the activist-driven civil rights movement archive. This website is an invaluable resource for the study of the movement. By using various forms of data that revealed some aspects of food in the movement, I deconstructed the archives, sources, and narratives to put certain pieces back together again to tell the food story of the Mississippi civil rights movement.

Book Organization

Chapter 1, "Food Denied, Food for Freedom: The 1962–1963 Greenwood Food Blockade," chronicles and analyzes the story of the Greenwood Food Blockade that occurred from November 1962 to May 1963. This story reveals how

Black activists and sharecroppers were blindsided by the use of food as a form of voter suppression by white elected officials in the Delta town of Greenwood in Leflore County. This move by the white elected officials instigated a six-month food crisis that exacerbated food insecurity in Black sharecropping communities across the county. In response, civil rights activists and organizations created an innovative food program known as "Food for Freedom." The Food for Freedom program represents one of the first manifestations of emancipatory food power in the movement. It was characterized by a translocal network of actors including activists, sharecroppers, community leaders, political figures, and organizations that came together to transform food into a symbol of freedom that could protect and feed those who were impacted by the blockade. This chapter shows how the Food for Freedom program, as a response to the blockade, brought food power politics not only to the center of the struggle for civil rights in Mississippi but also exposed the use of food as a weapon against the movement to the nation. Tensions surrounding the blockade reveal how the event is an entry point for the food story of the Mississippi civil rights movement that created space for new articulations of white supremacy and Black freedom.

Chapter 2, "Another Kind of Oppression: Civil Rights, Food Stamps, and the Segrenomics of the Lewis Grocer Company," documents and analyzes a forgotten 1960s food stamps campaign that mobilized white grocers and their affiliates in the Delta. Led by the Lewis Grocer Company, Mississippi's largest wholesaler-retailer at the time, the campaign began around the same time as the onset of the Greenwood Food Blockade and sought to use the federal food stamp program to transform food into an economic weapon against poor rural Black communities. Civil rights activists like Fannie Lou Hamer knew this, as she described the federal food stamp program as "another kind of oppression" that would perpetuate Black dependence on the white power structure in all aspects of life. This chapter reveals how the advent of the federal food stamp program in Mississippi was instigated by the president of the Lewis Grocer Company who wanted to protect the self-interests of white grocers and exert the company's domination over commercial food spaces in Black sharecropping communities. This level of food power was shaped by white supremacy in the context of food power politics in the Delta and was rooted in the history of the Lewis Grocer Company's role in the region's plantation economy which in turn shaped the food realties of Black sharecroppers from the late 1800s through the 1960s. The interactions between white grocery stores, plantation culture, and civil rights provide the necessary context for understanding how activists organized against the federal food program in the Delta and the reemergence of emancipatory food power in the movement.

Chapter 3, "Black Food, Black Jobs: Emancipatory Food Power and the North Bolivar County Farm Cooperative," examines the process by which the NBCFC generated emancipatory food power in the Mississippi civil rights movement. The NBCFC's process was realized in the creation of a local Black food economy that empowered Black sharecroppers and rural Black mothers to place their material needs at the center of the movement. In the face of a shifting post–1965 civil rights movement that collided with the onset of food stamps and changes in the agricultural economy of the Delta, the NBCFC's local Black food economy was a source of food security and economic mobility that brought hope to rural Black communities in the northern section of Bolivar County. Under the leadership of activist Mrs. L. C. Dorsey, the NBCFC continued the regional Black agrarian tradition of agency and self-determination in the production, consumption, and distribution of food. This chapter shows how this tradition shaped the emancipatory food power wielded by the NBCFC and their struggle to sustain their lives in the shadows of the collaspe of the Delta's plantation system and economy. The NBCFC's ability to operationalize a local Black food economy as a site for the production of emancipatory food power sets the stage for understanding how the food story of the Mississippi civil rights movement continues in the contemporary food justice efforts of rural Black youth of the NBCGFR in the Delta.

Chapter 4, "From Civil Rights to Food Justice: Black Youth and the North Bolivar County Good Food Revolution," fast-forwards to the present-day food story of the Mississippi civil rights movement. It examines how Black youth in the NBCGFR are extending the civil rights struggle for food and economic security initiated by the NBCFC to generate an updated version of emancipatory food power in the Delta. Many of the youth in the NBCGFR are descendants of Black sharecroppers in the Delta who navigated a plantation system that was designed to strip them of their agency and autonomy in the production, consumption, and distribution of food. While the geographic lines that demarcated large plantations in the region have disappeared, questions around food struggles in rural Black communities remain. Through agripreneurship, farming, and youth leadership development, the NBCGFR takes up these questions as they operationalize their vision for their growing food justice movement in the Delta. Working with Delta Fresh and local Black farmer-mentors, the NBCGFR builds on the past to build sustainable Black food futures where Black communities have the power to dictate when, where, and how they access food.

In the conclusion, I discuss how the food story of the Mississippi civil rights movement challenges us to think explicitly about how we understand the civil rights movement and how it can be used to enhance current struggles for food justice and food sovereignty in Black communities. This discussion clarifies how food power politics as a social struggle and theoretical framework pushes us to think critically about how power—in historical and contemporary contexts—shapes the food realities of Black people. It raises questions about emancipatory food power that point to the ways in which social change in Black communities involves the simultaneous process of dismantling oppression and building sustainable solutions in their fight against inequalities in and outside the food system. The conclusion ends by reflecting on how *Food Power Politics* creates a space to think critically about how the interaction between food and power in Black life offers us a way to rethink the past, navigate the present, and build a socially just and food secure future for all.

CHAPTER ONE

Food Denied, Food for Freedom

The 1962–1963 Greenwood Food Blockade

> Twenty-two thousand people in Leflore County, Mississippi, have been denied government surplus food because of attempts made by some to register to vote. The sharecroppers of the Mississippi Delta must receive relief or starve. . . . There has been no limit placed upon the means that have been used to destroy the Freedom Movement in the Mississippi Delta.
>
> —CHARLES McDEW AND WILLIAM "BILL" MAHONEY

> The winter of 1963 had been an exceptionally cold one in the Delta, and it had been a poor year for cotton pickers. . . . Commodities—surplus cheese, rice, flour, and sugar which were distributed free by the county as a supplement to often meager food supplies—were now crucial to fending off destitution. So when county officials halted the commodities program in reprisal for voter registration efforts, Leflore County Blacks saw what hadn't been clear to them before: a connection between political participation and food on their table.
>
> —BOB MOSES AND CHARLIE COBB

On the morning of Friday, November 9, 1962, the all-white Leflore County Board of Supervisors held a public meeting in the county courtroom in downtown Greenwood. Open only to white citizens, with approximately seventy people in attendance, the purpose of the meeting was to revisit the county's summer decision to not participate in the winter distribution of free food to poor people via the federal surplus commodities program.[1] Sam Block, Student Nonviolent Coordinating Committee (SNCC) field secretary in Greenwood, noted that less than 1 percent of the participants in the food program were white, and at the time, this federal food program was virtually the only way poor rural Black people who were cotton sharecroppers could access food.[2] As in other parts of the Delta and the South, the cotton season shaped all aspects of the lives of sharecroppers. The free food was crucial for them to survive the winter months with no cotton crop in the ground, and by that November, the cotton season was over, and several citizens approached the board of supervisors about reinstating the program.[3] White landowners were most likely the people responsible for asking for the program to be reinstated so that they could sustain their labor force during the off-season at no cost. But there was a conflict between those who supported the program and those who opposed it.

When the discussion about the program began at the public meeting, Supervisor Lewis Poindexter cited budgetary concerns as the primary reason for not administering the program that winter. Chief among those concerns were the costs of food transportation and labor to facilitate the program, and Poindexter suggested that it would not be financially feasible for the county to participate. Following Poindexter's comments, Mr. J. H. Peebles, then president of the Bank of Commerce in Greenwood, motioned to reaffirm the discontinuation of the federal food program. Carried by a vote of forty in favor, with twenty-nine voting against it, the board's decision was reaffirmed. While one county supervisor, board president W. J. Lipscomb, went on record in full support of the program, the majority vote to not reinstate the program ensured that a program that largely benefited Black sharecroppers was no longer supported that year.[4]

On the surface, the Leflore County Board of Supervisors' decision to halt the federal surplus commodities program appeared rational based on budgetary concerns. Yet when read against the context of the times, the decision sent shockwaves throughout the Mississippi civil rights movement. Activists conceptualized the county's decision as an all-out assault on ideas of democracy and a form of retaliation designed to punish Black citizens for attempting to vote. They framed this move as the onset of the "Greenwood Food Blockade," which lasted from November 1962 to May 1963 and produced high levels of food insecurity. By using the word "blockade," activists shifted the language of the movement and situated it within the long history of food power politics when opposing forces weaponized and withheld food in times of conflict and war. Indeed, this change in the language of the movement suggests that activists viewed the Greenwood Food Blockade as a deafening battle cry from their opponents. The blockade made it significantly clear to SNCC and other civil rights groups that the struggle for voting rights in general and the Mississippi movement in particular had entered a new phase. In the years leading up to the blockade, activists and their opponents articulated a local civil rights movement that engaged largely with national issues such as the right to vote and the integration of public facilities and schools. The onset of the blockade changed the rules of voter suppression and challenged activists to juggle both their commitment to voter registration efforts and an adequate response to the food question surrounding the blockade.

But the story of the Greenwood Food Blockade is not only about how the denial of food was used as a strategy of voter suppression. In a matter of weeks, activists gradually slowed down their voter registration efforts to transform food into a key site of action, organizing, and protest, igniting a nationwide food drive and program under the banner of "Food for Freedom." This innovative food program was designed to feed those impacted by the blockade and raise public awareness about the use of food as a weapon against the movement. The food program facilitated the development of an alternative, translocal, multilevel food network and distribution system that catapulted the racialized politics of food to the center of the movement. At the helm of this food network were lesser-known activists across the Delta like Vera Pigee of the National Association for the Advancement of Colored People (NAACP) who facilitated the logistics of the Food for Freedom program. While widely unknown in civil rights history, their efforts in operating the Food for Freedom program garnered the support of Mississippi civil rights leader Medgar Evers and national figures including Dr. Martin Luther King Jr., activist Bayard Rustin, Black comedian Dick Gregory, and actor Harry Belafonte. As such, Food for Freedom was empowering and demonstrated how food could be weaponized not only to oppress but also as a tool to contribute to the emancipation of Black people, even if temporarily, from their dependence on the white political power structure for food provision and to resist white supremacy.

The tensions surrounding the food question between the actions of the all-white Leflore County Board of Supervisors, which represented the local political establishment, and activists provide a front-row seat to how food power politics played out in the movement. To be sure, this was not the first time food power politics infiltrated movement spaces. Historian Bobby Lovett observed a food blockade in Tennessee when Black farmers attempted to vote in 1960.[5] Activists Charlie Cobb and Charles McLaurin witnessed the withholding of food from those who went to register to vote in 1962 in the Delta town of Ruleville in Sunflower County.[6] While such instances likely occurred in other counties, the Greenwood Food Blockade brought national attention to the political weaponization of food as movement activists and supporters mobilized to answer the cries for food.

Yet scholars treat and read the blockade as an isolated disruption to Black voter registration efforts in the Delta. Even though sociologist Charles Payne correctly identifies the blockade as representative of "a new plateau" for the movement, the event remains buried in the traditional framework of the 1960s struggle for civil rights.[7] This framework emphasizes interaction between national movement politics and local organizing traditions surrounding key issues such as voting rights, education, and public accommodations. At the same time, this framework de-emphasizes the significance of the blockade and by extension the centrality of food to both proponents and opponents of the movement. Such food power politics illustrate that there is much more to learn from the movement and how it shaped relationships between political participation and the food realities of "local people," as historian John Dittmer has called them, who reckoned with the power of food throughout the blockade.[8] When food power politics is used as a lens to read the Greenwood Food Blockade, it is clear that food reconfigured, even if only for a brief moment, the struggle for civil rights in the Delta.

This chapter offers a window into food stories of the movement that have yet to be told. It retells the story of the Greenwood Food Blockade that foregrounds food and the actors who used food to advance the struggle for civil rights in the Delta. Through an analysis of archival materials—including the SNCC papers, newspapers, correspondences, letters, reports, and memoirs—and historical scholarship, the chapter shows that food power politics preoccupied the crevices of the movement's strategic planning processes, reshaping the struggle for civil rights. In one sense, this chapter highlights how the blockade forced activists to consider what food meant to the Black sharecropping communities they organized in and illustrated just how far the white political power structure would go to eliminate any threats to their power over the region. In another sense, the blockade created a sociopolitical space for activists to tap into unforeseen streams of empowerment, recognizing the strength of networks with food at the center. As such, this chapter is instructive for understanding food power politics within a multidimensional civil rights movement.

Set against the backdrop of the intensification of racialized violent tensions, white landowners' opposition to civil rights activism, and the mechanization of cotton, which exacerbated the impoverishment and out-migration of Black sharecroppers and farmworkers, the chapter begins with a sketch of the food context out of which the Greenwood Food Blockade emerges.[9] This context is critically important in that it sheds light on often overlooked ways that food accessibility among Black sharecroppers and their families was shaped by white supremacist motivations and the agricultural economy of the Delta. Then, the chapter turns to the story of the Greenwood Food Blockade. This story of the blockade complicates the traditional framework of the movement to foreground the role of food in the movement and the actors who worked to mitigate the effects of the blockade. In this way, the story amplifies the role of poor rural Black communities, sharecroppers, local activists, and women who dictated the Delta civil rights agenda in tandem with national activists. The chapter concludes with thinking about how the Greenwood Food Blockade creates pathways for understanding the ways in which food power politics reshaped the Mississippi civil rights movement.

The Racial Politics of Uneven Food Access in Leflore County: The Context

Situated near the eastern corridor of the Delta at the confluence of the Yazoo, Tallahatchie, and Yalobusha Rivers, the Greenwood–Leflore County area was emblematic of what sociologist Rupert Vance described as the "cotton-culture complex" of the rural South. Built on the thesis that "the Cotton Belt may be regarded as a cultural area, and the cultivation of the cotton plant regarded as a trait of material culture," the cotton-culture complex shed light on the critical materiality of cotton production. "Among the most obvious of the material traits associated with cotton," Vance wrote, "are the food habits of the growers."[10] Such habits among poor rural Black sharecroppers were embedded in the area's culture and Jim Crow racial codes that maintained Black dependence on white authority, most visible in the Delta's cotton plantation economy. During the post–Civil War era, many rural Black people saw sharecropping as a step toward becoming independent landowners and worked on plantations to secure their right to land. But by the 1930s, this system was a de facto way of life, designed to maintain a subservient Black working class.[11] To do this, white plantation owners gave Black sharecroppers and tenant farmers cheap labor contracts to work and live on the land that included "furnishings"—capital for production, food, housing, and agricultural supplies, among other things.[12] Within this contractual agreement, Black sharecroppers accessed food in three intersecting ways.

First, they were forced by their employers to establish credit at plantation commissaries or grocery stores. To access credit, Black sharecroppers required white patronage as a form of validation to store owners, so they could purchase cheap staple foods that would sustain them with the credit given. As a result, they often suffered from hunger-induced malnutrition and relied on a "monotonous diet dependent on cornmeal, salt pork, field peas or beans and molasses."[13] Second, on some plantations, sharecroppers were also given access to a "truck patch"—small plots of land slightly larger than a garden space—to grow food for their families and communities during, and a little time after, the cotton season. On this plot, usually located on the side of a plantation shack, sharecroppers would plant vegetables and raise livestock such as chickens, hogs, and cattle. They would also plant "treats" such as sweet potatoes and use cows for fresh milk.[14] However, the use of the truck patch was often disrupted by the economic needs of white plantation owners to produce more cotton. During "good" crop years, when the market would cause the price of cotton to increase, plantation owners would collude with grocery or commissary store owners to raise the price of cheap staple foods and strongly discourage the use of the truck patch. Instead, sharecroppers were forced to forgo food production and plant cotton. Instances such as these, especially in the Delta, kept sharecroppers in poverty and solely dependent on white plantation owners for food provision, especially during "settlement time," when plantation owners took more than half of the profits from the cotton crop and money from supplies provided and totaled all the credit owed by sharecroppers.[15]

Third, to supplement the "furnish," Black sharecroppers would often use federal food programs, such as the federal surplus commodities program (and later, the Federal Food Stamp Program), which was supported by the Agricultural Adjustment Act (AAA) of 1933, as part of President Franklin D. Roosevelt's New Deal programs. Plantation owners relied heavily on these programs to feed their Black labor force during the winter months when the cotton crop had been harvested and no fieldwork was needed. In an effort to control agricultural prices and feed millions of hungry poor Americans during the Great Depression, the federal government purchased surplus foods to be distributed to these populations through county welfare agencies. In theory, the federal surplus commodities program was framed as a social welfare initiative designed to feed poor people foods such as canned meat, canned vegetables, flour, cornmeal, dry milk, cheese, and other nonperishable commodities. In practice, the program overwhelmingly benefited white farmers by providing price supports for them.[16] Moreover, states and counties had the option of whether or not to administer the programs, and in the Delta, the programs were controlled by county administrators who were plantation owners or businessmen who were active members or affiliates of the White Citizens' Council, the Delta-bred white supremacist organization. This organization, created in the wake of the 1954 *Brown v. Board of Education of Topeka* decision as a white response to civil rights activism, placed an economic chokehold on the Delta throughout the

1950s and 1960s.[17] Any Black sharecropper, farmworker, or employee discovered to be participating in civil rights efforts were forced, sometimes violently, to stop participating in efforts or be terminated from work.

When economic intimidation didn't work, food deprivation was used to ensure that Black sharecroppers would "stay in place" by not participating in civil rights efforts and by remaining dependent on the white power structure for their basic needs. Such instances, historian Greta de Jong posited, were part of a larger agenda of white supremacy that "encourage[d] African Americans to leave" the South so that "white leaders could avoid dealing with the social consequences of mechanization and minimize the threat of Black political power."[18] By the early 1960s, the social consequences and effects of mechanization began to significantly impact poor rural Black people who depended on the sharecropping system. Cotton production required more use of machines instead of Black labor, and many Black sharecroppers were forced off the land. As a result, sharecroppers were converted into day laborers or seasonal farmworkers who migrated to cities like Greenwood and traveled daily to work on plantations across the region. At the time, 100 percent of the Leflore County political offices were filled by white community leaders due to the fact that 95 percent of white people were registered to vote compared with less than 2 percent of Black people. These statistics were shaped by land ownership, which was deeply connected to regional electoral politics, and white people owned 90 percent of the county's land.[19]

Taken together, these demographics, coupled with the three intersecting ways that Black sharecroppers accessed food, reveal a civil rights food context that demonstrates how, as geographers Gloria Howerton and Amy Trauger argued, "uneven access to food is a function of intersecting social, political and economic factors."[20] Indeed, the prevalence of racial, social, economic, and political inequalities shaped the food realities of Black sharecroppers. This convergence created conditions by which over 22,000 Black people depended on the county's federal surplus commodities program while living in substandard housing and tar-paper shacks without floors or access to clean water, similar to plantation shotgun shacks—narrow one-story structures with rooms designed one behind another—that housed sharecroppers.[21] Closely observing this dire situation, groups such as SNCC and the Council of Federated Organizations (COFO)—the organization that represented all national, state, and local protest groups operating in the Mississippi including the state branches of SNCC, the NAACP, the Congress of Racial Equality (CORE), and the Southern Christian Leadership Conference (SCLC)—began organizing Black sharecroppers and agricultural workers around issues of political power.[22] Under the leadership of Mississippi NAACP president Aaron Henry, Bob Moses of SNCC, and Dave Dennis of CORE, COFO articulated a vision of liberation from the sharecropping system that required voting rights for those who worked the land and the group dominated the Mississippi civil rights agenda. COFO consistently documented acts of injustice and protested the dual organization of the South, which enforced white superiority and promoted Black inferiority.[23] Such efforts threatened the control of the all-white political establishment in the state.

To regain control, the all-white political establishment amplified its use of the tactics of economic reprisals and food deprivation as a way to disrupt civil rights efforts, especially in Black sharecropping communities. As activist L. C. Dorsey observed as the civil rights movement gained momentum in the Delta, "there was a subtle, gradual tightening down, you saw empty houses sitting out there because people had been let go, encouraged to leave. . . . There was this whole move to starve people out."[24] Even though the Black labor landscape of the state was rapidly changing due to the industrialization of cotton production, plantation owners held on to the sharecropping system so that they could continue to exert their dominance over Black sharecroppers, which profoundly shaped rural Black people's access to food. The racialized politics of uneven food access introduced new dynamics to the organizing tactics used by civil rights activists—forcing them to discuss white resistance not only as a form of physical violence but also as structural violence.[25] It is this backdrop of an unequal foodscape, compounded by changes in the Delta's agricultural economy and the intensification of racialized violent tensions in the wake of the fall 1962 crisis at the University of Mississippi when James Meredith was the first Black student admitted to the school, that perpetuated the circumstances and conditions that set the stage for the onset of the Greenwood Food Blockade.

Food Denied: The Onset of the Greenwood Food Blockade

The quiet decision made by the Leflore County Board of Supervisors to eliminate the federal surplus commodities program made the front page of the November 9, 1962, edition of the *Greenwood Commonwealth* under the headline "Leflore Won't Have Commodity Program."[26] To the mostly white readership of the newspaper, the article was major news that had no real impact on their daily lives. But for activists and the Black sharecropping communities, the headline intensified the struggle for civil rights in Greenwood. What made Greenwood so crucial was that it was the location of the national headquarters of the White Citizens' Council, which was just blocks away from the SNCC's Mississippi headquarters. The close proximity of these two opposing groups made Greenwood and the greater Leflore County area a major hotbed of both anti–civil rights and civil rights activities. In many respects, the Greenwood Food Blockade was a flashpoint in the Mississippi struggle for civil rights that incited a food crisis that emphasized Greenwood as a key battleground in the national movement.

Within a matter of months, by January 1963, the blockade had left at least 90 percent of the county recipients of the federal food program—totaled at over 20,000 participants—hungry and in need of food as retribution for voting rights activism in the region. "Many Negroes went . . . down to try to register, and white retaliation was proportionate," Aaron Henry wrote, "including standard reprisals of loss of employment, eviction from homes, denial of credit, and general intimidation."[27] Indeed, as Henry made clear, there were many "standard reprisals" that anyone who decided to join or support the movement could be at risk of encountering. Such "high-risk/cost forms of activism," as sociologist Doug McAdam put it, were to be expected in the movement.[28] But when food was introduced to the equation for civil rights in Greenwood, the rules of the struggle dramatically changed.

While activists in Leflore County were dealing with the blockade, their comrades in neighboring Sunflower County were dealing with a similar situation that winter. Drawing on a report about the Delta voter registration drive from SNCC field secretaries Charlie Cobb and Charles McLaurin in Sunflower County, SNCC's December 1962 *Student Voice* newspaper put it this way: "A new economic squeeze is being put on Negro citizens here. . . . Sharecroppers and day-laborers are finding it very difficult to obtain surplus government commodities."[29] Compounded by the fact that this was one of the coldest winters on record in the Delta, where at least two Black sharecroppers froze to death, the blockade was especially cruel.[30] Describing the winter conditions of rural Black communities and the need for food, SNCC organizers Willie Peacock and Sam Block in Greenwood sent a report to Executive Secretary James Forman in the organization's Atlanta office:

> These people here are in a very, very bad need for food and clothes. Look at a case like this man named Mr. Meeks, who is thirty-seven years old. His wife is thirty-three years old, and they have eleven children, ages ranging from seventeen down to eight months. Seven of the children are school age and not a one is attending school because they

have no money, no food, no clothes, and no wood to keep warm by, and they now want to go register. The house they are living in has no paper or nothing on the walls, and you can look at the ground through the floor and if you are not careful, you will step in one of those holes and break your leg.[31]

Such poor living conditions also created meager food conditions for poor rural Black people in Leflore County and across the Delta. Writing to Martha Prescod, a northern supporter in Ann Arbor, Michigan, Mississippi SNCC director Bob Moses vividly described the need for food in the area:

> We DO need the actual food. . . . Just this afternoon, I was sitting resting, having finished a bowl of stew, and a silent hand reached over from behind, [its owner] mumbling some words of apology and permission, and stumbled up with a neckbone from the plate under the bowl, which I had discarded, which had consequently some meat on it. The hand was back again, five seconds later, groping for the potatoes I had left in the bowl. I never saw the face. I didn't look. The hand was dark, dry, and wind-cracked, from the cotton chopping and cotton picking. Lafayette and I got up and walked out. What the hell are you going to do when a man has to pick up a left-over potato from a bowl of stew?[32]

These deteriorating living and poor food conditions were exacerbated by the Greenwood Food Blockade, and access to food via the federal surplus commodities program was crucial. As Charlie Cobb and Charles McLaurin concluded in their report, "Commodities are the only way many Negroes make it from cotton season to cotton season. If this is taken from them, they have nothing at all; and the success of our voter registration program depends on the protection we can offer the individual while he is waiting for his one small vote to become a part of a strong Negro vote. . . . The commodities are vital."[33] Aaron Henry summarized the entire situation going on in Greenwood and other parts of the Delta: "Many of the displaced people turned to the federal surplus food program, and it was clear that many would have starved without this assistance. But it was also clear to Leflore County officials . . . they [program participants] were either going to starve to death or capitulate to the pressures of the white community."[34]

Recognizing the link between an emerging food crisis and the struggle for civil rights in the Delta, Henry worked with SNCC and COFO to create a national food program one month after the blockade began. Operating under the banner of a program they called "Food for Freedom," this food drive provided a way for SNCC and COFO to articulate an early version of emancipatory food power in the movement. The Food for Freedom program was initially designed as a temporary solution that would lead to specific action toward correcting the food situation with three main goals: (1) to provide immediate aid to hungry Black sharecropping communities in the Delta, (2) to dramatize to the entire nation the plight of Black sharecroppers and their communities, and (3) to end the blockade.[35] To achieve these goals, SNCC and COFO created an alternative, translocal food campaign, network, and distribution system that operated at the national, regional, and local levels of the organizations to navigate food power politics.

Food for Freedom: Food Power Politics Takes Center Stage

In December 1962, just a few weeks after the beginning of the blockade, SNCC and COFO launched the Food for Freedom program. At the national level, then Howard University student and SNCC staff member William "Bill" Mahoney worked mostly behind the scenes as the architect of the food program. SNCC records reveal that Mahoney, communicating with people from Los Angeles to Chicago to Ann Arbor to New York City, developed a food network that secured not only food products but also medical supplies, clothing, and financial contributions to transport the supplies to those in need.[36] According to Mahoney, as he wrote to one northern supporter, "The food drive not only aid[s] the movement in the South, but also helps to communicate SNCC's program to people in the North."[37] He often used the Greenwood Food Blockade as a way to contextualize the Mississippi struggle to people in the North. As he and then SNCC chairman Charles McDew lamented in another letter to Congressman John Lindsay of New York, "Tens of thousands of Negroes in Mississippi have been denied government surplus food because some of them have participated in voter registration activity."[38] They wrote, "The Sharecroppers are not receiving wages or pay which would enable them to survive the winter. . . . The basis of the problem is related to automation and industrialization, and it is not a simple one. A major food drive may also bring to the forefront the need for a deeper, more meaningful solution."[39] By situating the growing food crisis in Leflore County and the Delta within a larger context of agricultural industrialization—against the backdrop of the social, economic, and political realities of Black sharecroppers—Mahoney and McDew's analysis made clear the complexity of the relationship between race, food, agriculture, power, and civil rights.

For the next several months, over 100 similar letters were sent out to groups and organizations across the nation that in some way restated Mahoney and McDew's analysis of food power politics. Churches were one of the first respondents to the need for food as Dr. Martin Luther King Jr. also spread the word about the food crisis in the Delta. "I am calling on supporters North, South, East, and West to gather staple goods in their communities through their churches to be sent to the Council of Federated Organizations (COFO). . .[in] Clarksdale, Mississippi," King proclaimed in a public statement.[40] College students, including two Black Michigan State University students, Benjamin Taylor and Ivanhoe Donaldson, also answered the call for food. For their efforts, Taylor and Donaldson were arrested by Mississippi police for attempting to deliver over ten loads of food and other supplies donated from communities in Ann Arbor, Michigan, and Louisville, Kentucky, that winter.[41] In southern California, a temporary group known as the "Compton Food for Freedom Committee" organized a "star-studded entertainment program" and benefit concert to raise food donations in support of the southern civil rights movement with an emphasis on Mississippi.[42]

In New York City, respondents to Mahoney's letter developed a Food for Freedom program that worked mainly with churches to secure over 50,000 pounds of food and clothing. This program even impacted the New York City borough of Manhattan's government. For instance, in April 1963, then borough president Edward R. Dudley declared April 6–13 "Food for Freedom Week."[43] Dudley's proclamation made clear that the Greenwood Food Blockade was an "inhuman program against a minority group which represents one out of ten United States citizens" that "brought thousands of men, women, and children in the Mississippi Delta to the verge of starvation in our land of plenty." As an indictment of the blockade, the New York City Food for Freedom Week was an effort to mobilize communities in the nation's largest city "to give maximum support to the Students Non-Violent Coordinating Committee [*sic*] and co-operating groups so that the fight by a minority for their Constitutional rights will not be hindered or stopped by near-starvation."[44]

National recognition from coast to coast brought in over 100,000 pounds of donated food and food products. Mrs. Vera Pigee of Clarksdale served as the director of the Food for Freedom program in the Delta and handled food distribution at the regional and local levels.[45] While Mahoney worked with churches, community groups, student organizations, and civil rights groups outside the South to secure food, Pigee organized the logistics and ensured that the food was distributed in Greenwood and other areas in the Delta facing similar hardships. As a local beautician, entrepreneur, and Coahoma County NAACP branch secretary and adviser to the organization's Youth Council, Pigee used her beauty shop as "an organizing site and a safe house for civil rights meetings," historian Françoise N. Hamlin observed.[46] Born into a family of sharecroppers in Tallahatchie County in the Delta, Pigee understood firsthand the realities of poor rural Black people dependent on the white power structure for their day-to-day needs. Growing up watching her mother Lucy Wright Berry be the leader of her family while "working the farm, raising livestock, growing vegetables, and exercising . . . a solid work ethic," Pigee developed her own leadership style in the context of what some scholars have described as "activist mothering" and "women's work."[47]

When read as just providing sustenance and taking care of the home, the work of Pigee's mother is often overshadowed or ignored altogether in that this work was to be expected of women. Such activities that are largely seen as the "invisible work," profoundly shaped the activist and mother that Pigee would become later. In many ways, Pigee represented the defining feature of activist mothering, which is the "overlap of mothering practices, political activism, and community work."[48] By using her beauty shop as a community space, site of political activism, and food warehouse, while providing "shelter" for activists and poor rural Black people, Pigee was emblematic of activist mothering and women's work. Pigee was also an example of how, as Psyche Williams-Forson argued, "working-class and poor black women who struggled to define themselves" in a society that overlooked them used food as a tool to shape their own lives and communities.[49] As Hamlin put it, "Pigee's role in the local movement shows that black women utilized their everyday social roles (in her case as a mother) to promote activism and radical change."[50]

In many respects, Pigee was representative of the many local Black women and other actors who did the invisible, behind-the-scenes work of leading and taking care of their communities and organizing efforts to achieve movement goals. As a key leader in the Food for Freedom program, Pigee worked alongside Aaron Henry, Dave Dennis, and Annell Ponder, who had been sent to Greenwood in the spring of 1963 by the SCLC to help organize citizenship schools.[51] Together, they developed and set up Food for Freedom distribution centers in conjunction with local Black communities in Clarksdale (Coahoma County), Ruleville (Sunflower County), and Greenwood (Leflore County). Since these three towns had become "the sites for a coordinated movement in Mississippi (sites of intense protest and voter registration)," political scientist Minion Morrison observed, these communities created the necessary space for the food program.[52] Each town selected community members, local leaders, and activists to designate and oversee the food distribution centers. In Clarksdale, Pigee and Henry selected the Haven United Methodist Church as the main food distribution center.[53] In Ruleville, civil rights activist and founder of the Freedom Farms Cooperative Fannie Lou Hamer used her home as a food for freedom checkpoint and regularly distributed food to her neighborhood.[54]

In Greenwood, Willie Peacock was named the chair of the SNCC Greenwood food relief committee and organized its food program. Peacock, a native of Tallahatchie County, which borders Leflore County to the North in the Delta, understood firsthand the blockade's impact on the conditions of Black sharecroppers in the area. He worked with community members to select the Wesley United Methodist Church as Greenwood's main food distribution center.[55] Located several blocks away from the headquarters of the White Citizens' Council, the Wesley United Methodist Church transformed their basement Sunday school room into a food hub. This hub was where older Black women such as Ella Edwards, Essie Broom, and Peggy Mayre worked with young women like Greenwood native Freddie Greene, who was too young to vote at time, to organize and distribute the food.[56] Many of these women were only identified and known by name in sources surrounding the blockade. Yet they played a critical role in securing and distributing food, which connected the local struggle to the national movement. Together, these women continued Ella Baker's "community organizing tradition" by cultivating agency through community food distribution designed to mitigate, and in some cases eradicate, the dependence of Black sharecropping communities on the white power structure for their most basic needs.[57]

While Willie Peacock provided the leadership for SNCC's Food for Freedom distribution program in Greenwood, Black women were the backbone of the entire operation in the city. Within two months from its inception in December 1962, the Food for Freedom program had successfully developed an active food distribution system and program that addressed the needs of those marginalized by the blockade. This web of organizing at the national, state, and local level not only provided sustenance for communities marginalized by the blockade but also was a tool of resistance to a racial hierarchy designed to dismantle Black insurgency in the state. It attracted national attention and received coverage by Black reporters such as *Jet* magazine's Larry Still, who wrote about the conditions surrounding the blockade and the importance of the Food for Freedom program in the February 21, 1963, edition of the publication.[58] But the most important local and national coverage came from the actions of prominent Black comedian

Mrs. Ella Edwards stacking cans of food donated through the Food for Freedom program in a Sunday school room of Wesley United Methodist Church, Greenwood, Mississippi, 1963. (Claude Sitton/ *New York Times*/Redux)

and entertainer Dick Gregory and his work with the Chicago Area Friends of SNCC group.

In late January 1963, as a member of the Chicago Area Friends of SNCC group, Gregory helped circulate a flyer with the words "GIVE FOOD for FREEDOM in Mississippi!" across the top of it, as part of a campaign to raise food for those impacted by the blockade. This ten-day campaign lasted from February 1 to 10 and was the first of many in Chicago. It raised over ten tons of food—including dried beans, rice, cornmeal, and canned meats—and other supplies across its thirteen "Food for Freedom collection depots," including several locations in communities on the South Side and West Side of Chicago.[59] Although Gregory had been involved in civil rights causes in Mississippi, such as the tragic Clyde Kennard case, he became heavily involved in civil rights in Mississippi and across the South after hearing the news of the blockade.[60] As one of the Chicago Area Friends of SNCC's most influential members, Gregory took the lead in ensuring that the food collected made it to the Food for Freedom distribution centers in the Delta. Using his celebrity status, he galvanized people in the Delta and across the nation around the relationship between issues of food, integration, and voting rights. With his unwavering confidence, Gregory became a moving target of the Mississippi white power structure, since his actions simultaneously increased the visibility of the Food for Freedom program and threatened the power of Mississippi's political establishment to maintain unequal conditions exacerbated by the blockade.

For example, Gregory publicly charged—across several national media outlets—the state's white power structure with stopping the federal surplus commodities program in response to an increase in voting rights demonstrations.[61] As a result, the white power structure forced the Mississippi Advisory Committee to the US Commission on Civil Rights to investigate Gregory's charges. Although the committee found "no racial issue involved" in the dismantling of the federal surplus commodities program in Leflore County, Gregory and other activists maintained their stance.[62] As a result, Gregory became the main culprit of "racial agitation" in the state, and the political establishment publicly charged him with "invading" the state with food.[63]

Dick Gregory's Mississippi "Food Invasion"

At a February 14, 1963, press conference held in Jackson, then Mississippi public welfare commissioner Fred A. Ross charged Dick Gregory and other "racial agitation promoters" with spreading "half-truths and outright lies"

GIVE FOOD for FREEDOM in Mississippi!

As you read this, thousands of Mississippi citizens face starvation because some of them dared to register as voters. In retaliation, Mississippi officials have withdrawn support from the U.S. surplus food distribution program on which these families must rely for subsistence during the winter.

Food for Freedom collection depots are located at:

Hyde Park
Ald. Despres
1217 E. 55th St.

Kenwood
Community Church
4608 S. Greenwood
Menonite Church
46th and Woodlawn

Woodlawn
First Presbyterian Church
6401 S. Woodlawn Ave.

South Side
Packinghouse Workers of Am.
4859 S. Wabash
Faultless Cleaners
205 E. 55th St.
L & L Cleaners
508 E. 43rd St.
Ernest's Chicken Shack
105 E. 51st St.
Shiloh Baptist Church
6201 S. May

Loop
Roosevelt Univ.
430 S. Michigan

Evanston
Democratic Org.
610 Dempster

Maywood
2nd Baptist Ch.
13th and Wash.

Lawndale
Cherokee Hotel
3307 W. Douglas

The hungry families of Mississippi appeal to all who support their fight for the right to vote to help them survive.

Volunteers bearing credentials will visit your neighborhood to collect your contribution of food or money. **FEBRUARY 1 - 10**

OPEN YOUR DOOR, YOUR HEART AND YOUR PURSE TO SUPPORT THE FIGHT FOR FREEDOM IN MISSISSIPPI!

Foods in greatest need are staples: flour, corn meal, rice, cereals, sugar, powdered milk, dried beans, cooking fats and canned meat products.

All contributions will be forwarded immediately to the Student Non-Violent Coordinating Committee which is spearheading the Mississippi Voter Registration campaign.

funds may be sent to

CHICAGO AREA FRIENDS OF SNCC
Charles Fischer,
treasurer
1316 E. Madison Pk.

for information
call: 493-2473

SPONSORING COMMITTEE (in formation)

Willoughby Abner
Mr. and Mrs. Edwin C. Berry
Dr. Leonidas Berry
Rev. Ulysses B. Blakely
Oscar Brown Jr.
Dr. and Mrs. Oliver Crawford
Hon. Leon Despres
Dr. Arthur Falls
Dick Gregory
Charles Hayes
Ralph Helstein
Prof. and Mrs. Walter Johnson
Misch Kohn
Laurence Landry
Russell R. Lasley
H. B. Law
Rev. C. T. Leber
Hon. Robert Miller
Rev. Owen Pelt
Rev. Howard Schomer
Rev. Douglas Still
Mrs. Fred Walker
Mr. and Mrs. Bernard Weissbourd
Dr. Quentin Young

Chicago Area Friends of SNCC Food for Freedom Flyer, circa 1963. (Chicago SNCC [Student Nonviolent Coordinating Committee] History Project Archives, [box 3, folder 4], Chicago Public Library, Woodson Regional Library, Vivian G. Harsh Research Collection of Afro-American History and Literature)

about hunger and the food blockade in the Delta. As a response to several inquiries from northern reporters about the Food for Freedom program, the press conference signaled the strong resistance of Ross and the state to the civil rights movement. "Dick Gregory, Martin Luther King, the Congress of Racial Equality, the Student Non-Violent Coordinating Committee, and similar racial agitation promoters are rendering a disservice to the Negro Population in Mississippi," Ross lamented to the press. "The cheap publicity generated by Gregory, and the gullibility of national news media . . . may result in the surplus food commodity program in Mississippi being seriously curtailed or wiped out entirely."[64] What angered Ross about the food drive had less to do with the food itself and more to do with the fact that such efforts laid bare the plight of Black sharecroppers at the hands of the white power structure in the Delta and attempted to disrupt the racial hierarchy of Mississippi. Such efforts placed a spotlight on the Greenwood Food Blockade, which acted as the catalyst for the Food for Freedom program. As a result, the racialized politics of food were at the forefront of civil rights tensions. Ross viewed such politics as part of a larger smear campaign against Mississippi, developed by activists and national media outlets in places like Chicago and New York.

Even prior to Ross's press conference, several prominent Mississippi newspapers, including the *Greenwood Commonwealth* and the *Jackson Advocate,* had already begun to run several stories reporting on what some described as Dick Gregory's Mississippi "food invasion" as a way to discredit the Food for Freedom program and downplay the blockade. For example, the Saturday, February 9 edition of the *Greenwood Commonwealth* ran its top story under the headline "Negro Here Hits 'Food Publicity.'" Written by reporter Thatcher Walt, the story denied that poor rural Black people and sharecroppers in Leflore County were suffering from hunger at the hands of the county board of supervisors. To support this claim, Walt used commentary on SNCC's food drive from a "Negro who asked not to be identified" who "came forward voluntarily." Walt wrote that his informant claimed that the food "isn't really needed" and that "nobody is destitute that we know of." The informant also stated that "the Negroes only object to the way publicity against Leflore County is being generated by statements of Dick Gregory." Walt concluded his article by writing, "This newspaper is satisfied that [the informant] speaks for a substantial group of Leflore County Negroes. He made the statement in the presence of several leading white citizens."[65]

Likewise, just one week later, the February 16, 1963, edition of the *Jackson Advocate* ran a story under the front-page headline "Dick Gregory Negro

Comic Invades State with Foods," where a reporter further denied Gregory's charge that the federal surplus commodities program in Leflore County was discontinued because of civil rights demonstrations. The reporter wrote, "County officials who are backed by the Mississippi Advisory Committee to the US Commission on Civil Rights deny any charges that the Surplus Food program has been withdrawn from Negroes because of voter activities. The program halted . . . because it was being abused."[66] What is interesting about the reports of program abuse uncovered by the Mississippi Advisory Committee is that they undermine the so-called budgetary considerations that the Leflore County Board of Supervisors used to end the county's surplus commodities program. Regardless of these conflicting reasons, a few days later, the *Advocate* ran another story on February 23, 1963, under the headline "Dick Gregory Food Invasion Turns Out to Be Laffing Stock." In this article, the reporter characterized Dr. Martin Luther King Jr. as an opportunist who "issued a nation-wide call for funds and food to help feed the thousands of starving Negroes in the state being victimized because of their efforts to register and vote by suffering the withdrawal of surplus Food Commodities." The reporter concluded, "Here in the state the facts stand out, and are well known by intelligent people of both races. . . . There is no known case of starvation of even one Negro anywhere in the state."[67] The constant denial of the blockade-induced food insecurity in the Delta and the targeting of Gregory, Dr. Martin Luther King Jr., and other "racial agitation" promoters exacerbated the conditions surrounding the blockade and cemented the foundation of the food crisis which local, state, and national actors struggled to navigate.

Despite the performative outrage of Mississippi's media and political establishment to divert attention from the effects of the Greenwood Food Blockade or ignore the event altogether, the Food for Freedom program tremendously enhanced SNCC's voter registration efforts. As Bob Moses put it when he wrote in his February 1963 "Letter to Northern Supporters" about the status of the Food for Freedom program, "The food drive you organized and publicized with the help of Dick Gregory and others has resulted in and served as the immediate catalyst for opening new dimensions in the voter registration movement in Mississippi. . . . The food is identified in the minds of everyone as food for those who want to be free, and the minimum requirement for freedom is identified as registration to vote."[68] What made the Food for Freedom program so important, according to Moses, had less to do with the food itself and more to do with how food could be used to support the movement. Indeed, food opened "new dimensions" in the movement as activists connected the Food for Freedom program to the over 150 Black people who went to the Leflore County courthouse in Greenwood to register to vote between February 25 and February 26. A few weeks later in March, over 400 Black people registered to vote in Leflore County, which was one of the largest voter registration turnouts in Greenwood and across any area in the South at the time.[69] Observing these new dynamics, Bob Moses concluded, "This is a new dimension for a voting program in Mississippi. . . . We don't know this plateau at all . . . but who knows what's to come next. The weather breaks in mid-April and I hope you will be able to continue to send food until then."[70] By recognizing the power of food, Bob Moses saw the food drive as a critical organizing strategy that had virtually been untapped in the Mississippi struggle for civil rights and throughout the national movement.

At the same time, activists used the Food for Freedom program as a mobilizing space to apply political pressure to federal government agencies to intervene and end the Greenwood Food Blockade. Activists in Mississippi and beyond worked together to simultaneously secure food and raise public awareness about the blockade. They even staged protests in Washington, D.C., at the US Department of Agriculture (USDA) and the US Department of Justice to build momentum.[71] Such protests culminated in the circulation of a report on Leflore County in early March 1963 written by civil rights activist Constancia Romilly. In the report, Romilly stated that at the behest of SNCC and other civil rights groups in Mississippi, "government action be taken to insure [*sic*] the sharecroppers of Leflore County surplus food and that if present rules prevent distribution of government surplus food to the needy, that the rules be changed with a stroke of the Secretary of Agriculture's pen."[72] Romilly's report contributed to the lobbying efforts of members of Congress from as far as Michigan and representatives of the NAACP in Washington, D.C., who petitioned federal intervention in the blockade.[73] Within days the US Department of Agriculture and Department of Justice opened investigations into the Greenwood Food Blockade and sent representatives to Greenwood to meet with the Leflore County Board of Supervisors.

"This Was a Time to Resist": The Greenwood Food Blockade Ends

On Tuesday, March 19, 1963, Mississippi public welfare commissioner Fred A. Ross and Department of Agriculture representatives James A.

Hutchins, director of distribution, and Russell H. James, area field supervisor, traveled to Greenwood to hold a special session with the Leflore County Board of Supervisors. The purpose of the session was to discuss a federal proposal to fund the reinstatement of the county's surplus commodities program as a way to remedy the food crisis instigated by the blockade. Yet the county board of supervisors opposed such accusations of a food crisis and maintained its position that there was "no actual need for food distribution."[74] Although Hutchins responded to the board's stance by sharing a report by the US Department of Justice that found a great need for surplus food in the area, the board continued to deny the crisis. The board believed that the report was fabricated by "professional agitators who had issued public releases that many Negroes were starving and hungry in the county."[75]

After several discussions about the report and the food problem, one member of the Leflore County Board of Supervisors asked what would happen if the county chose not to accept the USDA's proposal. Mr. Hutchins informed them that if they chose not to accept the proposal, the "Federal Government would move in, take charge of the program and distribute the commodities whether the Board of Supervisors agreed to it or not." Viewing this move by the federal government to intervene as a pending "invasion by Federal agents and probably marshals," the board acceded to the demands of civil rights activists and the federal government, ending the Greenwood Food Blockade. Within this agreement, the board was forced to administer the program "even though the Board is of the opinion that it is unnecessary," they stated in a press release, "and will have adverse effects upon the economy of the county and its general welfare." They concluded, "The Board of Supervisors calls upon all the citizens of the county to cooperate in its action in making this decision and assures all citizens that it was done in order to prevent Leflore County, Mississippi, and its citizens from being subjected to the ruthless invasion of Federal Agents."[76]

Angered by the decision of the board to accede to the demands of the civil rights activists and the federal government, Thatcher Walt ran a story the very next day under the headline "Pressured Supervisors Vote for Commodities" across the front page of the March 20, 1963, *Greenwood Commonwealth*. Below this headline were the words "This Was a Time to Resist," preceding an opinion column by Walt. Linking the decision to President John F. Kennedy's involvement in the struggle for civil rights, Walt concluded that the forced decision to reinstate the federal surplus commodities program "tends to prove that a naked political sword from the Kennedy arsenal in Washington has flashed into Leflore County to encourage the groups of racial agitators now operating here. . . . The power move by the federal government should have been resisted."[77] Reprinted beneath Walt's comments was the board's statement about the reinstatement of the program, which publicly ended the Greenwood Food Blockade. Two days later, in an internal newsletter, SNCC reported that the board's decision "came after protests at government agencies in Washington, a three-month campaign by SNCC to collect food and clothing for dispossessed Delta Negroes, and pressure from the Agriculture Department."[78] By March 22, 1963, the first shipment of surplus food was delivered and was scheduled to be distributed by the county around April 1, 1963.[79] The Greenwood Food Blockade had finally ended; however, SNCC continued its Food for Freedom program the rest of the year, recognizing the importance of being committed to addressing the day-to-day food and other pressing realities of Black sharecroppers, their families, and communities in the Delta.[80]

Conclusion

The Leflore County Board of Supervisors' forced decision to reinstate the federal surplus commodities program ended the Greenwood Food Blockade. For many activists and community members, this decision was "a great victory for those seeking to bring democracy to Mississippi," SNCC executive secretary James Forman remarked.[81] While the end of the blockade led to a significant increase in the number of participants in voting rights efforts, it also revealed the strength of transformative grassroots action and cross-geographic political pressure with food at the center. Motivated by the Food for Freedom program, such action profoundly reshaped the early days of the 1960s struggle for civil rights in Mississippi and throughout the nation. Indeed, all eyes were on the Delta between 1962 and 1963 as it became a breeding ground for a civil rights struggle that brought food power politics to the forefront of the movement.

In many ways, the end of the Greenwood Food Blockade demonstrated the power of organizing a multilevel food campaign, system, and program—Food for Freedom. What differentiated this program from previous initiatives is that it included actors from the bottom up and from the top down who envisioned a food program that would shield poor rural Black communities and sharecroppers in the Delta from the impact of sociopolitical struggle. At the same time, the food program allowed SNCC to link an isolated narrative of Black political inequality to the inadequacies of a federal program designed to feed poor people. This narrative made clear the often-overlooked relationship between food, everyday Black resistance, white supremacy, and state-sanctioned violence during the civil rights era. The narrative also revealed to the members of SNCC's leadership who were from outside Mississippi how entrenched Black food access was in the region's racial hierarchy. Due to the strong focus on securing voting rights as a path toward freedom, food was often ignored until the blockade. By connecting food and civil rights, activists used food—as sustenance and symbolism—through protests and programming, which resulted in the reinstatement of the federal surplus commodities program that ended the blockade.

Tremendously inspired by the mobilization of communities through food efforts across the nation in response to the blockade, SNCC used its annual leadership conference as a vehicle to place the food and economic concerns of Black sharecroppers at the forefront of movement politics. Led by William "Bill" Mahoney, who single-handedly worked out the logistics of the Food for Freedom program at the national level, SNCC's fourth annual leadership conference in November 1963 took on the theme "Food and Jobs."[82] At the time, it was the largest-attended conference in SNCC's history. Just months following the August 1963 March on Washington and less than a week after the assassination of President John F. Kennedy, over 500 participants traveled to Howard University for the conference. Noted Black author James Baldwin delivered the keynote address, and March on Washington deputy director Bayard Rustin discussed emerging perspectives in the movement.[83] SNCC chairman and civil rights leader John Lewis commented that the conference was a place to strategize around questions regarding "the economic deprivation of the disenfranchised Negroes in the South . . . [and] the programs available to bring about basic changes in the economic and political system which holds Negroes enslaved."[84]

Moreover, the "Food and Jobs" conference raised awareness about "some of the basic problems encountered by [SNCC] workers in the field: providing jobs and food for the people of depressed rural areas," the conference program read.[85] Recognizing mechanization as a major movement background variable that dramatically decreased the need for Black labor and agricultural workers, the conference placed a special emphasis on "specific problems of the small farmer . . . [and] the plight of the Negro in Mississippi."[86] Describing this particular situation as "The Agricultural Dilemma" at the conference, Fay Bennett discussed how sharecroppers were being displaced by machines.[87] As the national secretary of the National Sharecropper Fund, Bennett advocated for the need for SNCC to pressure federal agencies such as the USDA to work with rural Black agricultural workers to remedy issues that impeded their economic and social progress.[88] Inspired by such conversations, some activists organized Black farmers in Mississippi and across the South to run for county office in the USDA's Agricultural Stabilization and Conservation Service (ASCS) agency.[89]

In the months following the "Food and Jobs" conference, SNCC never developed a sustained interest in the politics of food at the national level. This was due, in part, to the fact that SNCC's food agenda was superseded by organizing efforts to prepare for Freedom Summer of 1964. At the same time, the successes of 1964 and 1965, which rendered racial segregation in public spaces illegal and earned Black people voting rights, respectively, marked another significant shift in the movement. On the ground in the Delta, though, the aftermath of the Greenwood Food Blockade lingered. Food power politics had cultivated a fertile soil for new articulations of unforeseen white opposition to the movement. Such opposition was motivated by the advent of the Federal Food Stamp Program in the Delta. As such, food stamps became another battleground for movement activists. Their opponents this time were a familiar yet largely overlooked powerful actor in the Delta's food environment: white grocery store owners. Such opposition to the movement became clear during the onset of the Federal Food Stamp Program, signed into law by President Lyndon B. Johnson in August 1964, that altered the rules of the Mississippi civil rights struggle yet again. This time activists were confronted with how food power in the context of food stamps, demonstrated in the relationship between white grocery store owners and powerful white politicians that represented Mississippi at the federal level in Washington, D.C., shaped intense levels of food insecurity in Black sharecropping communities in the Delta. As the national struggle for civil rights celebrated legislative victories surrounding the Civil Rights Act of 1964 and the Voting Rights Act of 1965, activists and the Mississippi communities in which they worked situated food stamp policy as a focal point of the movement, illuminating a new dimension of oppression with food at the center.

CHAPTER TWO

Another Kind of Oppression

Civil Rights, Food Stamps, and the Segrenomics of the Lewis Grocer Company

> These people have been trying to trick us a long time. A few years ago, they were shooting us; so what they decided to do is to starve us out of the state. So overnight, after they redistricted us and done all this kind of crap, they decided in Sunflower County to give us [food] stamps. Now, they know if a man wasn't able to buy, goes to pick up his free food with fifty cents, how in the world can he buy a stamp? So this is another kind of oppression.
>
> —FANNIE LOU HAMER

In November 1962, as civil rights activists organized in response to the Greenwood Food Blockade, the Delta-based Lewis Grocer Company, Mississippi's largest wholesale grocery corporation at the time, launched a campaign to influence the state's white political power structure to implement the Federal Food Stamp Program in Mississippi. This campaign was designed to mobilize 400 store owners—who received their supply from the Lewis Grocer Company—to indict the state and federal government for attempting to put the region's commercial food industry out of business through the distribution of surplus foods. The campaign began when Morris Lewis Jr., president of the Lewis Grocer Company, penned a November 15, 1962, internal memo to the company's grocery retailer clients, describing the distribution of surplus foods as "a disgrace to the county, the State of Mississippi, and the Federal Government" that forced "the Federal Government to enter the food business in competition with tax paying food retailers and wholesalers in the state."[1] Lewis, a pioneer in the nation's commercial food industry and leader in the economic development of the Delta, virtually controlled the entire commercial food environment of the region. He was also a financial supporter of the Mississippi legislature-sanctioned Mississippi State Sovereignty Commission, an organization that worked to preserve segregation, protect the Magnolia State from federal intervention, and used public funds to support the White Citizens' Council, the Delta's emblematic white supremacist organization.[2] Therefore, to rectify the surplus food issue, Lewis concluded his memo with a call to action, empowering grocers in the Lewis Grocer pipeline to pressure their all-white local county board of supervisors to petition the state to request the Federal Food Stamp Program.

Lewis's internal memo dispatched his network of grocery store owners in the company's supply chain to overcome government competition through local government so that the food would be distributed through "proper channels"—established commercial food stores. Historian J. Todd Moye argues that white grocers like Lewis were angered by perceived government competition in food distribution because, in their eyes, "every commodity that the government gave poor blacks was a commodity off of which the grocers could not make profit."[3] While the Lewis Grocer Company's internal memo did not include any reference to race, Lewis's argument for how to get food stamps implemented in the state required white grocers to pressure their local county board of supervisors, who operated according to a rubric of white supremacy. Any legislative or policy changes, including issues such as food stamps at the local level, were decided through the prism of the region's racialized sociopolitical context—shaped by capitalism, representative democracy, and white supremacy. Situating the Lewis Grocer Company's disdain for the distribution of surplus foods within this racialized sociopolitical context reveals that the food stamp program was much more than a vehicle for increased profit.

In some respects, Lewis's internal memo echoed some debates surrounding the development of the 1939–43 food stamp program. In the beginning, as part of the planning stages for the 1939–43 food stamp program, the program was designed to solely aid farmers by providing another market for surplus food.[4] But the final operation of the program was framed by public discourses that situated federal food assistance as a form of unemployment relief during the Great Depression. Created by the US Department of Agriculture's (USDA) Federal Surplus Commodities Corporation (FSCC), the same agency that designed the federal surplus commodities program that distributed food to poor families and fueled the national school lunch program, among other federal food programs, the 1939–43 food stamp program proved to benefit not only farmers but also retail grocers.[5] Shaped by advocates of federal food assistance and key actors in the retail food industry, contrasting public discourses emphasized the inadequacies of the direct distribution of surplus farm products to poor families. Advocates of federal food assistance critiqued the surplus food program for its inability to ensure that poor people had consistent access to food and for the lack of nutritious food provided. In the eyes of the retail food industry, the distribution of surplus farm products to poor families created government competition that threatened the vitality of private wholesalers and grocery stores around the nation. Through strong lobbying power and efforts, the retail food industry influenced the federal government to authorize a federal food stamp program that enabled surplus food distribution to be facilitated through regular business channels.[6]

The significant difference between the food stamp program and other federal food assistance programs was that food stamps were a form of *indirect* food distribution. Instead of poor families receiving food directly from the government through direct food distribution schemes, such as the federal surplus commodities program, they were required to purchase paper stamps to procure food through economic transactions sanctioned by the government and facilitated by grocers and merchants. These transactions enabled grocery retailers to collect stamps and redeem them for cash from local banks or wholesalers, which contributed to additional income for the retailer.[7] In May 1939, the first Federal Food Stamp Program was initiated in Rochester, New York, and provided poor families with two separate yet interconnected food stamps—one orange and the other blue. Orange stamps were valued at one dollar each and were purchased by eligible families to buy any food, as long as the number of stamps purchased did not exceed their normal food purchases. In exchange for purchasing orange stamps, families received blue stamps for free. Blue stamps, valued at fifty cents each, supplemented orange stamps at a ratio of one blue stamp to two orange stamps and could only be used to buy foods outlined by the USDA as surplus. This two-stamp system cost the federal government $261 million and operated in almost half of the counties in the United States, serving an estimated 4 million people annually. The remaining counties continued to rely on the direct distribution of surplus food to provide unemployment relief for the poor.[8]

While the existence of the 1939–43 food stamp program was cut short by a reduction in the availability of surplus farm products due to World War II efforts and a decline in unemployment levels, the program set the stage for President John F. Kennedy's first executive order in 1961 that created the civil rights–era Federal Food Stamp Program. Beginning as a pilot program, the new food stamp program, known today as the USDA's Supplemental Nutrition Assistance Program (SNAP), replaced the two-stamp system with food coupons that families could purchase. Based primarily on household income, the cost of food coupons per family was specified by the USDA, and the program was administered at the local level by state welfare agencies that designed the criteria that deemed families eligible to purchase food coupons. The coupons could be used to purchase any food except those that were imported.[9] In 1964, the food stamp program became a key part of President Lyndon B. Johnson's War on Poverty when he signed the program into law under the Food Stamp Act of 1964. By signing the Food Stamp Act of 1964, Johnson continued the work of Kennedy and ensured that the food stamp program would be a permanent part of American life. According to Johnson, the food stamp program was one of America's "most valuable weapons for the war on poverty" that promised to "rais[e] the diets of low-income families substantially while strengthening markets for the farmer and immeasurably improving the volume of retail food sales." President Johnson envisioned food stamps as a type of currency that would give poor Americans more "freedom" by "using their own dollars" in their food purchases.[10]

From the perspective of civil rights activists such as Fannie Lou Hamer, though, the Federal Food Stamp Program was "another kind of oppression." Indirectly connecting the plight of Black sharecroppers to ongoing Black voter registration efforts, Hamer argued that the food stamp program contributed to the systematic undermining of Black agrarian social mobilization, self-determination, agency, and autonomy in the acquisition of food and in everyday life in the Delta. Hamer knew that local white elected officials would decide the terms by which the program would be administered without any consideration of the mostly Black participants. But if Black people had the right to vote, she argued, they "could elect the people that we desire to be in office [and] people wouldn't be starving in the Delta where we outnumber the white in places five to one. They wouldn't have to starve, hungry white children, hungry black children."[11] At the same time, Hamer knew that Black sharecroppers in the Delta's plantation economy would be unable to meet the income requirement to purchase food stamps to buy food, let alone control the process implemented to access federal food assistance. In a plantation economy, agricultural production configures the social, political, and economic life of a region, usually centered on a particular crop such as cotton in the Delta. This plantation economy, like others across the South, Katherine McKittrick argues, "thrived on the interlocking workings of violence, black dispossession, and land exploitation."[12] These interlocking workings simulated white supremacy and compounded the swift changes in the plantation economy that led to machines replacing Black hands—deeming Black sharecroppers and agrarian workers useless in the agricultural industry of the region. While the plantation economy surrendered its use of Black labor around the same time that the Federal Food Stamp Program was implemented in the Delta, the plantation as "an uneven colonial-racial economy" that "legalized Black servitude" continued to shape the economic lives of landless Black sharecroppers.[13] As such, without income and with no jobs in the plantation economy, it was virtually impossible for thousands of poor, rural Black people who were employed by plantation owners to meet the income requirement to purchase food stamps to buy food.

The National Association for the Advancement of Colored People's (NAACP) 1967 report *Mississippi: Poverty, Despair—A Way of Life* reinforced claims made by Hamer and activists regarding the food stamp program in the Delta. Based on evidence from 117 interviews and photographic documentation of conditions, the NAACP declared that the transition from surplus food to food stamps "was the greatest single threat" to Black sharecroppers and their families in the Delta.[14] They found that when the food stamp program was put into effect in the Delta, Black sharecroppers who were on food assistance became more food insecure because they were unable to make the minimum purchase of two dollars per person for food stamps. In Leflore County, for example, within two months of the start of the food stamp program, Black sharecroppers were among the 12,420 people who were dropped from federal food assistance in 1966 with no other means to access food. Across the state, 64,000 people were removed from federal food assistance in 1967.[15] The NAACP also reported that Black sharecroppers were at the mercy of the local departments of welfare and plantation owners to obtain stamps for food.

Scholars tend to approach questions surrounding the advent of food stamps and the ensuing food crisis during the movement along the same lines as civil rights activists and organizations—through the lens of how the legislation impacted communities and its consequences. They focus on rural Black communities, sharecroppers, plantation owners, welfare offices, and government officials. But what about regional white grocery companies like the Lewis Grocer Company? What role did they play in the advent of food stamps? What can we learn about the civil rights movement when we place white grocers at the center? Throughout civil rights history in general and Mississippi movement history in particular, white grocers remain relatively invisible in that they are only accused of raising food prices in the wake of food stamp legislation. To be sure, activists like L. C. Dorsey knew that the creation of the food stamp program, as she put it, "would benefit the merchants and not necessarily the families, and especially families that had no means of income."[16]

What must be added to this view of white grocers, and what this chapter shows is that white grocers in the Delta transformed food stamps into an economic weapon to maintain their control in the face of a changing agricultural economy and civil rights struggle in the Delta that threatened commercial food distribution. In other words, white grocers transformed food into an economic instrument to sustain profit-driven white control in regional food distribution. This form of food power demonstrates how what Noliwe Rooks describes as "segrenomics, or the business of profiting specifically from high levels of racial and economic segregation," operated in the Delta's commercial food environment.[17] This level of segrenomics allowed white grocers to reconfigure how the mostly poor rural Black families that were dependent on the plantation economy for income accessed food through federal food assistance in the region. In many instances, this created two different shopping experiences—along racial and economic lines. White patrons were treated as paying customers who were able to exercise autonomy in their food purchases and experienced an uninterrupted food shopping experience. In contrast, poor Black plantation workers were stripped of their agency in obtaining food at grocery stores and were forced to use food stamps, which allowed white grocers to regulate and limit the types of food that these Black patrons could buy and eat. As such, segrenomics perpetuated by white grocers was in direct conflict with what the civil rights movement sought to do—give Black folks the ability to control their entire lives.

I develop this argument through a case study of the Lewis Grocer Company's food stamp campaign that places the company at the center of the advent of food stamps during the civil rights movement. The campaign provides a view of food power politics from a top-down perspective in that it emphasizes the process by which food was weaponized against Black communities in their struggle for civil rights. It began with the November 15, 1962, internal memo written by Lewis; by 1964, the memo took on a life of its own as it moved from the hands of white grocers to the media to segregationist federal officials who represented Mississippi in Washington, D.C., who contributed to the passage of the 1964 Federal Food Stamp Act. When food stamps were phased into the Delta, the Lewis Grocer Company continued to be involved in food stamp politics as proponents of the civil rights movement denounced the program, producing a new level of conflict with the movement. But, as this case study reveals, the Lewis Grocer Company's food stamp campaign was part of a longer history of white supremacy in the Delta's food system that can be traced back to the development of plantation commissaries in the region. Geographically, the "plantation logics" of commissaries bring into focus the material ways in which Black sharecroppers on former slave plantations accessed food as central to their life on plantations.[18] Commissaries also provide a window into questions about how such spaces were maintained in tandem with businesses like the Lewis Grocer Company—hinting at an often-overlooked relationship between plantation culture and grocery stores. At the same time, commissaries were also spaces that produced uneven power, which, in the context of this chapter, adds a layer of complexity to narratives of the civil rights movement that sheds a critical light on hidden sources of power, in the hands of unlikely actors like white grocers.

Working with rarely used archival materials, newspapers, legislative hearings, correspondences, and scholarly sources, this chapter shows how such food power wielded by white grocers undermined not only the civil rights movement but also the ability of Black people to evoke agency and autonomy in food provisioning. The chapter begins with a brief history of the Lewis Grocer Company to demonstrate how white supremacy was produced in the Delta's commercial food system. This history narrates how the Lewis Grocer Company single-handedly transformed the Delta's commissary-based food system and ushered in the rise of grocery stores—rooted in the region's plantation economy and sharecropping system. Then, the chapter analyzes the Lewis Grocer Company's campaign for food stamps and traces the early history of 1960s food stamp legislation. This analysis illuminates how segrenomics shaped the advent of food stamps and, in effect, reshaped the civil rights movement in the Delta. To illustrate the impact of this campaign and the advent of food stamps in the Delta, I draw on the voices of Black women activists that shed light on the impact of food stamps in the region. The chapter concludes with a discussion on how the magnitude of the food power exerted in the Lewis Grocer Company's food stamp campaign shaped Black food conditions during the movement, clarifying the interaction between civil rights and food injustice. This interaction sets the stage for understanding the reemergence of *emancipatory food power* during the post-1965 Mississippi civil rights movement.

From Plantation Commissaries to Supermarkets: A Brief History of the Lewis Grocer Company

Established in 1896 as the Lewis-Herrman Company, a small grocery business in Lexington, Mississippi, the Lewis Grocer Company became a Mississippi-based wholesaler-retailer food empire in the early twentieth century. Built on the stomachs of poor Black sharecroppers and their families who depended on the plantation commissary system, the food empire was designed by Morris Lewis Sr. Lewis, a Jewish immigrant from Poland, was a prominent figure in the Lexington community and founded the Merchants and Farmers Bank and Trust Company in 1905, then the largest bank in Holmes County in the Delta.[19] This bank provided Lewis with the financial power to become a major player in the cotton economy of the region. The majority of his clientele were members of what Jamaican writer and cultural theorist Sylvia Wynter described as the plantation "manager class."[20] This class was a critical component of what Clyde Woods described as the Delta's "plantation bloc" that "asserted the superiority of the plantation system" and "the expansion of their monopoly over agriculture, manufacturing, banking, land, and water."[21] Indeed, Lewis was a textbook example of the plantation bloc's membership. For instance, in the early 1900s, Lewis was instrumental in the development of Lexington's electric light plant, water-works system, and sewage system. In the agricultural sector, Lewis was responsible for getting the town's first cotton compress and cotton oil mill. He also brokered several deals with major cotton firms in America and across Europe to increase the amount of cotton processed in Lexington.[22]

Due to his critical role in the development of Lexington in general and the region's cotton economy in particular, Lewis was friends with some of the most powerful politicians in Mississippi. These included two governors: James K. Vardaman, who was governor of Mississippi from 1904 to 1908 and administered Lewis's oath of US citizenship; and Edmond F. Noel, who succeeded Vardaman as governor in 1908 and served as counsel for Lewis in some instances.[23] Together, Vardaman and Noel were early architects of white supremacist legislation and discourses that profoundly shaped the civil rights movement. Vardaman, who was known as "the Great White Chief," repeatedly advocated for the lynching of "unmoral and debased negro" people as a way to maintain white supremacy and keep them in their "place."[24] Noel was the author of the 1902 Mississippi primary election legislation that laid the foundation for what was known as "the white primary" in the South. This legislation promoted Black voter suppression that systematically excluded Black people from political participation and only allowed white people to vote.[25]

To be sure, close ties between businessmen like Lewis and political figures such as Vardaman and Noel were not uncommon. Sociologist David James found that affiliations between politicians and businessmen were critical to the political economy of the South. The southern political economy contributed to the creation and transformation of the "southern racial state" that was "organized to defend the class structure of labor-intensive cotton agriculture . . . by white plantation owners, white farm owners, and their allies to discriminate against blacks."[26] What made affiliations between political and economic actors in the southern racial state so important, James argued, was that oftentimes the political futures of local officials were linked to the economic futures of white businessmen like Lewis. Indeed, Lewis's affiliations with Mississippi politicians and his role in regional financing and cotton production provided him opportunities to build his entrepreneurial capacity and revolutionize the commercial food business industry of the Delta.

By the early 1920s, Lewis facilitated two mergers with local grocery wholesalers that transformed what started as the Lewis-Herrman Company, a grocery retailer, into the Lewis Grocer Company, a grocery wholesaler. In 1915, the Lewis-Herrman Company merged with the Barrett Grocery company to establish the Barrett-Lewis Grocer Company. One year later, this company merged with the Gwin Grocer Company to form the Gwin-Lewis Grocer Company, and Lewis was selected as president of the company. Due to this expansion and change in leadership, the Gwin-Lewis Grocer Company opened a second store in nearby Greenwood in Leflore County. Sometime throughout this transition, Lewis bought out the Herrman portion of the original company. In 1922, the Gwin family assumed full responsibility for the Greenwood store, and Lewis maintained ownership of the Lexington store. This store became the first location and headquarters of the Lewis Grocer Company.[27]

The establishment of the Lewis Grocer Company allowed Lewis to expand and monopolize the commercial food industry in the region. First, in 1924, Lewis bought out the Ellis Brothers Wholesaler Company in the nearby town of Durant, which had a large warehouse with cold-storage technologies. The acquisition of this warehouse provided the Lewis Grocer Company with the technologies needed to handle some perishable products like meat and dairy products. Second, and more crucial, the late 1920s ushered in the Lewis Grocer Company's expansion into the Delta's plantation system and laid the foundation for the food empire built by Lewis. As a grocery wholesaler and prominent banker, Lewis embedded the company within the Delta's plantation system through two profit-maximizing mechanisms. First, as a banker, Lewis financed loans that enabled white planters to cultivate cotton crops and sustain the region's economy. Second, as a grocery wholesaler, Lewis was the largest food supplier for the plantation commissary stores. These arrangements forced most plantation owners to be dependent on the Lewis Grocer Company for the survival of their cotton operations and to sustain the mostly Black labor class of sharecroppers. At the same time, Lewis depended on the plantation system to make a profit, which also made the company susceptible to shifts in cotton market failures and fluctuations.[28]

In *Human Factors in Cotton Culture,* sociologist Rupert Vance found that banker-merchants like Lewis assumed the majority of the risks involved in cotton production, since 40 to 80 percent of farm loans were administered by local banks, and 50 to 90 percent of their grocery wholesaler contracts were with plantation commissaries.[29] Among these two mechanisms, the plantation commissary store was the major operation of the Lewis Grocer Company. This store was a critical component of the geography of the plantation in that it facilitated the distribution of food to Black laborers, operating as the main grocery store for Black sharecroppers. The commissary store was, as Jacqueline P. Bull described in the 1952 article "The General Merchant in the Economic History of the New South," a central part of a system of rural stores "of several types, often making it hard to draw the line and to classify them in definite groups. There was the store at the crossroads, the plantation commissary, and the store in the small town. . . . The stores themselves were almost as uniform in outward appearance as if they had been assembled by modern prefabrication. The interiors were similar only in that they housed an almost endless variety of merchandise which was sold over heavy counters and stored on shelves, on tables, and in bins."[30] As a significant structure in the traditional iconography of the plantation, the commissary store was also the site where plantation owners and their labor negotiated the "furnishings" agreement, in which white grocery wholesalers like the Lewis Grocer Company dictated the contractual terms that provided the plantations with food within this agreement.[31]

In *Deep South,* Allison Davis, Burleigh B. Gardner, and Mary R. Gardner found that there were three ways plantation owners fulfilled the furnishings agreement.[32] The first was through plantation commissary stores. These stores allowed plantation owners to provide food purchased from a wholesaler and extend it to their laborers on credit. Second, if the plantation did not have a commissary, the food purchased from the wholesaler would be distributed by the plantation owner. "As a third alternative," Davis, Gardner, and Gardner found, the plantation owner would send Black laborers "to a store at which he had credit, with a written order for certain rations."[33] In some instances, the plantation owner would escort Black sharecroppers to the stores, as Myrlie Evers observed in *For Us, the Living.*

Building on the observations of her husband, slain civil rights leader Medgar Evers, Evers described what she saw as a regular interaction between plantation owners and Black sharecroppers in the securing of food. "We would be shopping for groceries on a Saturday night, and Medgar would point out a plantation owner huddled with the storekeeper as the sharecroppers made their weekly purchases of meal and flour and lard," she remembered. As the shopping continued, the plantation owner would regulate what the Black sharecropper could buy. Even if the sharecropper wanted to purchase "cookies or a pound of bacon," the plantation owner would forbid such purchases. In response, Evers wrote, the sharecropper "would meekly accept the command, taking, in effect, what he was permitted to take, feeding his family what the plantation owner decided he should feed them."[34] In all these cases, particularly in the Delta, Morris Lewis Sr. was the main grocery wholesaler, catapulting the Lewis Grocer Company into financial success throughout the 1920s and 1930s.

In many respects, the Lewis Grocer Company was a critical player in sustaining the plantation system of the Delta. By providing food to plantation owners for them to give to their sharecroppers, the Lewis Grocer Company ensured that white landowners stayed in control and promoted what Kimberlé Crenshaw describes as "symbolic" and "material" subordination among poor Black sharecroppers in the region. Crenshaw writes that "symbolic subordination refers to the formal denial of social and political equality to all Blacks. . . . Material subordination, on the other hand, refers to the ways that discrimination and exclusion economically subordinated Blacks to whites and subordinated the life chances of Blacks to those of whites on almost every level."[35] Indeed, the Delta's plantation system was a breeding ground for such inequality, and food was at the center of it. The food allowed plantation owners to virtually control every aspect of rural Black life at the time, and the Lewis Grocer Company was responsible for supplying food to keep the system going.

But the Lewis Grocer Company had more than just food contracts with plantation commissaries. During the 1930s and 1940s, they created their own agricultural supply stores that would provide farmers with everything needed to cultivate cotton successfully. Each store provided sharecroppers with pick sacks, bags, ties, fertilizer, veterinary medical supplies, insecticides, nails, and other hardware items. Of course, the stores also carried flour, molasses, sugar, lard, meal, black-eyed peas, and salt pork.[36] These staples were central to the "Three M's" diet of "meal, molasses, and white meat" that was shaped by the food realities of Black sharecroppers. This diet was cheap and nutritionally inadequate. It contributed to the high levels of hunger linked to the plantation labor conditions that forced Black sharecroppers to "make do" from season to season.[37] Such deplorable food conditions persisted as the Lewis Grocer Company continued to build its food empire and expand beyond nourishing the Delta's plantation system.

The development of agricultural supply stores marked the beginning of a set of business decisions and changes in leadership that set the stage for the Lewis Grocer Company to be the largest grocery wholesaler in Mississippi and one of the nation's largest food distributors. In the mid-1930s, Lewis moved the company's headquarters to the Delta town of Indianola, the seat of Sunflower County in the heart of the Delta cotton country and the birthplace of the White Citizens' Council. The Lewis Grocer Company rebranded itself as a company that would provide farmers with everything needed to cultivate cotton successfully. At the same time, Lewis promoted his two sons, Morris Lewis Jr. and Celian, to president and executive vice president of the company, respectively. As president of the Lewis Grocer Company, Morris Lewis Jr. single-handedly revolutionized the grocery business in the Delta and across the South. After graduating from the Wharton School of Finance at the University of Pennsylvania in 1932, Morris Lewis Jr. returned home to Mississippi to work for his father. Four years later, he assumed the position of president redundant.[38]

Amid Morris Lewis Jr.'s early leadership of the company, the Great Depression began to take its toll on the agricultural sector of the Delta. In response, white farmers created the Delta Council, an organization designed to control the region's agricultural economy and economic development initiatives. This organization, of which Morris Lewis Jr. would later serve as president from 1969 to 1970, supported the mechanization of the agricultural landscape of the Delta from its inception through the civil rights era.[39] This shift toward mechanization was the beginning of the end of the sharecropping system. During this time, the Lewis Grocer Company was doing well, grossing almost $2 million in annual sales. But recognizing that the sharecropping system would eventually be nonexistent, the Lewis Grocery Company abandoned its agricultural supply stores in the 1940s and transitioned into the food retailer and supermarket business.[40] But before Lewis could expand the company's portfolio into the supermarket business, the United States entered World War II, and he and his brother joined the service, both working in supply chain management and food distribution in the Pacific.[41]

During World War II, Morris Lewis Jr. served in Hawaii and rose to the rank of major in charge of the post exchange (PX).[42] Celian also served as a major but in the Pacific Theater, and as a commanding officer in New Guinea and the director of food distribution for the US Army in the South Pacific.[43] Morris and Celian were likely appointed to these posts because of their work in supply chain management, and this experience allowed them to gain significant skills in the management and distribution of food and other items at a global level. On military bases, Celian controlled the system of commissaries throughout the South Pacific. In terms of function, military commissaries resembled plantation commissaries in the Delta and served as the central site for military personnel to access food and household items. The PX, where Morris Lewis Jr. was the manager, supplied other goods and items such as clothing. Undoubtedly, this experience shaped the Lewis brothers' outlook on food distribution, and once the war ended, they used their skills to transform the commercial food business in the South.

When the Lewis brothers returned to the Delta after the war, they arrived in a new Delta and regional food environment. Amid the backdrop of a growing civil rights movement and the increasing mechanization of cotton production, the plantation labor that they had depended on in the early years and throughout the Depression was rapidly dwindling. Around the same time, the civil rights movement in the Delta was gaining momentum with activists and local Black community leaders heavily organizing Black sharecroppers as the region's sharecropping system was transforming. As machines replaced Black bodies in the cultivation of cotton, many plantation owners found it no longer feasible to provide a commissary on the plantation, and many Black sharecroppers found themselves hungry and without work. As such, not only did mechanization disrupt the lives of Black sharecroppers and their families; it also decimated the plantation commissary system, which facilitated Black food accessibility. While mechanization was not necessarily a grave concern of the Lewis Grocer Company, the latter, as it pertains to the commissary system, forced the company to reconfigure its business model.

The larger question faced by the Lewis Grocer Company in the early years of the post–World War II era was how to sustain its control over the commercial food industry in the Delta, given that the system from which it profited tremendously was virtually collapsing. The answer to this question was the development of their supermarket chain: Sunflower Food Stores. Likely drawing on their management experience in World War II, the Lewis brothers, in many ways, seemingly replicated the military system of food distribution to commissaries by opening up the line of Sunflower Food Stores.[44] While they had considered the idea in the latter years of the Depression, the war years disrupted the plan. In addition, while they were abroad, national chains were attempting to move into rural areas to expand their own wholesaler-retailer merchandising systems. Such moves threatened small rural retailers who couldn't cover costs associated with working with large national chains.

By creating the Sunflower Food Store chain, the Lewis Grocer Company secured its future as a Mississippi food empire. The company's wholesale operation saved rural grocery businesses that depended on the regional economy. The Sunflower food stores, once an emblem of the Delta, provided a space for the Lewis Grocer Company to impact the food realities of poor rural Black communities directly. These stores were located in predominantly poor rural Black communities in plantation counties of Mississippi, as well as in Arkansas, Tennessee, Louisiana, and Alabama. In the Delta, the clientele of these stores were mostly former Black sharecroppers or white patrons who were mostly women. But due to the collapse of the sharecropping system, Black sharecroppers found it hard to patronize the stores. Instead, those still working on the plantation or living in the surrounding areas depended on the free food distributed by the federal surplus commodities program. Those who suffered from economic reprisals for civil rights involvement depended on food relief programs organized by civil rights groups.

By the 1960s, the federal surplus commodities program and food relief programs were regularly used by poor Black sharecroppers, the same clientele on whom Morris Lewis Jr. and his affiliates depended. For landowners who were also businessmen, these programs greatly impacted their ability to control food distribution. As grocery merchants continued to despise the program, the federal government was piloting a food stamp program that Lewis saw as the ultimate solution to what he viewed as a power imbalance in the commercial food industry. In fact, the Lewis Grocer Company saw the federal government in direct competition with grocery merchants.[45] While civil rights activists denounced the Federal Food Stamp Program as another way to control poor rural Black people, the Lewis Grocer Company initiated a successful campaign to get food stamps to Mississippi.[46] This forgotten campaign played a major role in the legislation being passed at the national level and set the stage for the 1960s Delta hunger crisis that reshaped the Mississippi civil rights movement and the national war on poverty.

The Lewis Grocer Company's Food Stamp Campaign

The Lewis Grocer Company's campaign for food stamps began when Morris Lewis Jr. sent a November 15, 1962, internal memo to the company's 400 retailer customers. This memo was designed to caution his clients about what he saw as a growing threat to their businesses and the "American business system of free enterprise": the federal surplus commodities program.[47] Written within days of the onset of the Greenwood Food Blockade and a similar problem in Sunflower County, home to the Lewis Grocer Company's headquarters, the internal memo set the stage for the Lewis Grocer Company's wide-reaching food stamps campaign. The memo also illustrated how food power was articulated and manifested in the advent of food stamps in the Delta. This single document provides a window into this forgotten campaign of the Lewis Grocer Company and how the food power wielded by the company created food conditions that shaped the civil rights movement in Black sharecropping communities in the Delta. This campaign was rooted in the Lewis Grocer Company's then-president Morris Lewis Jr.'s disdain for any program, federal or local, that sought to distribute food outside of what he saw as the "proper channels" of food distribution—established commercial food outlets or stores that had food contracts with them.

In a larger sense, Lewis's disdain for the federal surplus commodities program was rooted in the fact that he saw the program as a major threat to his control of the state's commercial food industry. "As an independent businessman . . . I want to write you a few lines about one of your major competitors and its plans for taking some of your business," he wrote his retail consumers in the internal memo. "This competitor is the State of Mississippi, which is taking business from you through the furnishing of commodities by the Department of Public Welfare."[48] What angered Lewis the most was that, in his eyes, taxpayer dollars were being used to put the commercial food industry out of business. "You support your government through taxes," he stated, "and are forced to stand by and see your tax money being used to put you out of business . . . contributing to a situation that encourages government to seek and acquire business from ligitimate [*sic*] tax payers." He continued, "[While] we object to power continuously being concentrated in our Federal Government . . . we are contributing to the building of a tremendous bureau and new system of distribution that could easily expand" and, he lamented, "requesting the Federal Government to enter the food business in competition with the tax paying food retailers and wholesalers in this state." To remedy such "a sad state of affairs," Lewis suggested, the state "should immediately apply to the Federal Government to secure the Federal Food Stamp Program."[49] This solution suggested by Lewis required local county boards of supervisors to exert their power and petition the state to allow them to switch federal food assistance programs. In plantation counties across the Delta and certain parts of the state, plantation owners and businessmen dominated the boards, which gave them the power to dictate food access among the majority Black population of sharecroppers and farmworkers who worked as day laborers.

Most plantation owners in the Delta, though, initially resisted and rejected federal intervention via the food stamp program. As Lewis contended, "the only objection I have heard is from some who state that they oppose [food stamps] because they are conservative people and oppose the expansion of government in business affairs." In the Delta, he wrote, "we find some of the most 'conservative' land owners permitting their labor to participate in the free commodity program."[50] Interestingly, Lewis's words reveal that he was not necessarily anti–federal intervention in the context of food distribution. In fact, he was pro–federal intervention as long as the intervention ensured that he and other white grocery store owners would maintain control. It is important to note that both the surplus commodities program and food stamp program were federal programs designed to get food into the hands of poor people. But the way in which food got into the hands of the Delta's poor population of mostly Black sharecroppers and their families mattered to Lewis. Thus, the only way he saw to mitigate the perceived loss of control in the distribution of food was to support the food stamp program legislation. This legislation would allow him to force poor people in general and poor Black folks, in particular, to use food stamps to purchase food at white grocery stores, especially in the Delta.

But Lewis's internal memo was just the first step in his campaign for food stamps. Three days after he sent the memo to his retail customers, it was picked up by and made the front page of several major newspapers in the Delta. For instance, the leading article in the November 18, 1962, edition of Greenville's *Delta Democrat-Times* commented that Lewis had "coupled a strong attack on the commodity distribution program with a suggestion that the federal food stamp plan take its place."[51] Another article in the November 22 edition of Indianola's *Enterprise-Tocsin* stated that Lewis "sees a growing threat to the free enterprise system in the vast amount of commodities being given out by the federal government . . . as a substitute for the commodity handout, the food stamp plan whereby the needs of those requiring assistance could be met through the stores."[52] Both newspapers had a large white readership that included some of the most powerful people in the region and were likely targeted by Lewis to galvanize local county officials and white grocery retailers to pressure the state to adopt the food stamp program. While Lewis maintained that the initiation of a food stamp program was the responsibility of the local power structure, he also knew the importance of joining arms with federal officials who represented Mississippi in Congress. While the media attention to the food stamp program garnered considerable local support for the program, Lewis's ability to go beyond the media to the federal level was critical and the final step in securing the program in Mississippi.

From the Delta to Washington, D.C.: Food Stamp Politics

On November 27, 1962, Lewis sent the memo that he wrote to his retailers to his close friend Senator James O. Eastland, the infamous segregationist known by his friends as "Big Jim," who represented Mississippi in Congress.[53] Five days later, Eastland notified Lewis that he had received the memo and agreed with the points Lewis made. "I certainly think there is logic in what you have to say," Eastland wrote; "I will be glad to check into this and see what can be done."[54] Strategically, Lewis could not have asked for a better person to support his campaign for food stamps. Eastland, who proudly lived up to his reputation as "the voice of the white south," used his power and influential political status in Senate to sustain white supremacy.[55] He was also a wealthy farmer who owned a large, 5,000-acre cotton plantation in the heart of Sunflower County on the outskirts of Doddsville, roughly twenty miles north of the Lewis Grocer Company.[56] During the 1950s and 1960s, Eastland once served as chair of the Senate Subcommittee on Agriculture and Forestry in 1955 and served as chair of the Senate Judiciary Committee from 1956 until his retirement in 1978, where he worked viciously to block every single civil rights bill that came to the committee.[57] J. Todd Moye remarked that Eastland "went so far as to boast to white Mississippi audiences that he had his tailor sew special, deep pockets in his suit coats: the place where civil rights bills went to die."[58] Such power wielded by Eastland made him one of the most influential senators in galvanizing southern congressmen who were committed to maintaining white supremacy in the social, economic, and political order of the South.

Eastland's power also made him a key figure in major political decisions, including the legislation surrounding the federal food stamp bill of 1964, which he coauthored.[59] Amid congressional debates surrounding food stamps in the spring of 1964, Eastland and President Lyndon B. Johnson likely talked regularly about how to garner congressional votes to get the legislation passed. While the majority of the southern congressional establishment in the House supported food stamps, some also opposed the legislation because it would give the federal government additional power over the southern states. Concentrated power at the federal level was a major point of tension just three weeks before the food stamp bill passed the House on April 8, 1964, and deeply worried President Johnson. Due to his concerns about the tensions and the possibility that the food stamp bill would not pass the House, President Johnson talked to Senator Eastland to get some help from Mississippi because of the power that the state wielded in the South. Although Mississippi had only five members in the House—Jamie Whitten, William Colmer, Thomas Abernethy, Arthur Winstead, and John Bell Williams—these men dominated powerful committees. In the context of agricultural committees that played a key role in the Food Stamp Act, Abernethy and Whitten wielded the most power. Representing the state's predominantly white first congressional district, Abernethy chaired the Agriculture Subcommittee on Research and Extension, ranked sixth on the House Agriculture Committee, and was a ranking member of the agricultural subcommittees on cotton, dairying, and consumer relations. Whitten, who went on record stating that civil rights legislation was a "destructive package . . . forced upon the White majority by the armed might of the United States," represented Mississippi's majority Black second congressional district that included Eastland's plantation and encompassed the Delta counties.[60] He was also the long-standing chairman of the powerful House Agriculture Appropriations Subcommittee that allocated funds for the food stamp program.[61] Together, Abernethy and Whitten worked to ensure that their white constituents would benefit the most from agricultural legislation.

But the Food Stamp Act was a point of departure for Abernethy's and Whitten's commitments based on the racial makeup of their districts. This departure became clear in a March 18, 1964, phone call between Eastland and President Johnson regarding political struggles surrounding the wheat-cotton bill and the food stamp bill in the House.[62] "Now I'm gon' tell you 'bout my state," Eastland told Johnson. "In areas with a big nigra population where they give [food] commodities away, the merchants want [food stamps]." While speaking about the merchants who had aligned with the Lewis Grocer Company's food stamp campaign, Eastland alerted Johnson of a potential problem with getting food stamp legislation passed in

Mississippi. There is one issue in Mississippi, Eastland told Johnson, "we have congressional districts like [Thomas] Abernethy's of small white farmers and every little town has got several garment plants" where "they don't want any government at all" because "they got no nigras there." Worried about what these conflicting views could do to the House vote, Johnson still believed that Eastland could get him the help he needed as he bluntly asked, "Can't you get us some help on food stamps in Mississippi?" Eastland immediately answered, "Why, sure! That's what I was talking about. My merchants are for it in the nigra areas. You see, they haul commodities in there and give 'em out." He continued, "Now you take the niggers on my property. They got plenty of money, but every damn one of 'em line up and get commodities. The merchants in that area want food stamps because they get a cut out of it. You see what I'm talking about. Well, in Abernethy's area you don't have that and the merchants will oppose it. So it puts him on the spot. Now I'm going to try to work on him."[63]

The phone call between Eastland and Johnson reveals that food stamp legislation was not entirely designed to feed poor people. In fact, for Eastland, the food stamp program was all about white profit at the expense of poor Black people in Delta. But the absence of a majority poor Black population and an economy built on Black plantation labor made districts like Abernethy's more committed to keeping the government out of all their affairs. This was because those districts did not have a large Black labor force that would be dependent on federal food assistance because of an economy that rendered them poor and without reliable access to food. In contrast, plantation-based districts like Whitten's needed federal food assistance for Black labor, but only if it benefited the white power structure. As such, the Delta's white power structure targeted poor rural Black sharecroppers, farmworkers, and their families for the food stamp program so that they could remain dependent on the regional white power structure for everything.

The food stamp bill passed the House on April 8, 1964, with Abernethy, along with John Bell Williams of the state's third congressional district, voting against the legislation. Whitten, Winstead, and Colmer voted for the legislation because their districts were dominated by large white farmers who relied on federal assistance and white grocers to feed their labor.[64] Two months later in June, the food stamp bill passed the Senate with amendments. Among the amendments put forward, two impacted poor Black sharecropping communities in the Delta the most. One was the amendment that virtually abolished the federal surplus commodities program. Speaking about this amendment on the Senate floor, segregationist senator Allen Ellender of Louisiana, who was chair of the Senate Subcommittee on Agriculture and Forestry at the time, stated that this first amendment to the food stamp bill "prohibit[s] the distribution of federally owned foods to households under the authority of any other law in any area in which a food stamp program was effective, except during emergency situations."[65] The ultimate purpose of this amendment was to "phase out the presently operating free food distribution programs as the food stamp program expands."[66]

A second amendment gave all the authority to the states to dictate the food stamp program. "To initiate the program in any State," Ellender explained, "the State agency responsible for the administration of federally aided public assistance programs would submit to the Secretary for approval a plan of operation for the food stamp program in its State, specifying the various political subdivisions in which the program would be effective, the standards to be used in determining the eligibility of applicant households, and other details." Therefore, "the State welfare agency would be responsible for the certification of all applicant households and would be required to use the same care and diligence that it uses in other programs administered by it."[67] This amendment gave the Delta's white power structure full domination over when, where, and how poor people could access food through the federal food stamp program. Legally, the decision to get food stamps in a county would be up to the boards of supervisors and the State Department of Public Welfare, which is exactly what the Lewis Grocer Company's food stamp campaign fought for. The passage of the food stamp bill, with the amendments put forward on August 11 and the signing of the bill into law on August 31, marked a critical turning point in Lewis Grocer Company's campaign for food stamps. Although the law was in place, the next step was to ensure that Delta counties would apply for the program, making it the responsibility of local white power structures to pressure the state to implement the program.

Food Stamps Come to the Delta

In 1965, as the Lewis Grocer Company merged with SuperValu, Inc., the federal food stamp program was gradually phased into Mississippi.[68] This merger enabled the Lewis Grocer Company to increase their annual sales from $3 million to almost $38 million that year and expand the company's grocery and financial portfolio.[69] At the same time, the Lewis Grocer

Company's food stamp campaign was gaining momentum on the ground as the federal food stamp program made its way to the Delta a year later in 1966.[70] Coahoma County was the first county in the Delta to implement food stamps and soon thereafter the Lewis Grocer Company's campaign had influenced other grocery merchants in the region to petition for their respective county to switch over to the food stamp program.[71] For instance, Lewis was known for spreading the gospel of food stamps all over the Delta, including at his local country club in Indianola, where he and his affiliates would discuss the sustainability of small white grocery store owners struggling to survive in poor rural Black communities.[72] It was in those segregated spaces where Lewis and his peers aligned themselves with the politics of fear and victimization and strategized to get the food stamp program, which caused other retailers throughout the region to write Senator Eastland. For example, in Tallahatchie County, Vernon T. Brett of the family-run Brett Wholesale Grocery store wrote Eastland urging him to prioritize the county's request for food stamps in the context of Black farm labor and federal food assistance. "I doubt seriously if there is another county that would be helped economically any more than this county," Brett explained. "Our large population of farm labor which is practically supported by the commodity plan, is putting retail grocers out of business very fast."[73] In Sunflower County, the Ruleville Chamber of Commerce wrote Eastland asking for his "full support for the Food Stamp Program in lieu of the present system of food distribution to welfare recipients."[74] In their eyes, as president of the chamber of commerce, C. M. Dorrough Sr. wrote, food stamps "would permit the recipient to have a choice for food he needs that he does not have now" and "assist the merchants who are being deprived of the business . . . and maintain a better economic balance in the community."[75] Echoing President Johnson's rationale for the federal food stamp program, Dorrough's words reveal that the economic balance that the Ruleville Chamber of Commerce hoped to maintain was designed to ensure that white grocery merchants remained in control of the commercial food system. Feeding poor people in the Delta, especially Black sharecroppers, was simply a by-product.

This line of thinking and strategy was also promoted by the media. For instance, the morning edition of the Mid-South Network's Radio WONA (Winona) did a four-part series on food stamps titled "Super—Supermarkets (The Problem)" in March 1966.[76] The purpose of the series was to discuss the differences between the surplus commodities program and food stamps in the context of President Johnson's War on Poverty. While the reporter at-

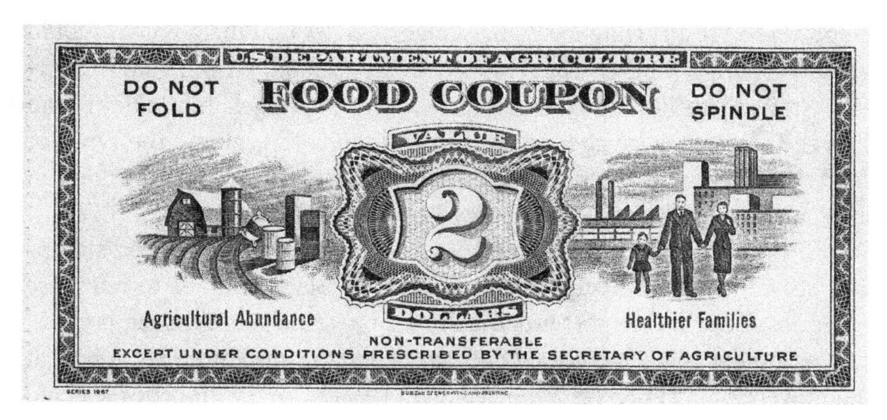

Food stamp coupon, 1967 series. (US Department of Agriculture)

tempted to give listeners "a factual basis upon which to decide" whether they were for or against the food stamp plan in Mississippi, it was clear that the station was influenced by white grocery store merchants. "In the cause of ending poverty . . . the first casualties have been the food merchants," the reporter remarked early in the first segment on March 30, 1966. Rather than beginning the segment with a comparison of the two federal food assistance programs, the series began with an indictment of the surplus commodities program in two counties in the region. Describing the locations where surplus commodities were distributed as large "Government Supermarkets in direct competition with privately-owned grocery stores," the reporter continued to discredit the commodities program. "The concern of these merchants and civil leaders is not to deprive anyone of the legitimate help that they need but rather to handle it in such a way as to not create more poverty and problems than are cured." Relying on a statement from an informant, the reporter concluded, "As one man said . . . what good is it to help one family from going hungry when in doing so you put another out of business and add them to the poverty rolls."[77] The entire four-part series on food stamps commissioned by the Mid-South Network's Radio WONA included similar informant statements and featured political figures from Mississippi like US Representative Jamie Whitten to demonstrate legislative support for the food stamp program in the state. It also received praise from Senator James Eastland who wrote that the series was "the most accurate and most objective analysis" of the federal food stamp program.[78]

Yet the strong praise of the federal food stamp program by white proponents of the legislation in the Delta failed to acknowledge, or ignored altogether, the fact that the food stamp program exacerbated hunger and empowered the all-white local government offices that dictated who could get food stamps or other welfare funds to access food. Drawing on a report from staff at Sunflower County Progress, historian Angela Jill Cooley found that the social service agency used food stamps to regulate the types of food that poor rural Black people could purchase and eat.[79] As the county-level agency that ran the Emergency Food and Medical program (EF&M), Sunflower County Progress helped poor people gain access to food stamps and provided financial support for poor rural Black families to purchase groceries. But this support was much more paternalistic than supportive. For example, Cooley recounted one case when the all-white EF&M staff at Sunflower County Progress "reported that they paid for the groceries selected by a beneficiary family, and the family purchased roast beef. The staff considered roast beef to be too expensive compared to bologna or neckbones, on which they thought beneficiaries should subsist. As a result, program officials started selecting and purchasing food for needy families." Cooley concluded that "the sole concern seemed to be price, and perhaps the quality of food to be fit for a poor black family. The EF&M staff made no mention of the preference, nutrition, or autonomy of the community members they served."[80] In other cases, historian Mark Newman pointed out, white landowners "often certified their workers' income" at county welfare offices, "which determined their eligibility for food stamps, and thus retained a powerful influence over the workforce." Beyond welfare offices, "some grocery owners accepted food stamps only for the most expensive brands of food and . . . raised prices when the county entered the food stamp program."[81] These types of experiences maintained white supremacy in everyday Black food access in the Delta. In response, civil rights activists used such experiences to carve out a space in the movement agenda to address racialized problems surrounding food stamps in the region.

Food Stamps at the Center of the Mississippi Civil Rights Movement

In January 1967, civil rights activists in Mississippi circulated a report titled *What You Should Know about Food Stamps*. In the report, activists provided data on how the federal food stamp program operated in Mississippi and ways to organize against the program. The report also outlined inequalities associated with the program. For example, the report found that some white grocery store owners would only accept food stamps for high-priced food items. At the local government level, county boards of supervisors failed to hold public meetings to educate poor rural Black communities about the food stamp program and voted for the food stamp program without consulting those communities that would be most impacted by the change in federal food aid. At welfare offices, some Black community members were informed that their welfare aid would be at risk of being stopped if they didn't participate in the food stamp program.[82] Activists viewed such instances as proof that the federal food stamp program in Mississippi was just another site for the exploitation of poor Black people across multiple local community spaces.

In July 1967, the NAACP released a report exposing two major discriminatory practices surrounding the federal food stamp program in the Delta.[83] The first discriminatory act was observed on plantations. NAACP evidence reveals that some white plantation owners implemented a food stamp loan program, forcing their Black labor to use the stamps to purchase food. This program deducted the cost of food stamps used from the weekly income of Black sharecroppers and provided transportation to white grocery stores designated by the landowner.[84] The second discriminatory act occurred at grocery stores. Black sharecroppers who lived on plantations that did not have a food stamp loan program were at the mercy of white grocery store owners. The NAACP found that white grocery store owners had also instituted a food stamp loan process. For any Black sharecropping family unable to purchase food, the white grocery store owner would loan the family enough stamps to buy food. This food stamp loan process at white grocery stores required Black sharecropping families to repay the loan with an average interest rate of twenty-five cents on the dollar.[85] The NAACP concluded that these two discriminatory practices, among others, were part of a "programmatic and systematic eradication" of Black people in Mississippi "that blatantly denie[d]" them "the minimum basic necessities of life consistent with human dignity and survival."[86] What must be added to the NAACP's conclusion is that the two discriminatory practices also shed a critical light on the ways in which the white power structure in the Delta controlled when, where, and how poor Black people who were dependent on the structure could access food.

While both reports provide broad snapshots of the vivid details that shaped the everyday Black struggle with food stamps in Mississippi during the movement, public testimonies of Black women activists in April 1967 placed an analysis of the food stamp program at the center of the movement. This analysis took the spotlight on April 10, 1967, at the War on Poverty hearings before the Senate Subcommittee on Employment, Manpower, and

Poverty of the Committee on Labor and Public Welfare in Jackson, Mississippi, at the Heidelberg Hotel.[87] Chaired by Senator Joseph Clark of Pennsylvania, the subcommittee included New York senator Robert F. Kennedy, the brother of President John F. Kennedy. The *Clarion-Ledger* reported that the purpose of the subcommittee's War on Poverty hearings was to assess "the effectiveness of the Mississippi phase of President Lyndon Johnson's war on poverty . . . [and] determine by the hearings the success of the state poverty program and decide which of the programs should be continued."[88] But the Black women activists that were asked to provide a testimony saw the hearings as an opportunity to publicly illuminate how the federal food stamp program in Mississippi reinforced food inequalities in poor rural Black communities and perpetuated food insecurity.

On schedule to testify, among others, were activists Fannie Lou Hamer, Unita Blackwell, and attorney Marian Wright of the NAACP's Legal Defense Fund. Speaking about food and agrarian conditions in Sunflower County, Hamer stated, "People are hungry this evening because . . . the minimum wage . . . and not only that but when [the county board of supervisors] said they are going to replace commodities, the surplus food, with stamps, then somebody is going to starve."[89] Hamer strategically situated the food stamp crisis within the context of the minimum wage law of 1967 that required plantation owners to pay Black farmworkers one dollar per hour of work instead of the fixed payment of $3.50 per workday. On the surface, this law would seem to have benefited Black farmworkers. But in the quest for agricultural efficiency, along with the fact that white farmers in the Delta received federal funds to reduce cotton acreage, such costs to employ Black farmworkers did not readily fit the new economic model of the plantation system. According to James C. Cobb, "one estimate suggested that the new law put twenty-five thousand able-bodied hands in the Delta out of jobs, resulting in a net migration of twelve thousand from that region in 1967 alone."[90] This mass loss of jobs and displacement among Black farmworkers increased their dependence on federal food assistance through the federal surplus commodities food program. In response to these conditions, Hamer and other civil rights activists strongly opposed food stamps and organized a campaign in the late 1960s against it, circulating a petition asking for a free food program to be implemented in the county.[91]

In her testimony about the food crisis on plantations, Unita Blackwell went a little deeper than Hamer. Blackwell explained to the subcommittee, "Mechanization took over and the people don't have anything to do. . . . We have children who had never had a glass of milk . . . [and] the people in Issaquena County have sons that they are trying to scuffle and feed and . . . people is very angry because they can't eat. It is just that crucial."[92] Blackwell's testimony connected the plantation food crisis to mechanization that replaced Black labor with low-cost efficiency schemes that reconfigured cotton production practices in the region's agricultural economy. Such a shift in crop production practices was compounded by the fact that those who administered federal food and other poverty programs were mostly white plantation owners. Blackwell further explained that white plantation owners were "the same men that threw people off the place because they wanted to register to vote or they would send their children to the integrated schools and these kinds of things."[93] Recognizing this, activists in Issaquena County led by Blackwell were able to stall the onset of the Federal Food Stamp Program by getting over 200 registered voters to sign a food stamp program petition that was carried due to the 1967 local election year.[94] Blackwell concluded, though, that the only way folks would not be hungry or starve is if the federal government intervened and created some type of free food stamp program.

Building on the testimonies of Hamer and Blackwell, Marian Wright's testimony further emphasized how the switch from surplus food to food stamps perpetuated the financial inability of poor rural Black people in the Delta to feed themselves. "With the change to food stamps, one has seen several things. One has seen a great number of people saying we can not eat," Wright stated. When asked to elaborate on the difference between surplus food and food stamps, Wright explained: "Well, the difference that was brought about was, one, surplus commodities were free. At least, they could go down to the welfare or commodity office and get some food that, while not adequate, would at least keep them alive. Food stamps cost money. People with no income can't pay money."[95] Even families with little income were unable to buy food stamps.[96] The fact that a family was unable to pay the two dollars required to get some stamps reinforced the deplorable conditions by which poor rural Black people were forced to navigate in the Delta. In a larger sense, what Wright was getting at in her testimony was that the food stamp program did nothing to disrupt the economic arrangements and white power structure of the region. In other words, the rubric by which the program was administered sustained food insecurity among poor rural Black people in the Delta.

Taken together, the testimonies of Hamer, Blackwell, and Wright represented the ways in which Black women civil rights activists used the Delta food stamp crisis to align with a Black feminist politic put forward by Black women in the Combahee River Collective that evoked "black women's style of talking/testifying in black language" about what they experienced or witnessed "that is both cultural and political."[97] Their testimonies, borrowing from anthropologist Ashanté Reese and activist Dara Cooper, also reflected critical connections between "Black feminist freedom dreams and food justice possibilities."[98] Food justice possibilities ensured that poor rural Black people in the Delta would be able to control every aspect of their lives, including the most basic need of all: food. Hamer, Blackwell, and Wright understood that such possibilities must consider a food stamp analysis that is rooted in the civil rights movement. Collectively, their testimonies are also in direct opposition with the white power structure's analysis of food stamps in the Delta. As discussed earlier in this chapter, the white power structure argued for a food stamp analysis across two dimensions—food choice and the economic sustainability of white supremacy. This point is critical in that their analysis revealed how the use of food as an economic weapon was rooted in a larger scheme that politically weaponized food as a way to undermine the successes of the civil rights movement. The intended casualties of this particular weaponization process were poor rural Black people who had been sharecroppers. But rather than passively observe this crisis, Black sharecroppers staged protests that also brought the Delta's Black food crisis to the center of national civil rights conversations. Such protests shed light on how food continued to be a critical economic and political weapon in the struggle for civil rights in Mississippi.

Conclusion

What began as a memo written by Morris Lewis Jr. to his retailer clients soon transformed into a campaign for food stamps that shifted movement politics and reconfigured the civil rights agenda in the Delta. To be sure, when the Lewis Grocer Company initiated its campaign for food stamps in the fall of 1962, it was a critical part of a regional wave of food power in the Delta wielded by the white political and economic power structure to dismantle the federal surplus commodities program. Such sentiments were aligned with how other actors in the region's white power structure viewed the program but for different reasons. For political actors in the county board of supervisors in plantation counties, the dismantling of the federal surplus commodities program was designed as a way to punish mostly poor rural Black people who were sharecroppers who dared to participate in civil rights activism as discussed in chapter 1. For economic actors who were grocery store owners like Lewis, the dismantling of the federal surplus commodities program provided a space for them to maintain control of regional food distribution in poor rural Black communities. White grocery store owners, as major economic actors in the Delta, enlisted political actors to use the federal food stamp program as a site for the production of white profit built on the exploitation of poor rural Black people. Indeed, this level of exploitation maintained white supremacy that, directly and indirectly, impacted the civil rights movement.

Yet, insufficient attention has been given to how economic actors in general and white grocery store owners in particular impacted the movement. A shift in our prefigured gaze from the white political structure to the economic structure, at least in the Delta, uncovers how instantiations of white supremacy that shaped Black food conditions during the Mississippi civil rights movement were rooted in the region's transition from plantation commissaires to supermarkets. The brief history of the Lewis Grocer Company that this chapter lays out demonstrates this point and provides a theoretical space to think about connections between white grocers and remnants of plantation culture. This interaction between white grocery stores and plantation culture represents a neglected aspect in studies of the civil rights movement. Indeed, the plantation economy of the Delta was crucial to the success of the Lewis Grocer Company and played a major role in its ability to wield so much power and mobilize a successful campaign in support of the federal food stamp program in Mississippi. The Lewis Grocer Company's role in the sustainability of plantation commissaires and the rise of supermarkets in the Delta secured the future of the company as a Mississippi food empire.

In the face of a decaying plantation economy that caused the Delta's sharecropping system to collapse, the Lewis Grocer Company was able to use its status as a commercial food empire to thrive and increase its profit by millions. As the president of the Lewis Grocer Company, Morris Lewis Jr. knew that the only way to benefit from this collapse was to petition for the federal surplus commodities program to be legally replaced by the federal food stamp program. This transition from surplus food to food stamps reconfigured the Delta's food environment, making it virtually impossible to access food outside of commercial food spaces. It also created a hostile grocery shopping experience for poor rural Black people, as civil rights activists and organizations documented, who were forced to get food stamps and patronize white grocery stores to obtain food to feed themselves and their families. The Lewis Grocer Company's campaign for food stamps ignored these experiences of poor rural Black people at white grocery stores and acted in concert with opposition to the Mississippi civil rights movement.

But the Lewis Grocer Company's food stamps campaign is not only about how white grocers mobilized to control the ways in which poor rural Black people accessed food in the Delta which in effect undermined the struggle for civil rights. The Lewis Grocer Company's campaign is instructive and a window through which we can explore often overlooked or even considered actors and stories that contribute to our understanding of the movement. By placing grocery store owners at the center of the civil rights era, we can foreground how hidden sources of power strategized against the movement and aligned with overt opposition to the struggle. For example, the Lewis Grocery Company's campaign for food stamps did not intensify until Morris Lewis Jr. sent the letter to Senator James Eastland, a vocal supporter of white supremacy. Lewis Jr. knew that it would be beneficial to connect the campaign to Eastland's influence over President Johnson—in the context of food and agricultural legislation—and his ability to shape the political maneuverings of the South. While it was common for economic actors to work with politicians to push policy that benefits them, grocery store owners were often not considered as economic actors in the conversation surrounding the civil rights movement.

In this line of thinking, placing economic actors like the Lewis Grocer Company at the center of the struggle for civil rights in Mississippi sheds a critical light on an early moment in the history of the federal food stamp program when the food program worked against poor rural Black people. While the program in and of itself was designed to get food in the hands of poor people, how it was administered is what enabled the program to benefit those who controlled the terms by which the program could be accessed and used. This point is important in the context of the Lewis Grocer Company's food stamps campaign in that the campaign brings into focus how white elected officials and county agencies used food stamps to exert their power over poor rural Black people in the Delta. Although white grocery store owners in the Delta—via Senator Eastland—had already put their bid in to ensure that they would financially benefit the most from food stamp legislation, they were not the only actors in the white power structure who profited and gained power from the program. This distribution of food power in white power structure of the Delta helps us understand some of the reasons why the food stamp program of the 1960s failed to get food into the hands and bodies of poor rural Black people. Although the federal food stamp program has improved since the 1960s and now operates as SNAP under the

USDA, the Lewis Grocer Company's food stamp campaign sheds light on how past inadequacies of the program were compounded by intense struggles for civil rights and the rapid technological shifts in the region's agricultural economy.

As the next chapter shows, the confluence of ineffective food stamp programs and swift agrarian changes in the Delta provides the context by which to understand how emancipatory food power reemerged in the Mississippi civil rights movement. This version of emancipatory food power was articulated by the North Bolivar County Farm Cooperative (NBCFC) and differed from how activists situated the Food for Freedom program through the lens of emancipation during the Greenwood Food Blockade. Instead of creating a network to get food shipped to the Delta to feed poor rural Black communities, the NBCFC created a local Black food economy that empowered Black sharecroppers and their communities to use food as a critical source of security and economic vitality. Civil rights records detailing the Mississippi movement show that the development of the NBCFC's local Black food economy was part of a wave of southern Black farm cooperatives that envisioned a civil rights movement through the prism of Black agrarian traditions in the production, consumption, and distribution of food.

CHAPTER THREE

Black Food, Black Jobs

Emancipatory Food Power and the North Bolivar County Farm Cooperative

> The Cooperative was organized to help people survive. The trauma created by mechanized farming, minimum wages, and ineffective food stamp programs set the tone for the successful organization of an agricultural cooperative. People were hungry, and unemployed. Families were ill because of improper diets. . . . They wanted an opportunity to work and help themselves. They believed in the age-old philosophy of sharing. And they knew how to grow vegetables.
>
> —L. C. DORSEY

In September 1970, Mrs. L. C. Dorsey testified before the US Senate Select Committee on Nutrition and Human Needs in Washington, D.C. Dorsey was the leader of the North Bolivar County Farm Cooperative (NBCFC), a Delta-based Black food network of civil rights activists, sharecroppers, farmers, and health-care professionals founded in 1967. A key leader in the 1960s Mississippi civil rights movement and community organizer, Dorsey went to Washington to secure additional federal support for the NBCFC. Echoing the theme of the Student Nonviolent Coordinating Committee's (SNCC) November 1963 conference on food and jobs, Dorsey testified that the cooperative was born out of an effort to connect nutritious food and employment in poor rural Black communities: "You have to connect jobs and nutrition . . . that is, a job where a person can make a decent income to take care of needs." Dorsey argued, "If all of the families that the doctor saw in 1967, that had advanced malnutrition had had good jobs, they would not have been malnourished. There would have been money to buy food and the right kinds of food." Placing mothers at the center of this origin story, Dorsey continued: "If mothers that go to the grocery store with their meager food allowance had more money, it wouldn't be necessary to buy all the starches which constitute much of the black man's life in Mississippi. She could buy vegetables and milk. That is what started the farm co-op."[1]

In the beginning, the cooperative emerged out of the struggle for economic and food security in the everyday lives of poor rural Black mothers and their communities in the northern half of Bolivar County. "We didn't have anything but each other and our combined need," Dorsey further explained in her testimony. Now, she stated, "our membership has grown to 500 people, to 956 families. The food that we produced last year in our crop was 620.5 tons." At the time, the cooperative owned 347 acres of land, and through Dorsey's leadership and vision, the NBCFC operationalized a viable, comprehensive local Black food economy. This food economy included an autonomous rural farm, food education programs, a regional food distribution network, and other food-related enterprises. While this local Black food economy operated across 500 square miles in the Delta, Dorsey and her comrades didn't see these accomplishments as a success. "This isn't a success story," Dorsey cautioned the Senate select committee, "because it really is not the end of what we hope to achieve."[2]

What the NBCFC hoped to accomplish went beyond eradicating poverty-induced hunger and malnutrition in the rural South. In fact, the cooperative's central mission was to provide food and jobs for Black families. This mission was integral to the NBCFC's dreams of creating new ways of farming on the material remains of the Delta's plantation economy. Instead of being dependent upon crops that could not be used for food, such new ways of farming were community-driven and involved a large amount of acreage to grow food that could sustain rural Black farm families and sharecroppers. The ultimate plan of the NBCFC involved food production built on the development of an autonomous community that would be solely dependent on itself in northern Bolivar County. Yet these dreams didn't necessarily materialize, given that the cooperative had dissolved by the end of the 1970s. As a result, Dorsey commented years later that the community "never really got the potential of the co-op maximized." Of course, if we only look at the cooperative in the context of the civil rights movement, we could assume that it was a failed experiment, as what the organization hoped to achieve never came to fruition. But prominent historian Robin D. G. Kelley cautions us, when examining the history of social movements, to not ascribe value to movements or measure their results through the lens of success versus failure. Kelley writes, "Unfortunately, too often our standards for evaluating social movements pivot around whether or not they 'succeeded' in realizing their visions rather than on the merits or power of the visions themselves. By such a measure, virtually every radical movement failed because the basic power relations they sought to change remain pretty much intact. And yet it is precisely these alternate visions and dreams that inspire new generations to continue to struggle for change."[3] Looking back at the dreams and visions of the NBCFC, I argue that the cooperative was a success in that it cultivated an innovative Black food space for new communities, institutions, and leaders to take center stage in the latter years of the Mississippi civil rights movement that provide a blueprint for communities today.

The new actors and organizations that came out of the civil rights struggle in the Delta, Clyde Woods argued, "were not the creation of the SNCC, SCLC, CORE, NAACP. . . . They emerged from the daily lives and collective history of the people of the Delta."[4] In thinking with Woods, the NBCFC represents the type of organizations that were born out of the Mississippi movement and operated in the shadows of broadly publicized civil rights efforts. In fact, the NBCFC was one of the many manifestations of Black protest that emerged during the post-1965 civil rights movement as part of what Dr. Martin Luther King Jr. proclaimed in 1967 as a "new phase" of the civil rights movement. This new phase of the movement was characterized by "a struggle for genuine equality on all levels."[5] For Dr. King, this phase included a transfer of leadership from the hands of dominant civil rights groups to the hands of Black women and poor people in places like Bolivar County. These emerging leaders, like those in the NBCFC, desired economic freedom to feed themselves through landownership and the production of nutritious food while experiencing the benefits of the political and educational gains achieved in the first phase of the movement.

At the forefront of the NBCFC were Black women who were civil rights activists, sharecroppers, farmers, grandmothers, and mothers who comprised 70 percent of the charter members of the cooperative. These women were what sociologist Belinda Robnett defined as "community bridge leaders" in the civil rights movement "who worked primarily through a specific movement organization."[6] Theoretically, the women bridge leaders led their communities and articulated a civil rights agenda that transformed food into what philosopher Cornel West describes as "cultural armor" in Black life. West argues that throughout history Black people "create powerful buffers . . . to equip black folk with cultural armor. . . . These buffers consisted of cultural structures of meaning and feeling that created and sustained communities; this armor constituted ways of life and struggle that embodied values of service and sacrifice, love and care, discipline and excellence."[7] In other words, the NBCFC was a "cultural structure" that enabled the women and their communities to recast food as a shield against inequities around race, food, agriculture, and health. Food as a shield empowered members of the NBCFC to promote cooperative farming as a space for economic vitality, social cohesion, and freedom from the brunt of such inequities perpetuated by the sociohistorical context of the Delta. The region's sociohistorical context illustrated how Black life was shaped by food power in the hands of the Mississippi white supremacist economic and political establishment as examined in the previous chapters.

Drawing on the records of the NBCFC, archival materials, oral histories, US Senate hearings, and scholarship, this chapter argues that the process by which the NBCFC transformed food into a shield to resist inequities and promote economic development represents emancipatory food power in action. This process demonstrates how the NBCFC generated emancipatory food power as an extension of the struggle for civil rights and, in many ways, institutionalized the earlier movement ethos of the 1962–63 "Food for Freedom" program in response to the Greenwood Food Blockade.[8] At the same time, this process reveals the centrality of Black rural livelihoods to the manifestation of an evolving civil rights movement in Mississippi that reconfigured the leadership structure of the movement. While middle-class Black men, rooted in urban centers like Atlanta and Birmingham, were leaders of the larger civil rights organizations, Black women and poor rural people placed their lives at the center of the movement to empower themselves through smaller, yet powerful, institutions like the NBCFC. Food, as both nourishment and mechanism for Black freedom, was crucial to this shift in movement politics.

To emphasize these points, the chapter proceeds as follows. First, I describe the sociohistorical context within which the NBCFC was established. This section locates and documents the origins of the NBCFC in the development of a 1960s Healthy Food Rx program at the Tufts-Delta Health Center (TDHC) that predates contemporary efforts surrounding the relationship between food and healthcare in farm-to-hospital programs across the nation.[9] Then, the chapter examines how the formative phase of the NBCFC galvanized over 800 rural Black families to join the cooperative and build its innovative network that used food to promote agency and an optimal quality of life. This section necessitates a discussion about the role of L. C. Dorsey in the creation of the NBCFC, as she is representative of both the leadership that shaped the cooperative and the people it was designed to empower. The next two sections document the transformative and operational phases of the NBCFC, characterized by specific strategies used by the cooperative to build emancipatory food power via the development of a local Black food economy. These strategies were part of a larger goal of creating and sustaining autonomy and agency in the context of Black self-reliance and uneven race relations. The chapter concludes with thinking about the unrealized dreams of the NBCFC and how its legacy reshaped the civil rights movement and laid the groundwork for future Black food justice and food sovereignty efforts in the Delta.

"Food Was Our Number One Problem": Food Insecurity, Health Disparities, and Black Self-Determination in North Bolivar County

The development of the NBCFC is best understood within the context of food insecurity and health disparities in the northern half of Bolivar County that coalesced in the 1960s Mississippi civil rights movement. Amid food insecurity and health disparities, the sociohistorical tradition of Black self-determination persisted. Located on the banks of the Mississippi River just north of Highway 8, bounded by Coahoma County to the north and Sunflower County to the east, the northern half of Bolivar County was an important site for former enslaved people who sought refuge from the ills of racism. Their site of refuge was Bolivar County's all-Black town of Mound Bayou.

Founded on July 12, 1887, in the northeast corner of Bolivar County by Isaiah T. Montgomery and his cousin Benjamin T. Green, Mound Bayou was an oasis of Black self-determination.[10] As former enslaved men owned by Joseph E. Davis, the brother of Confederate president Jefferson Davis, Montgomery and Green envisioned a town that would sit on a piece of some of the richest soil in the Delta and be a place for free Black people to reside. In 1898, Mound Bayou was incorporated, and Montgomery became its first mayor. Around the same time, Mound Bayou also became known as a safe haven for Black landowners and farmers. By the onset of the twentieth century, the town "had become a progressive all-Black community striving to achieve self-determination in a land where Black self-determination was not accepted at all."[11] Mound Bayou had an all-Black government with a successful economy driven by agriculture and forestry as well as a thriving business district. In his article about Mound Bayou titled "A Town Owned by Negroes," Booker T. Washington found that the town was rapidly "increasing its facilities for doing business" and "acquiring all the machinery of a highly organized community."[12] Washington observed that at the time Mound Bayou had "a bank, three cotton gins, a telephone exchange, [and] a weekly newspaper" and was in the process of constructing its own water and electricity systems. Mound Bayou also boasted a public school and a Farmer's Institute as a source of agricultural education for Black farmers to promote practical production strategies and early farm demonstration work. The ultimate goal of the Mound Bayou's Farmer's Institute was to "help farmers keep their lands from white merchants."[13] As such, Mound Bayou was also known as a "Black fortress in the land where the white man had ordained himself to rule."[14]

Building on these origins, Mound Bayou continued to rely on the principles of self-determination and autonomy to develop responses to the social, economic, and political changes in the Delta. But by the 1960s, as the civil rights movement intensified in the Delta, the regional agricultural economy was in the process of rapid mechanization. While in the previous years Mound Bayou was able to survive such changes, this change detrimentally impacted the city's agricultural sector and devasted Black farmers and sharecroppers, especially those on large plantations that bordered the town in northern Bolivar County. While "life on the plantation was never good," Mrs. Pearl B. Robinson, a community activist and one of the key organizers of the NBCFC, explained, by the summer of 1967 it was unbearable. At the time, "food was our number one problem," and many communities were trying to find ways to get some type of food or federal food assistance.[15] L. C. Dorsey described this moment as a "traumatic period" that forced Black sharecropping families to navigate a thin line between life and death.[16] According to Dorsey, in her prepared statement before the US Senate Select Committee on Nutrition and Human Needs in 1970, three factors greatly contributed to this "traumatic period" in the lives of Black sharecropping communities.

The first factor was the mechanization of the Delta plantation system. As the gradual process of mechanization intensified, Black farm labor was replaced with agricultural technologies that were designed to promote low-cost efficiency in the production of cotton. Historian Valerie Grim, in her study of the impact of mechanization on Black farm families in the Delta and throughout the rural South, argues that this change in the structure of agriculture—from labor to capital-intensive farming—"created spatial reorganization on both the family farms and large plantations."[17] This spatial reorganization was motivated by the need for less human input in agricultural production and an increase in the use of chemicals and biotechnologies in the region's agricultural economy. The agricultural economics of mechanized farming, Grim shows, enabled white plantation owners to increase their agricultural productivity through capital while exacerbating the preexisting "social and economic problems of black sharecroppers, renters, tenants, and wage laborers who relied so heavily on labor-intensive farming to survive."[18] These racialized problems included issues of persistent poverty and Black dependence within an unequal system, designed to promote social, political, and economic inferiority among Black farmers, sharecroppers, and their families.

The second factor that contributed to the trauma of Black sharecroppers was the February 1967 revised federal minimum wage law. Compounded by the shift from labor-intensive to capital-intensive farming, the revised federal minimum wage law required plantation owners to pay their Black laborers one dollar per hour instead of the customary $3.50 per workday.[19] On the surface, this law would seem to have benefited Black sharecroppers in that they would receive more income for their intense labor. But in the quest for agricultural efficiency, along with the fact that white farmers in the Delta received federal funds to reduce cotton acreage, such costs to employ Black sharecroppers and their families did not readily fit into the new economic model of the plantation system. As a result, virtually no jobs were available to Black workers in the region's agricultural economy.

The third factor, as chapter 2 examined, was the change in the structure of federal food assistance—from surplus food to food stamps. The impact of this change cannot be overstated in that this shift detrimentally impacted the food realities of Black sharecroppers the most. At the time, L. C. Dorsey was working as a sharecropper and witnessed this shift firsthand. Dorsey remarked: "Our only source of food was surplus commodities—and that program had been cut off. A food stamp program had been implemented—but most people had no money to buy the stamps." As a result, Dorsey explained further: "We struggled to survive on top of that land—some of the richest land in the United States displaced—dispossessed, and unemployed, with nothing to eat, while our shacks fell apart and our privies crumbled."[20]

As if they were acting in sync, these three factors were at the center of the mid-to-late 1960s hunger problem in Bolivar County and most of the Delta that shifted the focus of the civil rights movement in the region and increased efforts of outmigration. While demographer Calvin Beale found that Black rural-to-urban migration authorized an estimate of 3 million Black people in the farming sector to leave the rural South, the hunger problem contributed to more instances of migration.[21] For instance, the Mississippi Freedom Labor Union (MFLU)—a group of Black farmworkers and domestic workers—was organized in the town of Shaw in southwest Bolivar County in 1965 to address poor working conditions and deplorable wages that perpetuated hunger, malnutrition, and starvation.[22] Working directly with activists in SNCC and the Delta Ministry, the MFLU represented a shift in movement leadership and politics that placed Black farmworker needs at the center of civil rights struggles. In 1966, over 100 displaced Black sharecroppers and their families occupied an abandoned air force base in Greenville, Mississippi, because, in their own words, "we are hungry and cold and have no jobs and no land."[23] Around the same time, national and local activists widely circulated reports and fact sheets documenting the deplorable conditions and circumstances that had become ubiquitous in the lives of Black farmworkers in the Delta.[24]

Of course, these demonstrations and reports contributed to the increase in civil rights campaigns designed to dramatize to the nation the structural inequalities at the intersection of food, economic inequality, and the environment. They also opened the door for new ways of addressing such inequalities through community-based public health interventions. In Bolivar County, for instance, such interventions were facilitated by a partnership between poor rural Black communities and the TDHC. This partnership set the stage for the development of the NBCFC. The TDHC (which is still operating today as the Delta Health Center in Mound Bayou) was organized in 1966 by an interracial group of activist doctors in the Medical Committee for Human Rights (MCHR). This group included white activists Dr. H. Jack Geiger and Dr. Count Gibson, physicians at Tufts University Medical School, and Dr. Robert Smith, a Black activist and physician in Jackson, Mississippi, who served as the head of the southern branch of the MCHR.[25] The group selected Mound Bayou as the site for the TDHC as a way to protect it from white opposition to the movement.[26]

From the beginning, most of the staff of the TDHC were local civil rights activists and Black health professionals from outside the Delta and included John Hatch, a native of Kentucky, who was the director of community health action at TDHC and the first director of the NBCFC.[27] TDHC staff members were hired using funds from the Office of Economic Opportunity (OEO), the agency that administered antipoverty programs under the banner of President Lyndon B. Johnson's War on Poverty. At the core of the TDHC was Geiger's idea that the center would promote optimal public health among poor rural Black communities by practicing social medicine that situated "the real problems of ill health among the poor" in the context of "the social order" of a community.[28] Social medicine, in a place like Bolivar County, translated into food. Amid sociotechnical changes in the area's agricultural economy that perpetuated outmigration, unemployment, and unprecedented levels of food inaccessibility, food as social medicine was crucial.

Studying the realities associated with such conditions in 1970, Geiger found that the median income for Black families in the northern Bolivar county area was about $900 per year, which was roughly $2.45 per day. This median income figure equated to "about 75 cents a day per person for each family member for everything, clothing, food, shelter, all of the rest, let alone medical care." Geiger also noted that the majority of Black homes were "not fit for human habitation," the main water sources were contaminated, sanitation was nearly nonexistent, and "13 percent of the black families reported eating only one meal a day, and that had pitifully little protein content."[29] The common diet of poor rural Black families, a document produced by the TDHC stated, "consist[ed] of grits and syrup for breakfast, pecans (if available) and fatback (if available) mixed with grits for lunch and fatback in dried beans or greens, rice and syrup for supper."[30] At local stores, the prices of these foods were so high that poor rural people would use whatever income they had on food with not much left for anything else like soap, clothes, shoes, and other necessities.[31] Even after spending all of their money on food, Kenneth L. Dean, then executive director of the Mississippi Council on Human Relations, found that many Black families still suffered from starvation in that their bodies were "being denied proper sustenance" and "the systems of the body that must be maintained in order to ward off disease and infection" were "denied the necessary food elements."[32]

Recognizing the vivid food and environmental realities of the context in which they worked, doctors at the TDHC began stocking their pharmacy with food as a first step toward addressing this problem, especially among children. "We decided that wherever we saw children in that circumstance," Geiger stated in an interview, "we would provide them with food; so much milk, so much eggs, so much meat, so much vegetables . . . by writing them a prescription for food; this food literally as an Rx."[33] This Healthy Food Rx program was one of the first of its kind to implement initiatives around the idea of "food as medicine."[34] Although an earlier public health project in the area recommended food as treatment for rural Black people, as historian Susan L. Smith observed similar practices in the Depression-era Mississippi Health Project, an initiative created by the historically Black Alpha Kappa Alpha (AKA) Sorority, Inc., the TDHC went a step further.[35] Instead of only recommending food, they partnered with local grocery stores in Black communities where they had developed neighborhood health associations to fill the prescriptions and bill the pharmacy for it. This food Rx program was extremely beneficial to TDHC patients but was almost immediately met with resistance from the OEO. Geiger remembered when a representative came to visit the center and questioned the program. Given OEO funding regulations, the representative informed Geiger that the food Rx program was illegal and that the pharmacy was for medicine and "for the treatment of disease." Geiger responded to the representative, "That's right, and the last time we looked in the book for specific therapy for malnutrition, it was food."[36] However, Geiger saw the food prescriptions as a temporary solution to the food crisis in the area, and with the OEO watching the program, there would need to be a more sustainable food program in the long term.

The Formative Phase: L. C. Dorsey and the Garden Project

In the wake of the OEO's discovery of the TDHC's healthy food Rx program, Geiger and John Hatch went to their network of neighborhood health associations and brought up the idea of a vegetable garden run solely by the communities. They saw the garden as a way for the people in the health associations to use the agrarian skills they already had in an effort to reshape their diets. Hatch remarked in an interview that he saw this as a great opportunity for Black agrarian people "sitting on top of the richest land in the nation, who were malnourished and had limited access to food, but who knew how to raise it".[37] Initially, many people were skeptical of the garden idea since many of them had no land. Viewing this as a major hurdle, Hatch asked L. C. Dorsey, whom he had hired as a community outreach worker at TDHC, to be the community organizer and coordinator for the garden in the fall of 1967.[38] In many respects, Dorsey was representative of the Black sharecroppers and rural Black mothers in particular who lived in the northern section of Bolivar and organized the NBCFC. She was an activist who was the daughter and wife of sharecroppers. She intimately understood issues of poverty, food access, and hunger, especially in the context of her gendered relationship with food.

Born Lula Clara Warren on December 17, 1938, Dorsey was raised in the cotton plantation system of the Delta by her mother, Mary Frances Davis Jones, who was from Alabama, and stepfather, Will Jones.[39] The first eight years of her life were spent on a plantation in the Delta town of Tribbett in Washington County, and by the time she was seventeen she had lived on plantations across Leflore, Sunflower, and Bolivar Counties.[40] Growing up, Dorsey never knew she was poor in the sense that she believed that all Black people lived on plantations and her family always had food. "I never knew we were poor. . . . I thought all black people lived as we did, all over the country, and all over the world, because our world was that plantation."[41] Living out in the rural world of plantations, Dorsey's mother and step father relied on survival tactics to feed their families. Such tactics included fishing, hunting, picking berries, and canning fresh fruits for jelly in the winter along with muscadines. For Dorsey, these tactics enabled her family to be food secure in a time when folks on other plantations were not able to be as resourceful. Whenever a family was running low on food, Dorsey stated that they would depend on a "network of support on the plantation" that would share vegetables grown in their gardens and excess sources of meat, including rabbits. This network operated in the spirit of "oneness," Dorsey made clear, "and the fact that even in our oppression we were brothers and sisters, with love for each other and concern for each other."[42] In other words, the network of support cultivated mutual aid strategies surrounding food, among other things, and was crucial to the sustainability of Black life on plantations.

But the time between Dorsey's childhood in the 1940s and the onset of her work as a civil rights activist in the mid-1960s was shaped by what she described as a "cycle of poverty." In 1956, as the plantation economy began to disintegrate before her eyes, Dorsey dropped out of high school and got married to a Black sharecropper from a nearby plantation. Within ten years, Dorsey had six children and was forced off her plantation due to the mechanization and chemicalization of the cotton plantation system.[43] From the plantation she moved to the Delta town of Shelby in north Bolivar County and found herself living in a condemned home with her children and husband. During her time in Shelby, Dorsey's husband found a job in town making thirty-six dollars a week and expected her to take care of the home, as he strongly believed in traditional gender roles. While her father and mother collectively took care of the home when Dorsey was a child, in her household her husband refused to fish, pick berries, or hunt to supplement their meager household diet. "My role was to cook, clean up, and take care of the kids," Dorsey recalled.[44] Dorsey was responsible for using what little income her family did have to get food. She even worked long hours picking and chopping cotton, while taking care of the home. In this situation, she fully recognized that she never had full control of the food supply given that every part of her life was dependent on some other mechanism. Feeling the brunt of food insecurity, Dorsey found herself hungry most of the time and it hurt more when her children were hungry too. As she put it: "It's one thing to be hungry yourself, it is an entirely different thing to know that your children are hungry, and to put them to bed knowing they're hungry, and listen to them cry themselves to sleep. It is even more devastating . . . to have the older children, who are only ten or so, be just as hungry but try not to let you hear them cry."[45]

Hearing the hunger cries of her children forever changed Dorsey. From that point on, she was determined to change her situation. This decision coincided with the climax of the national civil rights movement. Between the passage of the Civil Rights Act of 1964 and the Voting Rights Act of 1965, Dorsey was recruited to the movement by Annie Devine and Victoria Gray of the Mississippi Freedom Democratic Party (MFDP). By 1967, when she was hired by Hatch at the TDHC and subsequently selected as a community organizer for the NBCFC, she had been trained in movement politics by Fannie Lou Hamer and was a teacher in Head Start.[46] She had also been active in groups like the Delta Ministry, the Southern Christian Leadership Conference (SCLC), MFDP, the National Council of Negro Women (NCNW), and the Lawyers Constitutional Defense Committee.[47]

Dorsey's life and civil rights movement experiences undoubtedly guided her organizing approach to galvanizing displaced Black sharecroppers to join the garden project and her future work as the director of the NBCFC.[48] She saw this work as integral to the civil rights movement as she realized that for those on plantations, "the right to vote, the right to go into any café or restaurant or hotel was really kind of empty without a job . . . without the money to eat."[49] Once commissioned by Hatch to garner community support for the garden, Dorsey recruited a committee of mostly local Black activist women like herself, including Bernice Trigg, Willie Mae Osbourne, and Lucinda Young. This organizing committee of Black women canvassed door-to-door to convince families to sign up for the project. They went from plantation to plantation "knocking on doors," and many of the "people responded to the food concept."[50] Most likely appealing to the experience of the poor rural Black mothers in securing food for their families and explaining to them their similar situations, Dorsey and the women were able to recruit over 800 families to join the garden project. As a result, they soon realized that the garden project would not be large enough to accommodate the food needs of the families.

In response to the overwhelming support for the garden, John Hatch called a community meeting on December 9, 1967. The purpose of the meeting was to discuss transforming the garden project into a cooperative. Held in an almost abandoned theater in downtown Mound Bayou, the meeting was attended by sixty-four community members. Hatch began the meeting by discussing how he envisioned a cooperative project that would be owned, operated, and administered solely by the community. Following Hatch, others spoke about the logistics surrounding organizing a cooperative. Speakers included Dr. Rupert Seals, then a professor of

Mrs. L. C. Dorsey and two women in the North Bolivar County Farm Cooperative organizing, 1968. (Photo by Dr. Doris Derby)

agriculture at Iowa State University, who spoke about the amount of land needed to feed the families who signed up for the garden project, which was about 100 acres. Dr. Roy Brown, the medical director of the TDHC, spoke about "the medical value of food" and "the needs of pregnant women and children for protein and green vegetables."[51] After Brown's presentation, Hatch opened the meeting for questions and conversation. During this part of the meeting, Dorsey recalled, it was obvious that people in attendance were excited about the cooperative idea as they "talked about raising food in little gardens and sharing it with each other."[52]

For many of the attendees, the cooperative was just a "big garden" or large truck patch, Dorsey remembered, since the "people did have a natural history of working together and cooperating both in the agricultural development and growing of crops, but also just in living and surviving."[53] This natural history that Dorsey pointed out was part of a Black agrarian and cooperative tradition linked to the work of Frederick Douglass, Booker T. Washington, George Washington Carver, and W. E. B. Du Bois.[54] At the center of this tradition was land, and many of the people at the meeting were deeply concerned about land as well as the money and equipment needed to achieve their goals. In response to these concerns, two Black farmers from the area who were in attendance, Ed Scott and David Delaney, offered land, and others began to offer equipment, such as tractors or any resources they owned to support the project. Others volunteered to work the land and operate the equipment, since all of them had been tenant farmers or sharecroppers who had already acquired the skills needed to farm.[55] By the end of the meeting, the attendees strongly endorsed the cooperative idea, and within a matter of weeks the NBCFC was organized.

What began as a garden project, pitched to Black families by L. C. Dorsey and her organizing committee, had transitioned into a cooperative that allowed Black sharecroppers and their families to pool resources together to grow food. At the same time, the cooperative created the necessary space for them to use food to protect themselves from disparities in access to nutritious food and jobs. As such, Black sharecroppers and their communities were working toward making emancipatory food power a reality in their community through their collective work in creating and sustaining a local Black food economy.

The Transformative Phase: From Garden Project to Cooperative

Building on the momentum from the December 1967 meeting that transformed the garden project into the NBCFC, the attendees hit the ground running. Their ultimate goal was to be a self-sufficient local Black food economy. To build this local food economy, this phase required attendees to translate their excitement for the opportunity to create their own garden project into an organization. First, they needed to secure some type of funding or resources to purchase seeds for their vegetable operation. While they had been given land and equipment to cultivate a crop, funding was crucial to purchase seeds. As L. C. Dorsey explained after that first meeting in December, "We had . . . people to work, equipment to work with, and land to get started on, [but] we didn't have any money for seeds and nobody had any vegetable seeds in the amounts that we were talking about that we would need . . . for large acreage, so then the problem came of how we were going to get money to do the seed and fertilizer."[56] In response to this critical issue, John Hatch was able to secure $5,000 in start-up funds from a private Tufts University donor to begin the cooperative farm.[57]

Over the next three months, the cooperative took considerable shape and an additional 200 families applied for membership to join the cooperative.[58] As community volunteers worked day and night to plant sweet potatoes, which were the NBCFC's pilot crop, attendees from the first meeting designed the cooperative's financial and organizational structure. Overwhelmed by how the cooperative was growing, the NBCFC selected a temporary board of directors. The temporary board was commissioned to lay the foundation for the cooperative until the interested communities could elect their own board members.[59]

Led by Mr. William Finch, a former sharecropper from the Delta town of Symonds in Bolivar County, the board accomplished a number of things.[60] First, the board selected John Hatch as the cooperative's first director and Mr. John Brown, a farm manager at the nearby Abe Miller plantation, to manage the farm.[61] Second, they limited its membership to families that had a household income of no more than $1,000 and required each family to pay fifty cents to join the organization.[62] However, no family would be turned away if the family was in dire need of food. Third, the board drafted bylaws and the NBCFC was incorporated in April 1968, making it the first chartered Black cooperative in the state of Mississippi.[63] Fourth, according to an early organizational chart of the cooperative, the NBCFC's membership was separated into ten, at first, and then twelve farm co-op associations—one association for each community in the NBCFC's food network—that made up its general assembly.[64] Specifically, the NBCFC's food network included the following communities with an association: Rosedale, Gunnison, Symonds, Pace, Winstonville, Shelby, Mound Bayou, Alligator, Duncan, Round Lake, Beulah, and Perthshire. Each association selected a local group chairman and two other community members to serve on the cooperative's board of directors, which allowed the cooperative to be democratically controlled. Once the cooperative board of directors was elected it would then nominate

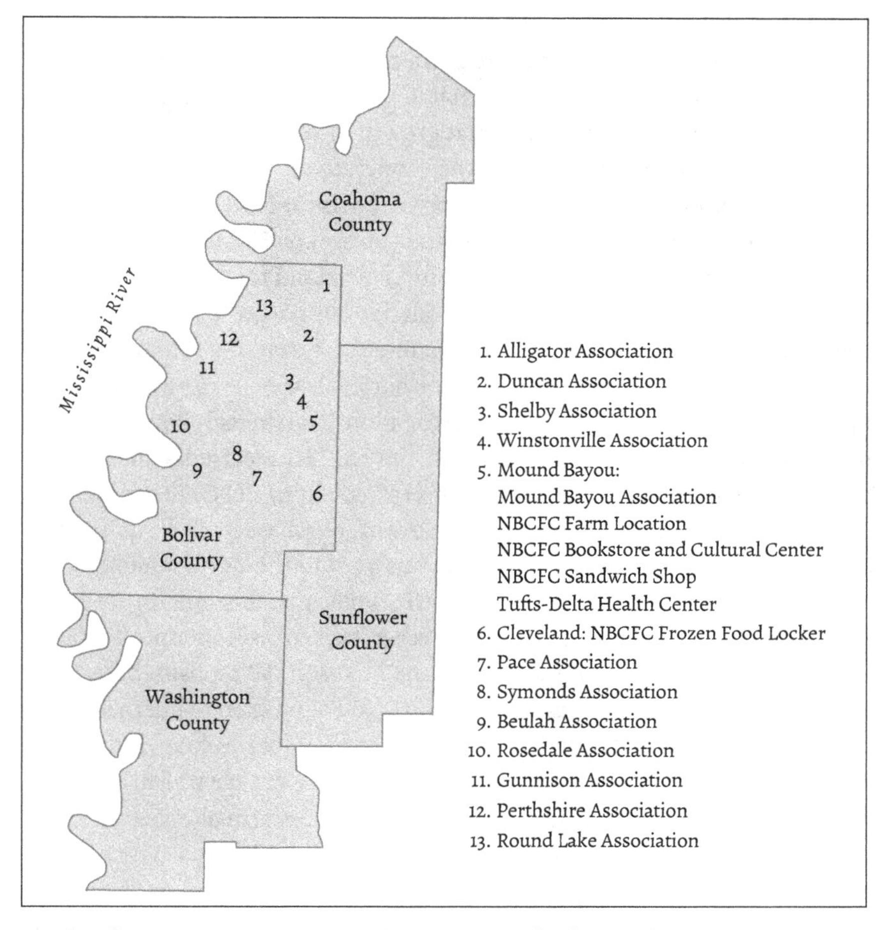

North Bolivar County Farm Cooperative community food network, 1967–68.

officers such as chairman and vice-chairman, for example, pending the approval of the general assembly.

At the board level, the following three committees were created to organize its efforts: the management committee, organizing committee, and technical assistance committee. Members of the management committee were responsible for identifying and securing equipment and land to ensure that the cooperative would be operational. The organizing committee worked to build local community capacity to support the full development of the cooperative. The technical assistance committee worked with university staff members from the agricultural college at Mississippi's 1862 land-grant institution, Mississippi State University, and personnel from Iowa State University, to learn additional production techniques to grow crops efficiently.[65] Among these committees, Hatch saw the work of the management committee as critical to the potential growth of the NBCFC because of its role in securing land as the basis of the cooperative.[66]

Aligned with an analysis of land being the basis for Black freedom and justice as put forth by Malcolm X in 1963 and Fannie Lou Hamer in 1970, Hatch realized that the cooperative would need to own land for production and to build its local food economy.[67] While outside support was secured to start the cooperative, Hatch and the NBCFC members saw this foundation as a way to build their survival capacity. Such survival capacity, however, would take time, so Hatch looked to the OEO for additional funds following the cooperative's incorporation. In May 1968, the NBCFC received a "nutritional demonstration grant" in the amount of $152,000 from the OEO through the TDHC, which allowed it to hire a full-time staff, purchase its own equipment, and hire a farm manager.[68] This grant was vital to the development of the cooperative, but the members of the NBCFC knew that this funding was temporary and that they would need to find other ways to be economically viable. As such, they also received funds from the Madison, Wisconsin–based civil rights group Measure for Measure and the Ford Foundation to purchase their own land, which would serve as a strong foundation for the cooperative.[69]

By the beginning of the summer of 1968, the cooperative was ready to begin its first crop year. This first year of the NBCFC's farm allowed the community to expand the meaning of civil rights by building a type of food democracy that placed the ideas and needs of community members at the core of an emancipatory vision. This operational phase also made space for new ideas, leaders, and projects to emerge and for the cooperative to move toward its goal of full autonomy beyond the purview of its relationship with the TDHC, which was always a critical part of its plan. In many respects, this phase made real the collective dreams of many displaced Black sharecroppers and farmworkers who attended the December 1967 meeting.

The Operational Phase: Nourishing a Local Black Food Economy

According to the NBCFC's articles of incorporation signed in April 1968, the purpose of the cooperative was to "promote the general welfare of agriculture in North Bolivar County . . . [and] enable members of the Association and others situated in the same geographical area to cooperate in the pro-

John Hatch with a cooperative member on the North Bolivar County Farm Cooperative Farm, 1968. (Photo by Dr. Doris Derby)

ductions [*sic*], processing, packing, distribution, financing and marketing of agricultural products."[70] Due to OEO funding stipulations, official membership in the cooperative was restricted to families that fell under the office's established poverty level, which was $800 per household.[71] As such, out of the 900 families that applied for membership in the initial campaign for the cooperative, only 698 families were considered members during its first crop year.[72] While this restriction did not keep the NBCFC from feeding all those in need, it undoubtedly fueled its quest to become self-sufficient and operate its own local Black food economy. The anchor of this economy was the NBCFC farm that framed the cooperative's employment, production, distribution, education, and food service activities.

Employment

The NBCFC's workforce was all Black and composed of mostly poor rural people who represented the families that made up the cooperative. Due to mechanization and racism, many of the younger Black population in the area had migrated to Chicago and other northern cities to escape such conditions that left many Black people jobless and hungry. As a result, the majority of the poor families that made up the Black population that the NBCFC worked with were headed by men or women who were at least sixty-five years old and responsible for raising their youngest children and grandchildren. In addition, senior citizens who lived alone or senior couples found work with the NBCFC. As a result, over 90 percent of the workforce had less than a high school education.[73] To work at the cooperative, though, formal education was not a requirement. Instead, as L. C. Dorsey wrote in the 1969 NBCFC report, "the only skills needed were a strong back and nimble fingers."[74] All other skills would be obtained through various trainings and educational activities. The poorest families in the area, the households with an income of less than $200 per family member, were prioritized for employment.[75]

By creating multiple job opportunities, the NBCFC provided employment for over 300 Black families. These included the farm, the cooperative main office, a sandwich shop at the TDHC, a frozen food locker, a senior citizen and worker hot lunch program, a Black bookstore and cultural center in Mound Bayou, and the community co-op stores. Due to the NBCFC being financially backed by the OEO in its first few years of operation, those who obtained employment from the NBCFC received ten dollars per eight-hour workday, which equaled the $1.25-per-hour minimum wage at the time. This payment structure was important in that those who worked for the NBCFC had been sharecroppers who were accustomed to barely making three dollars per ten-hour workday, which amounted to thirty cents an hour for their labor. This income was mostly used to purchase food and other essential household items. Recognizing this, the NBCFC's payment system was a wage-food credit system in that the workers would receive four dollars in cash and six dollars in food, which was their ten-dollar payout for the workday. Others worked for eight dollars a day depending on their hours and were paid three dollars in cash and five dollars in food. Therefore, the cash could be used to purchase other things beyond food that each family needed to survive.[76]

The NBCFC's budget played a major role in its ability to pay its workers a living wage and improve their economic and food realities. As cofounder Pearl B. Robinson remarked toward the end of the NBCFC's second growing season, "We are eating better and some of us make $8.00 and $10.00 a day working on the farm."[77] During the first three months of operation, all work was voluntary and no one received any wages or salary until the OEO's support became available. This support, supplemented by membership dues and funds generated from the other enterprises, was the foundation of the NBCFC's budget. During the first full growing season in 1968, $97,850 was paid out in wages, with over 70 percent of the labor budget going to workers in the field. The second growing season saw a reduction in wages paid out to $90,000 due to changes in the farm production plan as the cooperative transitioned some of its land to cotton, soybean, and pea production to offset additional farm costs. Regardless of budgetary constraints and farm plan changes, the NBCFC remained committed to ensuring that most of the budget would support workers in the field and the farm enterprise.[78]

Production

Juxtaposed against a sea of cotton and soybeans, the production activities of the NBCFC operated within the intersecting processes of farm planning, land resource acquisition, and the production of fresh produce. At its peak, the NBCFC owned 427 acres of land and farmed over 1,000 acres of leased land. This land produced a variety of fruits and vegetables such as cabbage, broccoli, cucumbers, cantaloupe, watermelon, carrots, navy beans, pinto beans, and a host of others on rich Delta soil.[79] The NBCFC also maintained a peach orchard and planted pecan trees that allowed it to diversify its crop selection. The peach orchard, which started producing fruit in 1973, provided multiple job opportunities for cooperative members.[80] Beyond vegetable and fruit production, the cooperative also engaged in food-making. The NBCFC's food-making activities consisted of the production of low-cost, high-protein noodles made on-site in the cooperative's largest building constructed with funds from the Noodles for America foundation and the OEO.[81] Such production activities occurred on several tracts of land that made up the NBCFC farm, which was the cooperative's principal enterprise and anchor of their local Black food economy. The production-planning process of the NBCFC occurred in three phases, which ensured that it would meet its goal of "freedom from hunger and unemployment" in the area.[82]

First, the cooperative board surveyed poor rural Black communities across north Bolivar County to find out what kinds of foods they would likely eat if grown on the farm.[83] For these communities, this was one of the first times that poor rural Black people who had been sharecroppers had the opportunity to actively decide what types of food they wanted to put in their bodies. For many decades, the plantation system made these decisions for these communities through "furnishings" or federal food assistance programs. What made the cooperative's food plan different from federal food assistance, John Hatch remembered, was that those "existing programs were geared primarily toward avoiding starvation and were not doing very much to build survival capacity."[84] By asking the communities what they wanted to eat and in effect grow, the NBCFC gave poor rural Black people agency in the production, consumption, and distribution of food.

After building a list of foods from the community surveys, the NBCFC collaborated with doctors and nutritionists at the TDHC to identify foods that could be grown on the Delta's fertile soil. Separated into four groups, the foods selected from the list contributed to a proper nutrient-rich diet that could counter the many instances of malnutrition among the poor rural Black communities.[85] The first group included foods that were sources of protein such as peanuts, lima beans, snap beans, and southern peas such as black-eyed peas. The second group contained foods that were a good source of critical vitamins and included cucumbers, okra, tomatoes, sweet potatoes, and greens such as turnip, mustard, and collard—key foods in the southern diet. The third group consisted of staple foods that were carbohydrates, such as Irish potatoes and corn. The last group was made up of fruits such as watermelons, which many of the community members enjoyed, especially during the summer months. Among these foods, peanuts, lima beans, tomatoes, sweet potatoes, turnips, and other field greens were highly recommended for production on the farm.[86]

With a food and growing plan in place, the second step in the process of developing the farm was to acquire suitable land for production beyond the acres that were donated by Black farmers at the December 1967 meeting.[87] The land donated, which was approximately 128 acres across multiple tracts, was used to test the cooperative's ability to grow the foods identified by the community.[88] While the NBCFC did not own this land, the donated land was critical to the early successes of the cooperative and set the stage for the expansion of the farm. For instance, this land yielded over 1 million pounds of food that the NBCFC produced in its first growing season.[89] Recognizing its ability to grow food at this level, the cooperative wanted to secure its own land so that it could build infrastructure to scale up and have one tract of land as a base. In 1968, the cooperative was able to make a down payment on its first piece of land, a forty-acre lot, with the help of funds raised by the Measure for Measure organization.[90] With funds from the Ford Foundation, the cooperative acquired its largest piece of land—a 307-acre plot—that provided the space for the cooperative to build its base and infrastructure.[91] With this purchase, the cooperative now had 347 acres of land to support its growing local Black food economy.[92]

Cooperative member holding snap beans on the North Bolivar County Farm Cooperative Farm, 1968. (Photo by Dr. Doris Derby)

The third step in this process was to obtain the necessary resources and infrastructure to work the land and grow food. During its first growing season, the NBCFC relied on equipment loaned to them by Black farmers in the area. They also relied on agricultural merchants who assisted with equipment to plant certain test crops, including potatoes. While this was a crucial foundation for the cooperative and critical to the major successes of its first year of operation, it was not sustainable. This became evident during the NBCFC's second year of operation when it purchased its own land. Due to this increase in acreage, the NBCFC purchased state-of-the-art equipment that included four tractors, a small vegetable seed planter, and an air blast sprayer machine, which was one of only three in the entire county at the time. In addition, the NBCFC created its own irrigation system to support its production capacity and ensure that the vegetables the NBCFC wanted to grow would be able to survive the extreme Delta heat during the summer. It also was critical to the NBCFC's nonfood crops such as cotton and soybeans that offset costs associated with community-based food production.[93]

Undoubtedly, the equipment and irrigation system made the NBCFC one of the most advanced Black cooperatives in the South and allowed the organization to substantially expand during and after its second growing season. Drawing on what it called its "labor reserves" of over 300 families in the area, the NBCFC also built infrastructure on its land, which included the renovation of an on-site home for the farm manager and his family. The NBCFC even built a large shed for storage, processing, and packaging. Such infrastructure was critical to the sustainability of their local Black food economy and allowed the NBCFC to minimize costs and operate at optimum efficiency as cooperative members worked to realize their emancipatory food power dreams through tangible means.

Distribution

The NBCFC's food distribution system was made up of a frozen food locker, a system of community cooperative stores, innovative marketing ventures, and farm-to-institution distribution programs. The idea of the frozen food locker came about during the NBCFC's first growing season. At the time, the cooperative was faced with the question of what to do with surplus food produced on the farm and how to store it for year-round availability, especially during the winter months. John Hatch presented the frozen food locker as a solution to the surplus food problem at the August 2, 1968, meeting of the cooperative and reported that the cooperative had secured a one-year lease to use the former Hatchcock food locker in nearby Cleveland, Mississippi. In many respects, the food locker was a critical investment by the NBCFC and had the capacity to store up to 100,000 pounds of food. The locker came with state-of-the-art technology to process, flash freeze, store, and package all of the fresh produce from the farm. Such technology also enabled the NBCFC to flash freeze locally produced meats for its members and patrons. Although the NBCFC did not have a meat operation, it purchased the meats from farmers and wholesalers in the area.[94]

What made the frozen food locker impressive was that it also had space to operate like as a discount grocery store. L. C. Dorsey remembered that

Cooperative members working the land at the North Bolivar County Farm Cooperative Farm, 1968. (Photo by Dr. Doris Derby)

the discount grocery store allowed NBCFC members to get "more food for their food dollar than the grocery store."[95] The frozen food locker had regular business hours throughout the week with a full staff that included an on-site butcher and offered access to a variety of foods.[96] Mrs. Lucinda Young, one of the founders of the NBCFC, recalled that the cooperative's frozen food locker had "neckbones, and steaks, and hams—cured ham, fresh ham—turkey wings . . . , southern peas, lima beans, string beans, squash, [and] tomatoes," all available for purchase at discounted prices for members.[97] Noncooperative members could also purchase food from the frozen food locker. If any members or nonmembers were unable to store their meat in their homes, the frozen food locker provided space for them to store their meat and vegetables at a reasonable price, while cooperative members received discounts on locker spaces.[98] The ability of the frozen food locker to offer food at a discounted price and a place to store food made it one of the NBCFC's most innovative operations.

But for those without transportation or means to set up a way to get to the frozen food locker in Cleveland, the NBCFC distributed food through a system of co-op stores in each community it represented. Each store was a separate food retailer and was managed by one member of that community.

Selected by the community, the store manager was employed by the NBCFC and worked with the cooperative's garden committee to coordinate the transportation of food from the frozen food locker or farm to the store. In this way, the NBCFC frozen food locker and farm operated collectively as a wholesaler and the cooperative stores as retailers. As semiautonomous community food retailers, the stores also managed food deliveries for members who could not travel. Prices for food were decided based on community need in consultation with the NBCFC board of directors. As a result, the prices at the stores were cheaper than grocery stores in the area. For instance, dried beans were normally sold at local stores for between twenty-five and forty-five cents a pound, but at the cooperative stores the beans were sold for between ten and fifteen cents a pound.[99]

In addition to selling food, the cooperative stores also carried other items. For example, the Winstonville community cooperative store sold used clothing to members at low prices as well as gave free clothes away to those in dire need.[100] At this location, the store manager worked three half-days a week and was responsible for selling the items. At other locations, stores sold items collected by the NBCFC such as "books, canned goods (fruits, meats, etc.), clothing, shoes, pots, pans, baby items, soap, and other toilet articles."[101] Some stores even sold furniture to families who lost their possessions in fires and other situations. "The whole concept was to sell these things," L. C. Dorsey stated in an interview, "and create a job for a person in that community and at the same time have a person who was part of the organization be able to look out for . . . the people in that community."[102] As such, co-op stores provided a critical food access point but also served the community in ways beyond food procurement.

While the frozen food locker and network of co-op stores were the main points of food distribution for the NBCFC, the cooperative also sold fresh produce in innovative markets beyond the Delta. Vegetables produced by the NBCFC could also be found on the tables of families as far north as Chicago and Detroit and as far south as New Orleans.[103] The reasons for shipping food to these cities were not solely based on the "marketing potential" of this type of distribution but aligned with "the concept of addressing hunger nationwide," L. C. Dorsey remarked in an interview.[104] The founders of the NBCFC well understood that hunger was not just an issue that Black folks in the Delta were experiencing but something that impacted Black communities nationwide. Their explicit marketing ventures included okra contracts with food processors such as Winter Gardens and other small farmers in the area.[105]

Additional foods produced by the NBCFC were used to facilitate farm-to-institution relationships cultivated by the cooperative in collaboration with schools, education programs, and the TDHC. The NBCFC's work with educational institutions and programs included distributing food to three public schools, two Head Start programs, and one local Catholic school. Working with the TDHC, the NBCFC distributed food to the health center's social service department and emergency food program. In some cases, the NBCFC distributed food to malnourished patients who received food prescriptions from the TDHC. Specifically, the formal farm-to-institution relationship between the NBCFC and the TDHC reflects an earlier instantiation of what we know today as farm-to-hospital programs.[106]

Education

The educational arm of the NBCFC facilitated a multidimensional approach to community education at the intersection of agricultural education, outreach programs, and food literacy. The NBCFC agricultural education program was designed to build on preexisting agrarian knowledge among cooperative members and translate it into large-scale food production. Skills developed in the program could be used to enhance Black life on the land and prepare cooperative members for jobs in the agricultural industry. In many ways, the NBCFC agricultural education program aligned with what Amber Dailey, Carol Conroy, and Cynthia Shelley-Tolbert describe as "the basic core of agricultural education instruction" that "consists of three intracurricular components: 1) classroom instruction, 2) experiential learning through supervised experiences, and 3) leadership activities."[107] In partnership with faculty members and staff from Mississippi State University's Extension Service and their Department of Horticulture the NBCFC agricultural education program offered courses on the most up-to-date farm management techniques, including pest management, soil conservation, and planning for food production.[108] NBCFC members also worked with faculty and staff from Atlanta University, Iowa State University, and Michigan State University to generate additional courses that would provide technical assistance on the farm.[109]

During each growing season, the courses were held every two weeks and were open to the entire community as well as small independent farmers throughout the area. During these courses, participants would also visit the farm to connect new agricultural concepts to what they were seeing on the ground. This manifested into two positions being created by the cooperative in crop health and management.[110] Although the cooperative exclusively focused on Black farmers and their families in the northern section of Bolivar County, they believed in sharing their resources with anyone who needed them. For instance, the knowledge obtained from these courses was used to provide technical assistance to the NCNW community gardening program and Fannie Lou Hamer's Freedom Farms Cooperative in neighboring Sunflower County as well as other Black cooperatives in the Delta and Arkansas.[111] The NBCFC also worked with the Federation of Southern Cooperatives (FSC), of which it was a member, to develop workshops in the region.[112] By working with FSC, the NBCFC articulated its emancipatory food power project as local and regional. Emancipation could not be achieved unless everyone in their purview engaged in economic practices that would uplift poor rural Black communities impacted by the regional agricultural economy throughout the South.

To this end, the NBCFC had an expansive outreach program that organized multiple economic development conferences in the South. In 1968 alone, the cooperative conducted five economic development conferences, two in Mound Bayou, two in Atlanta, and one in Memphis.[113] At each conference, participants were given the opportunity to discuss how large-scale vegetable production could be used as the base for rural Black economic development. The idea of food production as a base for Black economic development could be viewed as part of what the Black economist and creator of the Emergency Land Fund, Robert S. Browne, described as the "Black Southern Strategy." Historian Alec Hickmott argues that Browne's strategy placed land at the center of rural Black struggles by "linking space to race and the broader history of the region's economic development" to promote "a rural development agenda that envisioned African American landholders at the center of a more equitable and prosperous economic landscape."[114] For cooperatives in the late 1960s like the NBCFC, food production was also at the center of this rural development agenda. But food production was not just about growing food on Black-owned land as a way to ensure its economic capacity to survive; it was also about creating a food system that could produce food literacy.

Conceptually, food literacy is the competency in food skills and practices that empower an individual or community to correct improper diets and promote life-giving nourishment. Melissa Bublitz and colleagues argue that food literacy extends beyond just nutritional knowledge in that it facilitates the ability to understand "declarative types of knowledge" that allows one to identify both a specific food and the nutrients it provides the body and to understand "procedural knowledge" that provides a set of skills to cook the specific food.[115] In the case of the NBCFC, the purpose of the food literacy component of the educational arm of the cooperative was to enhance the cooking and life skills of poor rural Black mothers.[116] The NBCFC likely targeted this population given the fact that these mothers, whether voluntarily or involuntarily, took on the responsibility of feeding their families and communities. Sociologists Patricia Allen and Carolyn Sachs characterize this responsibility as the "socio-cultural" food domain that contributes to how women's relationships to food are defined. The socio-cultural domain represents women's "ties to family and also maintains cultural traditions that are at the heart of many women's identities."[117] For Black mothers in the NBCFC, this responsibility included not only cooking the food but also growing and harvesting the food on the cooperative farm.

The Black mothers of the NBCFC, in many ways, were key agents of change in the transition from improper diets to life-giving diets in their community, especially among children. This task was extremely hard given the influence of the plantation system on the diets of poor rural Black communities in the Delta. Most families had become accustomed to a diet that included the overconsumption of starches that led to the prevalence of diet-related illnesses."[118] While culturally appropriate foods like collard greens and sweet potatoes were known, other vegetables grown on the farm such as spinach and carrots were less known by the families. As such, the NBCFC food literacy program assisted Black mothers as they learned about ways to expand beyond plantation-based eating habits by providing them with the skills and practices needed to have agency in nourishing their families. These skills included learning new recipes. The cooperative asked Pauline Holmes, a Black nutritionist at the TDHC and resident of Mound Bayou, to develop recipes for the mothers of the NBCFC that would expose them to new ways of cooking with familiar and unfamiliar foods to incorporate into their diets.[119] Holmes, who was president of the Mound Bayou Civic Club at the time, held a degree in nutrition from Ohio University.[120] Her standing in the local community and formal training in nutrition made her the perfect person to create food literacy programming for the NBCFC that accounted for declarative and procedural types of food knowledge among cooperative members.[121] The NBCFC food literacy program took seriously the realities of poor rural Black mothers in the area, and all recipes were designed for food that the mothers would receive from the cooperative. Holmes even went a step further in that she often went into the homes of Black mothers in the communities to do cooking, canning, freezing, and storage demonstrations using food from the farm.[122] Herman Johnson Sr., a longtime Mound Bayou resident who was affiliated with the NBCFC, remembered the classes that Holmes taught. In an interview, Johnson said that Holmes "would go around the county to the communities and teach people how to cook foods that we grew on the farm—she would teach people how to take beans from the field, cook them, mash them together, and make bean burgers."[123]

While the cooperative knew that it would take time for the mothers to adjust to the new recipes, they knew that this type of intervention would promote some type of autonomy in food preparation. But the autonomy that the NBCFC sought to promote complicated their emancipatory politics in that the work of the cooperative was not necessarily concerned with disrupting gender roles in the context of the kitchen. Indeed, the NBCFC food literacy program was deeply gendered. Poor rural Black mothers in the area were similar to L. C. Dorsey in that many of them were forced to nourish their families in households that subscribed to traditional gender roles. As such, emancipation didn't necessarily mean that poor rural Black mothers would be emancipated from their assumed role of ensuring the nourishment of their household and community.

Despite these gender-based blind spots, the NBCFC food literacy program was a crucial part of the cooperative's educational arm. Black mothers obtained the skills to contribute to the mitigation of poor health outcomes associated with the previously racialized lack of access to nutrition. In many respects, the NBCFC food literacy program reshaped what food preparation entailed for poor rural Black mothers and produced a model for new ways of cooking with limited resources. The program even reached beyond the NBCFC's community base and was designed to uplift any community that needed assistance in the Delta.

What is important about the educational arm of the NBCFC is that it was designed to *build* on the skills that community members had already obtained. For instance, those who participated in the cooperative's agricultural education program already had agrarian knowledge and attended the courses offered to expand their knowledge base and learn new skills. The outreach programs provided a space for the NBCFC to collaborate with other groups to build a regional emancipatory food power project that promoted Black autonomy in the production, consumption, and distribution of food.

The food literacy program considered that poor rural Black mothers took on the responsibility of feeding their families and knew how to cook in the social context of the region. This is important in that many interventions in Black communities, then and now, create models that assume a lack of skills. The NBCFC assumed that members of its communities had agricultural and food skills and built on them, which made the educational arm of the NBCFC an important intervention.

Food Service

The food service operations of the NBCFC were farm-to-table efforts that provided food for the public and contributed to the building of managerial skills among the membership. Among these operations, the most innovative was the NBCFC sandwich shop. Located in the TDHC, the sandwich shop was a self-supported "pure business enterprise." Each day, two members of the cooperative who lived in the nearby Merigold community traveled to the center to prepare delicious sandwiches for hungry employees and visitors. The two members who ran the sandwich shop were full-time employees and managed the food plan and income of the shop. The sandwich shop was a thriving business that operated independently and provided a space for the NBCFC to enter the food business and create a consistent stream of income for two cooperative members.[124]

In addition to the sandwich shop, the NBCFC operated two hot lunch programs, one for senior citizens and the other for workers on the farm.[125] Using food donated by the cooperative, the purpose of the senior citizen hot lunch program was to address the lack of access to food and meals among senior citizens in the northern section of Bolivar County. Cooperative documents suggest that the food security of senior members of the community was a priority as the NBCFC always focused on ensuring that this population had access to nutritious foods. For instance, the cooperative created a health and welfare committee whose sole responsibility was to make sure that elderly cooperative members and any sick members had access to food.[126] The hot lunch program for field workers was administered during the summer months of the growing season and ran until near the end of harvest when the workday shifted and most workers worked through lunch. This program was managed by a member of the cooperative who lived in the Mound Bayou community. Selected by the community, this member would coordinate with the frozen food locker to procure fresh vegetables and meats to cook during the work week. The "simple, but nourishing and hot meal of meat, vegetables, and bread was offered at noon" each day.[127] This meal was crucial to the development of the farm in that it provided the workers with the energy needed to produce food on a regional level.

Unrealized Dreams and Lessons Learned

When looking through the records of the NBCFC, it is clear that the activities and enterprises that made up the organization's local Black food economy represented a preface to what the cooperative had hoped to achieve. The NBCFC had emancipatory dreams of scaling up beyond the sole focus on food production as a source of economic and food security for its membership. In fact, the pursuit of two projects haunted the cooperative: a commercial food-processing operation and the NBCFC farm supply store.[128] These two projects were heavily researched and pursued by the cooperative but were never realized. Yet, the very pursuit of these projects demonstrates how invested the cooperative was in creating future innovative ventures that would sustain its communities and offer additional opportunities to thrive.

For instance, the commercial food-processing operation was designed to facilitate the construction of an on-site canning operation that would create food products, including a line of canned soul foods. "The idea of a commercial food-processing business" managed by the NBCFC, one feasibility report stated, was to "use land as a base for a production facility that will not only help to feed the hungry but lead to sales and earnings which can help to transform the entire Mississippi Delta."[129] The commercial food-processing business would have enabled the NBCFC to create canned food products that were produced by Black people for Black people. As part of what can be seen as an early wave of Black creative thought that resembled the principles of the early 1990s "For Us, by Us," or FUBU, campaign, the NBCFC's potential canned soul food line would have created a market that did not exist for Black communities at the time.[130] While most grocery stores were marketing food to other ethnic groups, the tastes of Black people were left out in that no products were directly marketed to them. Recognizing that grocery stores, in the South and the North, failed to provide culturally appropriate canned foods such as beans, okra, tomatoes, and different kinds of greens that were central to the southern Black diet, John Hatch raised this question: "If you could market Chinese food and Italian food and Jewish food and Irish food in the grocery stores around the country why couldn't you market a food aimed primarily at the tastes of black people?"[131] While the NBCFC was at the forefront of this type of food marketing that preceded the development of food companies like the Black-owned Sylvia Woods Food Company in New York, this venture never materialized into a component of the cooperative's local Black food economy.

In addition to the proposed commercial food-processing operation, the NBCFC sought to develop a farm supply store primarily for its members and Black farmers in the region. While the farm supply store would have the capacity to serve all farmers, it targeted Black farmers who were unable to access the resources needed to work the land and make a profit from it. Writing in their OEO proposal titled "Establishing a Retail Farm Supply Store at a Low Income Farm Cooperative," representatives of the NBCFC stated that the proposed store "would sell fertilizer, seed, chemicals, tires, batteries, paint, farm equipment, and other general farm supplies."[132] Building on a model that was common among other FSC members, the NBCFC farm supply store would operate as an independent retailer and purchase all supplies from the FSC's purchasing program. In this way, the FSC served as a wholesaler of farm products, and the sales from the proposed store would "allow the cooperative to provide to their members fertilizer, seed and other items at equitable prices."[133] The supply of agricultural products would have been kept in one of the warehouses built on the NBCFC's land which would have expanded the infrastructure of the cooperative. But just like the commercial food-processing business, the NBCFC farm supply store didn't survive past the planning stages.

The unrealized dreams of the NBCFC in creating a commercial food-processing enterprise and the farm supply store took shape against the backdrop of the expected loss of federal funding from the OEO, which forced the cooperative to rethink its business model. The new business model did not include many of the existing enterprises such as the frozen food locker. Although the cooperative knew from the beginning that federal funding would eventually go away, it needed more than five years of funding for the development of its local Black food economy to be able to sustain itself. As one way to get ahead of the impact of the loss of federal funding from the OEO, the NBCFC had to intensify the economic capacity of its farm by scaling up. As a result, the cooperative increased its acreage in cash crops such as cotton and soybean. The production of these crops depended on the purchase of heavy machinery and labor trained to use the technologies. As such, this move toward producing more cash crops decreased the amount of labor needed on the farm, which decreased the number of jobs that the cooperative could offer its members.

In many respects, the cooperative mirrored the shift that the Delta's plantation economy had made which left thousands of Black sharecroppers hungry and without jobs. Indeed, the irony of this shift, albeit at the community level, was clear as internal conflicts and divisions between the leadership and the members of the cooperative came to the forefront and the membership dramatically declined by nearly 300 families.[134] "The co-op has been criticized as not being well-run, of being a plantation, and many other things," L. C. Dorsey wrote in 1971. She concluded, "Maybe we're guilty of all these things, but we started out to fulfill a need that was expressed by our members."[135] For many in the NBCFC, the shift toward the production of cash crops pushed the cooperative further away from its goals. But the shift toward this type of production was not a failure of the leadership or membership of the cooperative—they achieved their goal of providing food and jobs for poor Black families in north Bolivar county. The first five years of the cooperative enabled poor rural Black people who had been sharecroppers to rebuild their lives on the ruins of the plantation, but the dependency on federal funding crippled the NBCFC's vision of emancipation through food production. Given the context by which the NBCFC navigated, the NBCFC did not shift its business model due to the belief that its emancipatory dreams would not be realized. In fact, it saw the shift toward scaling up as a way to sustain its economy. For instance, the cooperative continued to produce food for its members and supply food through the cooperative stores. The only failure, in a sense, was the fact that it could not provide enough long-term jobs and opportunities to sustain its vision of being an autonomous Black community built on a local Black food economy.

Conclusion

This chapter documented the process by which the NBCFC generated emancipatory food power through the creation of a local Black food economy. What started as a simple idea to get Black folks some food to eat and jobs to work manifested into one of the most innovative organizations to be born out of the latter years of the civil rights movement in the Delta. Yet, the history of the civil rights movement in Mississippi and across the nation has remained silent on the impact of the NBCFC on the movement and the nation. The poor rural Black communities that got together to make the NBCFC cultivated a space for them to think beyond just voting rights and education as paths to freedom. This space was necessary given the fact that by 1967, the key legislative wins of the movement had not translated into meaningful change in these communities. But their commitment to Black freedom remained unwavering. Rather than waiting for the legislative wins to free them, the NBCFC became a site for them to extend the movement to capture their everyday struggles with food and economic insecurity. Indeed, the NBCFC was a fertile site for the articulation of emancipatory food power that insulated the poor rural Black communities from the conditions and realities of racial conflict that coalesced in the agricultural landscape of the civil rights movement.

The question of emancipatory food power was always at the forefront of the NBCFC's agenda, which is why the organization struggled as it got closer to operating without federal funding. While it is unclear when the NBCFC officially disbanded, the combined effects of unrealized dreams, loss of federal funding, internal conflicts, and the shift in the goals of the cooperative marked the beginning of the end of the NBCFC's local Black food economy. Throughout the 1970s and 1980s, the cooperative struggled to recover from the losses and regain its momentum and keep its land from local groups seeking to transform it into other enterprises. Wendell Paris replaced Dorsey as cooperative director when she left for New York to pursue graduate education in the fall of 1971, and Ronald Thornton became the farm manager. Both men were graduates of Tuskegee and early leaders in the FSC. Over the next decade, Paris and Thornton worked tirelessly to rebuild the membership and increase vegetable production on the farm.[136] But the cooperative never fully recovered from the unrealized dreams and other shifts of the early 1970s.

In the 1980s, the organization simultaneously dissolved and evolved into several local organizations based out of Mound Bayou. For instance, a few members of the cooperative went on to organize the Mound Bayou Farmers Cooperative, which would eventually become the area's Sweet Potatoes Growers Association Cooperative. Throughout the 1990s, this association supplied the raw sweet potatoes used in the former Glory Foods Mound Bayou Sweet Potatoes canned food line.[137] In the spring of 1995, Mississippi's 1890 land-grant institution, the historically Black Alcorn State University (ASU), leased forty-five acres of land from the North Bolivar County Development Corporation, a former subsidiary component of the NBCFC founded by the board of directors in 1972.[138] This tract of land, which was once part of the NBCFC's largest tract of land on the eastern edge of Mound Bayou, is now home to the Alcorn State University (ASU) Extension/Research Farm & Technology Transfer Center. In the spirit of the educational arm of the NBCFC, the Alcorn demonstration farm offers a number of courses on the production of vegetables and outreach services that primarily target Black farmers in the area. The ASU farm also specializes in the production, processing, and distribution of purple hull peas, a southern staple. The peas are processed at ASU's fresh vegetable processing plant in the Delta town of Marks, Mississippi, and distributed mostly to Kroger stores across the South.[139]

Remnants of the groundbreaking work of the NBCFC exist today, and its dreams of emancipation—through food production that offered both nourishment and economic security—provide a window into understanding the current strategies of groups that mobilize around the food justice movement in the Delta and across the nation. As the next chapter shows, a group of Black youth who call themselves the "North Bolivar Good Food Revolution" are setting the stage for a comprehensive local food economy in the area. Located just one mile down the same street where the NBCFC once operated in Mound Bayou, the group's farm space is an incubator for training Black youth on agricultural production and how to create a viable business operation through food that can sustain their communities and resist the overwhelming food inequalities that pervade their lives. The fact that Black youth in the area are engaging in this type of work cannot be overlooked. Most community work and research on food production in the Delta has focused on older Black farmers and how to enhance their operations. The Mound Bayou–based farmer organizations and the work of the ASU Extension/Research farm are evidence of this approach.

But the work of the Black youth–led North Bolivar County Good Food Revolution signals a shift in the future of food production in the area that picks up where the NBCFC ended. This is exactly what L. C. Dorsey imagined when she was asked in a 1992 interview what she would have done differently with the funds used to start the cooperative. She stated that she would invest the funds in Black youth groups and programs in the Delta "because I really think that is the future of this region. You really do have to work intensely with . . . young people, helping them understand and building skills and working in all of the sectors of the community . . . and get them to the point where as leaders they could go back and restore some of these lost institutions and values."[140]

CHAPTER FOUR

From Civil Rights to Food Justice

Black Youth and the North Bolivar County Good Food Revolution

> In a very real sense, the future of food is people. . . . This future was also written long ago. . . . And it is young black people who will lead the conversation on changing our food and farming systems.
>
> —SHAKIRAH SIMLEY

When the North Bolivar County Good Food Revolution (NBCGFR) was created in 2017, its lead adult organizers in the Delta Fresh Foods Initiative (regionally known as Delta Fresh) envisioned the group as a catalyst for a Black youth–led food justice movement in the Mound Bayou–Winstonville-Shelby area of northern Bolivar County. They intentionally situated the NBCGFR as a continuation of the civil rights struggle to end food insecurity in the Delta that was initiated fifty years earlier by the North Bolivar County Farm Cooperative (NBCFC) in 1967, as examined in the previous chapter.[1] Many of the organizers personally knew folks from the NBCFC like activist L. C. Dorsey, and as if they were rehearsing plays from her playbook, they recruited youth with the goal of making them leaders in the establishment of a sustainable and just local food system in their neighborhoods. In many ways, the rural Black youth of the NBCGFR are the young people that Dorsey imagined would be continuing the work of her and her comrades in the NBCFC. While there is no historical marker that indicates where the NBCFC farm once stood or events that commemorate the tremendous impact it made on the food and economic realities of Black sharecropping communities from the late 1960s through the 1970s, the NBCGFR reflects this important project. In fact, the NBCGFR farm is less than one mile down the street from where the NBCFC farm was located. Some of the youth in the NBCGFR are direct descendants of sharecroppers who once benefited from the NBCFC and shaped the plantation system and agricultural economy of the Delta.

Today, however, geographic lines that once separated plantations are blurred. The rise of global, corporate agricultural interests and agribusinesses in the South have drenched the Delta in over 2.5 million acres of soybean, cotton, corn, and rice.[2] Abandoned plantation shacks have been erased from the rural imagery of the region and replaced with large-scale agricultural companies, research centers, and farms that make the Delta an enduring symbol of the ingenuity of American industrial agriculture. Cotton has been dethroned by soybean, which is now the most important crop in the state. The Delta is home to roughly 78 percent of the state's acres devoted to soybean production, and the region represents 39 percent of state agriculture sales, making it the largest contributor to the state's agricultural economy.[3] The US Department of Agriculture (USDA) reports that the Delta has the top five counties with land in farms in Mississippi: Bolivar, Sunflower, Washington, Tallahatchie, and Yazoo. Across these counties, the producer population is 83 percent white and 15.7 percent Black.[4] Bolivar County has the most land in farms in Mississippi, approximately 409,242 acres with 70.7 percent of that land devoted to soybean production, and the farmer population is 69.5 percent white and 27.3 percent Black.[5]

Yet in the shadows of such agricultural abundance, members of the NBCGFR and their families and communities navigate a local foodscape with virtually no nutrient-rich food options. Sociologist Norah MacKendrick defines a foodscape as the "places and spaces where [people] acquire food, prepare food, talk about food, or generally gather some sort of meaning from food . . . including the institutional arrangements, cultural spaces, and discourses that mediate our relationship with our food."[6] Bounded by high rates of poverty, the local foodscape of the majority Black Mound Bayou–Winstonville-Shelby area is representative of foodscapes that can be found in small rural Black communities across the Delta.[7] These small rural Black communities are nestled between soybean fields and include gas stations like Double Quick that offer an abundance of greasy fried foods, snacks, sodas, and alcoholic beverages. Convenience stores like Dollar General, which stock their aisles with cheap and highly processed canned, packaged, and frozen food items, high in salt and sugar content, anchor this foodscape. To access fresh produce, residents are forced to search elsewhere for nutritious fruits and vegetables. Some residents drive at least three counties over to Spain's Supermarket in Grenada, about 140 miles roundtrip, to access affordable fresh produce and meats. Others travel roughly twenty-five miles north to Walmart in Clarksdale. The majority of the residents drive a little over ten miles south to Cleveland, Bolivar County's largest city and home to Delta State University. In Cleveland, there is a Kroger, Vowell's Marketplace, and Walmart. There are also over fifteen readily accessible fast-food restaurants including Zaxby's, Popeyes, and Taco Bell that line two miles of Highway 61 that bisects the town.

Speaking about the agricultural conditions and food circumstances that shape Black life in Bolivar County, Delta native Cora Jackson stated, "I think it is very ironic that the communities around us are very much flourishing with agriculture, yet there seems to be a shortage of food."[8] Put differently, the invisible color line that separates the region's flourishing agricultural landscape from the prevalence of extreme food insecurity and poverty characterizes what *Orlando Sentinel* reporter Jeff Kunerth observed in 1989 as the "Delta Paradox."[9] This paradox provides texture to alarming statistics that surround Bolivar County and the state. Recent data from Feeding America estimate that the county's food insecurity rate is 24.1 percent, more than double the national average of 10.5 percent.[10] The poverty rate is 36.6 percent, which ranks the county among the top 5 poorest counties in Mississippi.[11] Data available from the Mississippi Department of Health (MSDH) reveal that 13.3 percent of adults in Bolivar suffer from Type 2 diabetes, 42.6 percent were diagnosed with high blood pressure, and 35.1 percent were obese. As it relates to heart disease, which is the leading cause of death in Mississippi, Black residents in Bolivar have the highest heart disease death rate in the county.[12]

At the state level, Mississippi has the highest food insecurity rate at 15.7 percent and the highest poverty rate at 19.5 percent in the nation.[13] The Congressional Research Service (CRS) found that 43.4 percent of persistent poverty counties in Mississippi were located in the majority Black second congressional district that includes the Delta.[14] The persistent poverty indicator captures areas that have had a poverty rate of 20 percent or higher for the last thirty years or more. Social policy analyst Joseph Dalaker writes that these areas "experience systemic problems that are more acute than in lower-poverty areas."[15] Systemic problems in the context of such high levels of food insecurity in the Delta contribute to the fact that the Delta is known as the epicenter of the "Black American Amputation Epidemic" linked to the regional prevalence of diet-related illnesses such as diabetes, obesity, heart disease, high cholesterol, and hypertension (high blood pressure).[16]

In a larger sense, Black food and health disparities—demonstrated in the Delta Paradox—are fashioned by what activists are describing as "food apartheid." Black activist-farmer Leah Penniman defines food apartheid as "a human-created system of segregation that relegates certain groups to food opulence and prevents others from accessing life-giving nourishment."

Penniman argues that food apartheid produces "dire consequences" for Black communities that include "incidences of diabetes, obesity, and heart disease . . . fueled by diets high in unhealthy fats, cholesterol, and refined sugars, and low in fresh fruits, vegetables, and legumes."[17] By using the term "food apartheid," I want to emphasize that the Delta Paradox is a function of a regional system of racial segregation—linked to the legacy of plantation power relations—that forces poor Black people in general and Black residents in the Delta in particular to depend on a state agricultural system that rarely, if at all, considers their food needs. Instead, the state of Mississippi is preoccupied with supporting the agricultural ventures of its majority-white producers that make up over 85 percent of the state's producers, while importing an estimated 90 percent of its food for consumption from outside the state.[18]

Against this backdrop of food apartheid that conjures the legacy of food power politics and instigates an ongoing multilayered food and health crisis in the Delta, the NBCGFR struggles to resurrect past dreams of emancipatory food power that emerged during the civil rights movement. Such dreams push the youth to confront questions surrounding the construction of Black food futures—where Black communities have the full autonomy and capacity to imagine, create, and sustain a self-sufficient local food system designed by them. Black food futures for the youth can be achieved through food justice efforts, or as they see it, efforts that propel them toward food sovereignty where they have the power to use agriculture and food as vehicles to control their lives. The youth hope that such futures will provide a pathway to economic security and cultivate a new food narrative in the Delta that promotes optimal health outcomes for their communities beyond a paradigm of disparity. Delta Fresh, through the work of the NBCGFR, draws on the spirit of the NBCFC to extend the work of the civil rights movement by investing in Black youth so that the youth can invest in themselves and their food futures.

But the story of the NBCGFR is not simply about how the past shows up in the present. Their story demonstrates what happens when we invest in Black youth so that they can transform the future of their communities. Shawn Ginwright characterizes such investments as an "ecologically responsive approach to working with black youth." In *Black Youth Rising*, Ginwright writes that this approach represents a practice that "build[s] the capacity of young people to act upon their environment in ways that contribute to well-being for the common good." He concludes that with this approach "learning becomes richer and more meaningful when young people intervene in issues that shape their daily lives."[19]

In thinking with Ginwright, and building on social movement theory, the learning process by which the NBCGFR operationalizes a food justice movement is facilitated through what sociologist Kenneth Andrews describes as a "movement infrastructure" and political scientist Sekou Franklin theorizes as "creative organizing."[20] These two concepts can be used to clarify a long tradition of Black youth social movement activism that can be traced back to the 1930s and that continues through today in the contemporary surge of youth-based food justice activism.[21] Organizationally, a movement infrastructure is "composed of a complex leadership structure, multiple organizations that have centralized governing structures and decentralized affiliate groups, formal and informal activists, and a resource base (i.e., funders, patrons, contributors, etc.) that coalesce around the same problems."[22] Delta Fresh is a movement infrastructure of local farmers, city and state officials, churches, public health organizations, schools, colleges, and other related stakeholders that provide the base for the NBCGFR to co-develop creative organizing strategies—innovative actions and methods—that move forward food justice work in northern Bolivar County.[23] Franklin writes that youth-based movements rely on at least three creative organizing strategies: framing, indigenous resources, and positionality.[24] Framing enables youth to assemble narratives that provide explanatory power in understanding the particularities of a problem that their communities face. The strategy of indigenous resources pushes the youth to view themselves in relationship to other actors and preexisting networks and organizations that seek to solve the same problems or community issues—recognizing the strength of people power in movements. The strategy of positionality encourages the youth to see their voices as valid and at the center of community concerns in tandem with adult mentors and groups.[25]

This chapter shows that the creative organizing strategies of framing, indigenous resources, and positionality are entangled in the agripreneurship, farming, and youth leadership development activities of the NBCGFR. Commissioned by Delta Fresh, these three activities reveal how rural Black youth in the Delta are rehearsing a new version of emancipatory food power that is situated in the context of their food realities and futures. This new version seeks to create the world that their predecessors in the NBCFC dreamed of—a world where Black folks can be free to make their own food and community decisions. The activities of the NBCGFR are intergenerational dress rehearsals for Black food futures that they hope will translate into a model for rural and urban Black communities across the nation. In fact, an underlying goal of Delta Fresh in creating the NBCGFR was to use the northern section of Bolivar County as a pilot test for the development of a food justice project in a specific community, rooted in the lives of people on the ground in general, and Black youth in particular. They predict that the NBCGFR will inspire other communities to invest in youth through the production, consumption, and distribution of food. Agripreneurship, farming, and leadership development are potential sites for the staging of social change in a food system or a conduit for creating something new beyond what can be imagined amid current realities. They are sites that can provide rural Black youth in and outside of the NBCGFR with the pens to rewrite their own stories through emancipatory food power.

Drawing on interviews, primary sources, newspapers, and other forms of data, including media, this chapter begins with a brief sketch of the history of Delta Fresh to situate the organizational beginnings of the NBCGFR. The organizational beginnings of the NBCGFR culminated with their 2017 community food survey that set the stage for their food justice movement. The chapter then explores how the NBCGFR builds the capacity of Black youth through agripreneurship, farming, and leadership development. Together, these activities give the NBCGFR the tools that authorize them to effectively control their own food futures—through market mechanisms, intergenerational relationships with their community including Black farmers, and pragmatic life skills—and by extension, empower their communities to do the same. The chapter concludes with thinking about how the NBCGFR's food justice work continues the civil rights struggle for emancipatory food power and links the connection between the past and the present in struggles for food justice in Black communities. This link is crucial for the creation and sustainability of Black food futures envisioned by the NBCGFR.

Organizational Beginnings: The Formative Phase of the NBCGFR

The NBCGFR emerged out of the history of Delta Fresh and the communities that many of its organizers grew up in or had deep ties to. Founded in 2010, Delta Fresh is a vast, Black-led, interracial network of local food systems actors including activists, farmers, and organizations committed to establishing a region-wide food justice movement. The vision for the movement was to promote food equity and produce economic and health benefits in poor rural Black communities in the Delta. In the face of food apartheid, which produced a profound impact on the livelihoods of Black people and other marginalized communities in the Delta, Delta Fresh began with seed funding and technical assistance from WhyHunger, a US-based nonprofit that supports grassroots efforts to address hunger and poverty around the world. This partnership strengthened the capacity of Delta Fresh to galvanize preexisting local relationships between groups of people who were already committed to creating real change through food equity across the Delta's expansive and unequal foodscape. In a region that has been used as a laboratory by outside institutions and organizations to understand and attempt to remedy some of the nation's most pressing problems with no real change, relying on the strength of local people and resources was non-negotiable for Delta Fresh. Rather than operating from a passive position waiting for "outsiders" to "fix" them, as former Delta Fresh chairwoman Deborah Moore put it, the organization built its own capacity by leveraging social capital and financial resources to produce the results it wanted.[26]

Building on this assets-based approach, Delta Fresh hit the ground running. By 2015, it had created a board of directors and achieved 501(c)(3) status, which allowed Delta Fresh to apply for foundation, state, and governmental funding to support additional work.[27] It also created a successful web of community action plans that included the development of a movement infrastructure through local farms, school and church gardens, innovative growing techniques through high tunnel production, farm-to-school programs, community food programs, and health education. While Delta Fresh made some important gains during those first five years, it recognized that it did not have the full capacity or staff or community bandwidth to support all of the projects in meaningful ways. It also realized that a regional model would not be sustainable as a long-term starting point due to the particularities and politics of each community. Instead, Delta Fresh saw an opportunity to revise its approach and scale down to the local level within the region to build a model for a food justice movement that could be replicated across the Delta.

In 2017, the Delta Fresh board reconfigured the organization and decided to focus its efforts solely on Bolivar County as a testing ground for its food justice movement with Black youth at the center. This reconfiguration manifested into the NBCGFR project. Although youth had always been a key part of the project, one of the founding members said, "We felt that if we worked with children it would help to change their eating habits and so as they get older, they will be able to pass that knowledge down." Ultimately, "we want them to know about healthy food and where that food comes from."[28] To facilitate the NBCGFR project, Delta Fresh received funding from the Bolivar Medical Center Foundation to focus on the communities that most of its board and members were from—north Bolivar County, specifically the Mound Bayou–Winstonville-Shelby area along Highway 61.[29] At the time, the population of the area was 4,168 with 1,445 households. Approximately 98 percent of the population was Black, 0.8 percent was white, and the remaining 1.2 percent was Native American. The median household income was $21,209, and 46.4 percent lived in poverty.[30] Such demographics made it clear to the board that addressing food and poverty issues was a necessary starting point for the county.

The renewed attention of the board members to the area provided a way for them to recalibrate their commitment to food justice by developing a rural Black youth–based project that would "rebuild a robust, sustainable, and equitable local food system" in the area.[31] It is important to note that Delta Fresh envisioned the NBCGFR project as (re)building a local food system that was once a vibrant, self-sufficient local Black food economy. The area that the Delta decided to create this project in was chosen not only because of the close ties that the board has with the three communities. In fact, they chose the area because of its long, rich history of Black self-determination in the production, consumption, and distribution of food that included the early Black agricultural work of Mound Bayou's founders and the civil rights–era food work of the NBCFC. Speaking in the 2019 short documentary *Building the Future: North Bolivar Good Food Revolution* by Delta-born Black filmmaker Arthur Evans, Tyra Slaughter, a founding youth member of the NBCGFR, characterized the work of the group through the past. Tyra explained, "We are fixing to start growing our own food—like during the summertime, we were going out there and we were picking our own food . . . peeling and shelling and all that, packaging it up and then we started selling it on our own and I feel like that's the same thing that Mound Bayou did—they got out there and did what they had to do."[32]

Intentionally building on this history and the broader legacy of emancipatory food power in the entire region, Delta Fresh launched the NBCGFR in the fall of 2017.[33] The name of the group points to the need for "good food" among those who are most vulnerable and how a "revolution" could ensure food justice and produce real change through food. For one of the early youth members, LeBroderick Woods, the name represents "a paradigm change for the community. We've gotten so stuck on instant gratification—your Big

Macs, your quick meals and things of that nature. We've kind of gotten away from things we were raised on—the fresh produce and grandmama's cooking and things of that nature. So good food is not just good tasting, it's good for the spirit. It's good overall."[34] Another youth, Tonitria Hunt, put it this way: "The good food is the healthy food, and revolution stands for trying to change the area to something new."[35] Trayla Britton, one of the youngest members of the group, argues that the name emphasizes that "we're helping people find the solution to get out of eating bad food—helping them eat good food and providing it."[36] According to another founding youth member, Quantrell Holmes, "The Good Food Revolution, to me, is just coming up with a solution to solve mostly the biggest problem that I can see . . . not just in Mississippi, but in the world. That's what the Good Food Revolution is, trying to fix what the government has done wrong, not putting healthy foods in local neighborhoods, and not putting healthy foods in corner stores."[37]

Food justice activist Tanya Fields argues that the "good food" frame in the food justice movement adheres to the fact that Black people "just want to get better food in our communities and make sure that those who are the most impacted are the ones who benefit from the economic opportunities that it would bring."[38] The focus on those who are most impacted is at the core of the NBCGFR. The youth of the NBCGFR want their community and the world to change through food. They also see it as their responsibility to do this in their particular context. The youth see their work as a form of empowerment that enables them to work to shift power in the local food system and be a model for other areas like theirs. Oftentimes rural communities like theirs are forgotten and not considered in larger conversations about food security and justice throughout the nation that have mobilized around urban communities. Recognizing their own power in addressing their own community food needs, regardless of exposure, the NBCGFR project did not begin on a farm or with a group sitting around a table thinking about prescriptive solutions for the community. The NBCGFR began on the ground with a simple, yet complex action: the development of a community-based food survey.[39]

The development of the community-based food survey was an effort to ensure that before the NBCGFR considered creating any solutions to the area's food problems, it would take an intentional step to listen to the community and learn about its food concerns. For many decades, communities targeted by the NBCGFR had been left out of regional and national efforts to address food security concerns in meaningful ways. When they were considered, it was to benefit large organizations seeking information to create a larger dataset that captures the demographics of food insecurity. While such data are important, they obscure realities experienced by communities in the Delta. From the top down it could be assumed that many people in the Delta just don't want to eat healthy food, but as one of the youth in the NBCGFR learned, "people really [don't] have the money to buy healthy foods. Because it's so high versus going to get ground beef or getting something healthy is much higher. Or just going to McDonald's to get a burger off of the dollar menu versus getting a salad. . . . They would love to eat healthy but they just didn't have the money to."[40] Such circumstances and conditions were the catalysts for the development of the NBCGFR's community-based survey that would generate data that captured the real food security concerns of the NBCGFR's communities that moved beyond an outsider's perspective of the area. To do this, Delta Fresh used funding from the Bolivar Medical Center Foundation to support the survey initiative and connected the NBCGFR project to the Mississippi Food Insecurity Project (MFIP) at Mississippi State University.[41]

Founded in August 2015, the MFIP is a diverse group of scholars at universities in and outside Mississippi that works with communities in all eighty-two counties of the state to document food insecurity and provide resources for community-led research projects on hunger and local food systems.[42] The MFIP's work with the NBCGFR encompassed trainings in survey development and methods. While the MFIP worked with the NBCGFR to generate data for its own work as well, the NBCGFR designed the survey with its communities and administered it themselves. Based on a series of meetings with city officials, churches, organizations, and community members across the Mound Bayou–Winstonville-Shelby area, the survey instrument was ready in October 2017.[43]

After this process, the NBCGFR learned about issues of food access and food insecurity in local food environments while being trained to conduct neighborhood surveys. Instead of mailing the surveys out to the community, the NBCGFR decided to go door-to-door to conduct the survey. For four Saturdays in the fall of 2017, the youth in the NBCGFR wore green t-shirts with their logo on the back and armed themselves with clipboards and surveys to knock on over 1,000 doors.[44] At first, one of the youth told me, many of the households refused to take the survey, but the youth continued to go door-to-door in teams. The perseverance of the youth to get the data needed to enhance their community proved to be productive, beneficial, and enjoyable, as Tyra Slaughter put it. "I enjoyed it," Tyra said as she spoke about her experience with the survey project, "but it was something like you got to keep a pace to it. . . . It's people in Mound Bayou that I didn't know stay around here, and I got to meet a lot of people, then see my folks."[45]

The survey project not only operated as a way to gather data from the community, but it also worked as a way to raise awareness about the NBCGFR and demonstrate to the community that Black youth were concerned about their neighborhoods and the food that they eat. This point is crucial in that their community loved the fact that youth were taking control. As Tanielle Woods, another founding member of the NBCGFR, stated, "By us being young and Black, they see that we are trying to do something, something productive, positive."[46] Indeed, this project was something positive because it gave the NBCGFR the data it needed to begin to imagine what the future of food in the area would look like. By the end of the survey project, the youth were able to obtain 211 completed surveys, which represented nearly 15 percent of the households in the Mound Bayou–Winstonville-Shelby area.[47]

According to the NBCGFR's survey, 43 percent of the respondents reported that they were food insecure, and 62 percent indicated that they used convenience stores to purchase most of their food. As it pertains to diet-related illnesses, 33 percent reported that they had Type 2 diabetes and 54 percent had high cholesterol. Among the respondents who indicated that they had to make critical decisions regarding food purchases over a twelve-month period, 81 percent indicated that someone in the household had to choose between buying food or medicine, 71 percent chose between food and utility bills, and 59 percent chose between food and rent or mortgage. Despite such hardships, 69 percent of participants indicated that chemical-free or organically grown local food was important as well. The survey also found that 89 percent of respondents indicated that they would support a mobile market that provided fresh produce to the community, especially given the fact that no stores in the area sell produce in general and local produce in particular.[48] As Tanielle described her community of Mound Bayou, "[There] are no stores. We have a Bob's Express that sells fried chicken. But nobody around here in the Mound Bayou area sells fresh produce."[49]

More crucially, the survey revealed that community residents like Tanielle view their food environment through the lens of what anthropologist Ashanté Reese theorized in her study of the Black community of Deanwood in Washington, D.C.: "nothingness." Reese writes that "nothingness—empty, void" is a lens by which Black communities shaped by food inequities make sense of "how, where, and how often they accessed the groceries they nee[d] to feed themselves and their families."[50] For the residents in Tanielle's rural Black community, nothingness captures their sentiments. At the same time, nothingness provided a seemingly blank canvas by which the NBCGFR was able to critically imagine Black food futures built on the needs of its communities. Nothingness also made clear to the rural Black youth that if they wanted to change their community, they would have to do it themselves, and the survey project empowered them to do so.

Building on the momentum of its survey project, the NBCGFR worked with the MFIP to develop a final report and organized two local events to share the results publicly. The first event was a small community town hall in December 2017 in the Mound Bayou–Winstonville-Shelby area. During the town hall, the youth engaged in community discussions about how to translate what was learned in the survey into collective action. Recognizing that the majority of respondents overwhelmingly supported the mobile produce market idea, the NBCGFR asked the community members present if the market idea would be a great first step in a long-term community plan. Those present at the meeting enthusiastically reiterated their desire to support the mobile produce market idea, and the NBCGFR worked with the Delta Fresh board to purchase one. They unveiled the mobile produce market in March 2018 at the inaugural North Bolivar County Farm-to-Table community event held at the Lampton Street Church of Christ's Fred Clark Family Life Center in Mound Bayou. This large event was designed to both celebrate efforts put forth by the NBCGFR to bring locally produced food to the community and demonstrate that this project was invested in the sustainability of the area. The event was attended by community residents, city officials, regional leaders, and a host of other key stakeholders who discussed ways to support and enhance the NBCGFR. This event also marked the beginning of the NBCGFR's journey into agripreneurship.[51]

Agripreneurship in Practice: The NBCGFR Mobile Produce Market

On the first Saturday of June 2018, the NBCGFR hosted its first mobile produce market in Mound Bayou. This opening market allowed the members of the NBCGFR to see the importance of their work in north Bolivar County. In the six months prior to the first market, the youth hit the ground running. Beyond the two local events to raise awareness and mobilize their community around their project, the youth worked tirelessly to procure locally produced fresh fruits and vegetables to be sold at the market. The most crucial part of the six-month process included the building of mutually beneficial relationships with local Black farmers, institutions, families, and commu-

North Bolivar County Good Food Revolution Mobile Produce Market at the organization's headquarters, Mound Bayou, Mississippi, 2020. (Photo by author)

nity residents. These relationships allowed members of the NBCGFR to learn about local food logistics as they organized and planned the harvesting, packaging, marketing, pricing, and transportation of the fresh produce to be sold at the market. For instance, LeBroderick Woods received management training so that he could serve as the market's first manager. In his role as market manager, LeBroderick designated three mobile market locations in the Mound Bayou–Winstonville-Shelby area. In the beginning, the market alternated weekly between each identified location and was purposely near a community anchor such as a church so that community members could easily walk to the market or drive a very short distance to get to the fresh produce. LeBroderick also organized his peers into groups to work with and on local Black farms to create contractual agreements—set up by Delta Fresh—to procure local produce. Such agreements were decided individually between each farm and enabled the NBCGFR to secure a supply of fresh produce that would meet community demand.[52]

In a larger sense, the NBCGFR's mobile produce market continues the long tradition of food entrepreneurship in Black communities. Black food entrepreneurship is rooted in what geographer Bobby Wilson called the "formal black economy in America" that emerged during slavery.[53] Enslaved people who gained their freedom created social and economic relationships through the growing and selling of food, as well as other goods, in their communities in segregated sections of northern and southern cities. For example, these food relationships emerged in the mid- to late nineteenth-century Black economy in places like Washington, D.C., where "hucksters," those who grew and sold food on wagons or at street markets, engaged in mobile food business ventures to build economic security in their communities.[54] What makes the NBCGFR mobile produce market different from earlier forms of everyday Black food entrepreneurship, though, is that the market goes a step further. The market is not only a place for the building of social relationships through economic transactions. The NBCGFR mobile produce market represents an innovative outside classroom where the youth learn the logistics of local food marketing and the business aspects of agricultural production.

The learning component of the NBCGFR mobile produce market creates pathways for rural Black youth in the project to learn about the importance of agripreneurship and how it can be used to increase community access to affordable fresh food. While the concept of agripreneurship is often used to describe innovative agricultural ventures in developing countries, it resonates deeply within the work of the NBCGFR. According to Voliveru Sudha Rani, agripreneurship is a community-based approach to the direct marketing of sustainable agriculture. This type of agriculture "denotes a holistic, systems-oriented approach to farming that focuses on the interrelationships of social, economic and environmental process."[55] Situated along this line of thinking, the agripreneurship arm of the NBCFGR trains the youth to be social entrepreneurs of their local food system. David Bornstein writes that social entrepreneurs are individuals who have the transformative capacity to generate systemic change through "new ideas to address major problems[,] who are relentless in the pursuit of their visions [, and] . . . who will not give up until they have spread their ideas as far as they possibly can."[56] Indeed, the ultimate goal of the NBCFGFR is to be an example for their region and eventually the world. But for the NBCGFR, the first priority is working alongside their community to change the food realities of their families and residents in the area.

In a 2019 interview with the Mississippi Public Broadcasting (MPB) network, Tanielle described the mobile produce market as "seed-to-consumer."[57] While, on the surface, the seed-to-consumer description put forth by Tanielle may not be new in that other communities have similar projects across the nation, this idea goes beyond just the marketing and selling of fresh okra, tomatoes, potatoes, peas, cabbage, and watermelon that ends in an economic transaction. Instead, the transaction is just one small step in the NBCGFR's holistic approach to building a mutually beneficial relationship that seeks to enhance the social, economic, and physical health of their families and communities. The relationship is solidified as soon as the seed is put in the ground. What makes this moment so important is that the youth know that the seed will open up an entire new world to their community. While many of the residents had grown up on the land, they had become dependent on grocery stores and gas stations that accept the US Department of Agriculture's Supplemental Nutrition Assistance Program (SNAP) benefits, formerly known as the Federal Food Stamp Program, to purchase food from outside of their communities. As a result, many of them viewed the process of getting fresh food as complicated and extremely stressful. The presence of the mobile market in the community makes it easier to purchase fresh produce in one specific area. Such a shopping experience at the market, one patron commented, "helps us a lot to get everything we need in one place. It is very economical and healthy."[58] The fact that food is affordable and healthy is a critical part of the NBCGFR's larger goal of creating and sustaining a local food system in the community.

But this larger goal does not begin with community members accessing and purchasing fresh produce at the market and end with an economic transaction. Each market location offers a relational experience in that community members and other consumers have the opportunity to learn about the food production process and how to cook certain foods through demonstration and cooking classes at local churches.[59] "We basically tell the stories behind the food," Tyra Slaughter remarked when talking about the cooking demonstrations.[60] These stories are most likely shared in a commercial kitchen in a local church fellowship hall, which is a cornerstone of many Black churches. As the "greatest social institution" in Black life, as sociologist W. E. B. Du Bois once wrote, the Black church plays a major role in rural Black communities across the South and especially in the vitality of north Bolivar County.[61] Many of the early supporters of the NBCGFR were pastors and stakeholders associated with local churches who recognized the importance of creating a healthy congregation through systemic change.

Reverend Dr. Heber Brown III, founder of the Black Church Food Security Network (BCFSN), writes that "Black Churches have the leverage, standing, and resources needed to develop the systemic solution to food insecurity that gets to the root of the problem."[62] In this line of thinking, the youth see their cooking demonstrations at churches as an intervention for their mostly older patrons who like to use the fresh produce in the preparation of soul food. The demonstrations are a space to build what social scientist Abigail R. Lawrence-Jacobson describes as "intergenerational community action." Lawrence-Jacobson writes that intergenerational community action represents "older adults and youth working together to address a community issue of mutual concern" that "contribute[s] to older and younger people's empowerment and sense of shared responsibility for the well-being of the other generation."[63] While many of the older generations know how to prepare the food, the demonstrations are designed to promote alternative ways of preparing southern vegetables using more herbs coupled with less meat, sugar, and salt. By transforming the church kitchen into a creative space to reimagine the use of culturally appropriate vegetables with older generations, the youth are able to also learn about their community. They have even conducted such classes at local festivals to attract other demographics. They have also used consumer SNAP education programs to demonstrate how these food benefits can be used at the market. The consumer education programs also increase the community members' awareness of how to use their SNAP benefits in places other than traditional grocery food outlets.

To be sure, the youth recognize the tremendous impact that the market has made on their community. Based on the almost immediate successes of the first season of the market and community support, the youth realized that the community needed a local space to buy fresh food and build social relationships that promote systems-level change. This approach aligns with sociologist Thomas Lyson's notion of "civic agriculture" that "embodies a commitment to developing and strengthening an economically, environmentally, and socially sustainable system of agriculture and food production that relies on local resources and serves local markets and consumers."[64] This commitment is extremely important to the youth in the NBCGFR, and the mobile produce market and related activities are only short-term solutions. The ability to create and manage the community-designed mobile produce market not only enhanced their capacity for agripreneurship but also gave them the capacity to dream bigger.

What started as a simple idea based on community feedback related to the need for food evolved into an important aspect and asset in the community. The youth envision the next steps as working toward building permanent infrastructure like a small grocery store to complement the mobile market and scale up their production. "I hope [the mobile produce market] grows to us having our own market here, and it being a consistent thing throughout the week—not just a Saturday event," LeBroderick stated, "that it's something that can be prominent and it lasts through seasons—summer, winter, fall, all of the above. That it's our own Walmart or grocery store here in Mound Bayou."[65] Another one of the youth said that it would be great if we had "closer markets, closer grocery stores. Maybe grocery stores that sell things, two-for-one deal with lettuce. Instead of selling it, maybe a pick five on a lettuce or actually you get two lettuces, or you get a bundle deal of vegetables or something like that."[66]

The fact that the youth in the NBCGFR are thinking about permanent infrastructure that provides consistent access to nutritious food is important. For them, the infrastructure would demonstrate the power of the community, especially given that those who own the corner stores that sell cheap and highly processed food to their community don't look like them. Speaking about the corner stores and changing the products offered at those locations, Tyra told me, "We got to want change for things to start changing. If we step up and say, 'We don't want this in the store. We're going to close this store down.' We have the power to do anything." She further stated, "Majority of everybody here is Black, and it's just the people in the [corner] store that's not the same color. They don't stay here. If we want to do something, we can get rid of all that stuff. And then we can get fruits and vegetables and fresh meat and stuff like that, and put it here, where we stay."[67] Tyra also suggested, knowing that building infrastructure and shifting power in who owns stores in the community would take a while, the NBCGFR could create contracts with local corner stores to sell its produce through some type of pilot program in the future.

In looking at the NBCGFR's agripreneurship model, food is both nourishment and an entry point for the youth to begin to dream bigger collective dreams. Indeed, as Ashanté Reese asserts, "food is never just about food," and the NBCGFR's agripreneurship model makes this clear.[68] This model extends beyond the traditional view of larger agricultural businesses that often solely focus on profit over people. The collective dreams of the youth in the NBCGFR transport them to a time when Black food futures exist indefinitely and all of their community is healthy. These Black food futures (re)introduce the generations to self-sufficiency generated in the past that reverberates in the present. At the center of these futures is a critical space for youth to learn about farming as well. For the NBCGFR, being young plays an important role in the NBCGFR members' ability to see changes in their lifetime, and those changes begin with farming.

The NBCGFR Farm Project

The NBCGFR's farm project is built on a farm internship program that enables members of the NBCGFR to rotate between working on the NBCGFR youth farm and local Black farms. The project empowers NBCGFR members to immerse themselves in local food production and receive agricultural training under the supervision of local Black farmer-mentors who grow fresh produce in the area.[69] Partnering with the nearby Alcorn State University (ASU) Demonstration Farm, the project offers opportunities for the youth in the NBCGFR to apply cutting-edge scientific agriculture to the production of fruits and vegetables.[70] The NBCGFR farm project also provides travel opportunities for the youth to build connections with other youth groups with similar commitments to transforming their communities through the act of growing food. For instance, during the first three years of the NBCGFR, the youth traveled to New York, Hawaii, and California, where they worked with a variety of crops on farms and exchanged best practices with other youth that allowed them to network and contribute to a growing youth food justice movement across the nation.[71] Such experiences were designed to expose the youth to different methods of food production that could be used as they build their own farm.

In many respects, the NBCGFR farm is a collaborative incubator space that serves as an outdoor laboratory for the agricultural training of NBCGFR members. Located on ten acres of donated land alongside Martin Luther King Drive, which bisects the town of Mound Bayou from east to west, the farm stretches across two neighboring plots and is managed by Chris Johnson, a local Black farmer in Cleveland. The first plot is seven acres and is owned by St. Gabriel Mercy Center. The other plot is three acres and is owned by local Black farmer Mr. Larry Haywood. During my time in Mound Bayou, the three acres of land donated by Mr. Haywood were the only part of the NBCGFR farm that had been cleared for food production. On this land, Johnson teaches the youth how to use chicken fertilizer for the soil and operate a chemical-free drip tape irrigation system. He challenges the youth to discover their passion for agriculture and gain the skills needed to produce food for

Quantrell Holmes mowing between crop rows on the North Bolivar County Good Food Revolution Farm, Mound Bayou, Mississippi 2020. (Photo by author)

their families and communities. Under Johnson's guidance, the youth learn how to grow fresh culturally appropriate produce that is aligned with the eating traditions of Black community members such as cabbage, watermelon, sweet corn, tomatoes, cucumbers, purple hull peas, butter beans, okra, and a variety of peppers. The youth even got the opportunity to grow broccoli and squash. While growing these foods presents a challenge for many of the youth who have never farmed before, Johnson constantly reminds them that farming in and of itself is a learning experience and that they shouldn't be concerned about getting it right the first time.[72]

But for other youth like Larry Mims II, who grew up around farming and working in his late grandmother's large fresh vegetable garden, growing food on the NBCGFR farm means something deeper. When asked to explain why he enjoys working on the farm, Larry stated: "You can thank my grandmother for that, because she loved that. She loved her garden. . . . She grew tomatoes, carrots, and then she grew potatoes and butter beans. . . . I would do the watering. I loved gardening with her, because literally that's just something with me and her just to bond, just to talk and everything." For Larry, growing food symbolizes the moments he spent with his grandmother: "I feel like, when I'm farming, I keep having memories of doing it with my grandmother. Me and her did it all the time. We did it nonstop. We just had this real bonding. Every time I'm gardening or just farming, I just think of her nonstop. Can't stop, won't stop." Larry's memories of gardening with his grandmother contribute to the myriad of experiences some of the youth in the NBCGFR have had with farming.[73]

Building on the different farming experiences of the youth the NBCGFR farm internship program is a critical part of their development as young farmers. This program facilitates intergenerational mentorship through relationships with local Black farmer-mentors that transform their land into a classroom to teach different aspects of farming. For Black farmer-mentors like Mr. Larry Haywood, working with local Black youth through agriculture had been a dream of his prior to even being connected with members of the NBCGFR and giving them their first piece of land to start their farm. Known as the community "watermelon man," Mr. Haywood explained in an interview how he got involved with the NBCGFR: "A couple years ago, my neighbor and I was talking about planting some peas, because the top vegetable crop here and around this community is purple hull peas, and we were thinking that . . . we could get young people involved in making money during the summertime." But Mr. Haywood and his neighbor didn't know where to start until they were introduced to Judy Belue, then executive director of Delta Fresh, and the members of the NBCGFR. After meeting Judy and some of the youth, Mr. Haywood thought that it would be great to partner with them to create summer farming opportunities for the NBCGFR. In his mind, he and his neighbor would provide the land and vegetables "and the kids could take part in the harvesting and learn how to do the farming and . . . growing their own food." After that first summer working with the youth, Mr. Haywood joined the efforts of the NBCGFR as a Black farmer-mentor. In his capacity as a mentor, Mr. Haywood found joy in the fact that he was a part of a project that he believed would outlast him. As he put it: "Me, going out on the top end to see young people coming in on the bottom end, to me, that kind of brings joy to my heart to know that they'll be [and] this process will be going on once I'm gone and I think that's just great."[74]

Many of the Black farmer-mentors, borrowing the words of Mr. Haywood, hope that the NBCGFR will grow tremendously so that it can "supply healthy, farm-raised, chemical-free food for the entire, at least, Mississippi Delta, . . .

and encourage people to start eating it at a younger age."[75] Mr. Haywood's sentiments are aligned with Black farmer-mentor Mr. Artman Jackson's who sees the farm internship program as the foundation for a new generation of Black citizens who are healthier and less dependent on cheap and highly processed foods. Mr. Jackson, a retired teacher from the Mound Bayou Public School District, specializes in the production of okra and has produce contracts with local grocery stores. When asked what he thought was the goal of the NBCGFR farm project, Jackson responded, "Well, the end product would be a healthy generation. You know if we can get to the point to where we are not so dependent on processed foods, I think that would help our health problems."[76]

For other Black farmer-mentors like Robbie Pollard of the Delta town of Marks, who comes from generations of Black farmers in Mississippi, the NBCGFR farm project is not only about remedying food-related health problems but also "build[ing] wealth through food . . . on some of the richest, sandiest soil in the world," he told me. "We want to be able to help [the youth] understand that you can make a living growing produce, that it can be profitable . . . with the right equipment and training outlets."[77] Although Pollard's farm is about one hour northeast of Mound Bayou, he travels once or twice a month to the NBCGFR farm to help the youth develop their general farm infrastructure. The youth work with Pollard to build raised beds and initiate food production in their newly constructed high tunnel. They also learn about sustainable agricultural practices and the business aspects of community-based agricultural production. On some occasions, the youth also travel to Marks to work with Pollard on his farm to gain additional agricultural experiences and help him with planting and harvesting.

In many respects, intergenerational mentorship in the farm internship component of the NBCGFR cultivates other forms of intergenerational community action that lie at the heart of the NBCGFR farm project. According to Judy, Black farmers like Chris Johnson, Larry Haywood, Artman Jackson, and Robbie Pollard "are the real backbone of the project . . . invaluable men [who] are real heroes to me. I feel it is fortunate, even providential, that we all have the opportunity to work together to try to transfer the skills to these young people." For Judy, the purpose of the mentoring relationships between the Black farmers and members of the NBCGFR is to demonstrate to the youth "and to help them understand the transformative power of real food to promote a sense of empowerment, self-sufficiency, potentially better health and economic benefits—real game-changers."[78] Indeed, the intergenerational relationships go beyond just mentorship in the production of food. These relationships also help the youth navigate their own lives.

For example, when speaking about the impact of working with Mr. Jackson had on their lives, three members of the NBCGFR spoke highly of him. Tonitria stated that Mr. Jackson was the most "influential person" in her life.[79] Reggie stated that "Mr. Jackson taught me a lot while we were on the farm. . . . He didn't just leave us out there to just work. There's things he do, he taught at the school, it's a lot of stuff he do that I could look into doing one day. Things like farming . . . just caring about people and helping other people."[80] Reflecting on his many interactions with Mr. Jackson, Quantrell said that Mr. Jackson "really taught me a lot of stuff that I wasn't planning on learning. I was just planning on going out there, throwing stuff in the ground, covering it up, and coming back home. He actually taught me how it's done, why we're doing it, and the point of us doing it."[81] For Tonitria, Reggie, Quantrell, and others, working with Black farmer-mentors like Mr. Jackson empowered them to recognize that working on a farm goes beyond the act of growing food and requires a level of care for the land and people.

For other members of the NBCGFR like Tyra and Tanielle, intergenerational mentorship in its farm project has inspired them to pursue agriculture at the college level. Both members interned on the ASU demonstration farm, learned about the sustainability of local food systems, and gained skills in detailed farm management and local crop planning. These experiences cemented Tyra's and Tanielle's decisions to major in agriculture in college. For example, Tyra knew from the first moment she visited the ASU demonstration farm when she was a freshman in high school that she wanted to major in agriculture. During that first visit, she met Mr. John Coleman, interim farm manager at the ASU farm, which changed her perspective on agriculture. Looking back at that moment, Tyra remembered in an interview that "Mr. Coleman showed me all these different things and told me what they do and how they help around here. It was something that really caught my eye."[82] What Tyra liked the most about the farm was that it was designed to help Black communities in general and Black farmers in particular grow their own food and transform it into a source of income. For Tanielle, interning on the ASU farm and working with Delta Fresh to create the NBCGFR caused her to change her intended major. In an interview, Tanielle stated that she was originally going to major in physical therapy but working out on the farm and "getting more involved with agriculture . . . really made me change my mind." She continued, "I actually never thought about agriculture until I joined Delta Fresh. We actually had a class at school, but I didn't take that class, I took business. I just never really thought of it. I never paid attention to the field. I never found it interesting until I joined Delta Fresh."[83] Such changes in the minds and life trajectories of the youth are a critical aspect of the NBCGFR farm project and demonstrate how the NBCGFR can be a pathway for youth to consider careers in agriculture and farming.

To be sure, though, not all of the youth in the NBCGFR enjoy working on the farm or plan to major in agriculture. But they understand the importance of farm work and recognize what's at stake. For instance, when asked did she like working on the farm, Trayla immediately responded, "I don't like it. I don't like it at all. But you have to do things to get somewhere. Because if we don't plant the food, how are we going to sell it, how are we going to get it out to the people to understand that we're trying to make food affordable to grow so who else is going to do that. So I go out there and I do it and sometimes it makes me happy when we accomplish actually growing a product. I get happy because I feel that, oh, we did this together. We're doing something; we're making progress."[84] What the NBCGFR farm project teaches the youth is that sometimes you have to do things you don't like to do to get where you want to go. At the same time, the NBCGFR farm project teaches the youth that it is their responsibility to take care of their community. As such, the ability to see through the process of growing food for the community creates a sense of accomplishment among members of the NBCGFR that can translate into other parts of their lives. It is the other parts of their lives, in the context of self-care, that the youth leadership development activities of the NBCGFR seek to interrogate by connecting the youth's relationships with food, farming, agripreneurship, and overall individual and community health.

"A Game Plan and a Strategy": Youth Leadership Development through Care for Self and Community

Through leadership development efforts, the youth in the NBCGFR learn to embody the capacity and power to produce Black food futures filled with two sites of care: self and the community. Such efforts, which are mostly planned activities or discussion-based sessions at the NBCGFR headquarters in Mound Bayou, are designed to "bring food justice coupled with self-care to the forefront for the young people," Judy told me.[85] The "self" in what Judy described means the personal and the "care" captures the interaction between the personal and the community. Therefore, self-care is not selfish in that it is concerned solely with the individual. Rather, it is care that gives the youth the necessary space to change themselves as they are working to change their communities. This form of care among Black youth, Shawn Ginwright writes, "is more than simply trusting relationships and mutual expectations and bonds between individuals." Instead, this care "moves beyond coping and surviving and encourages black youth to thrive and flourish as they transform community conditions."[86] For many rural Black youth in general and the youth in the NBCGFR in particular, survival has been a way of life, especially in the context of such extreme food injustices. "If you want to see what food injustices feel like, look like, and sound like, look at the youth from these communities," Katrina Sanders told me in an interview.[87] Known as "Miss Katrina" by the youth, Katrina is Judy's assistant and coordinator of the NBCGFR youth leadership development efforts. She works tirelessly to empower the youth to look beyond their present food situations and place themselves at the center of their project and growing food justice movement. This repositioning of self to the center challenges the youth to consider their own relationships with food in relation to their lived experiences and collective responsibility to care for their community through food. To reposition themselves, Katrina argues, all the youth need is "a game plan and a strategy."

When asked what she meant by "a game plan and strategy," Katrina told me that she uses this language because she views herself as a coach. "And I'm a pretty good coach," she jokingly remarked during one of our conversations. "If I can tell them a plan that will work, that this strategy works, [and] it will score every time . . . it empowers them more. And it's a win-win for me. . . . If they can do that, they can win at life." Indeed, Katrina takes this role seriously because she wants to see the youth win in life and to recognize when they win, the community wins. Katrina sees each designated leadership activity or workshop as "practice" where the youth work to learn about themselves and every aspect of their lives. Food is used as the key piece of equipment for each "practice" and is always the starting point for conversations about personal and emotional health, community sustainability, familial issues, and larger societal problems that show up in their community. As Katrina put it, food is "a connector to so many bigger issues . . . in the South and in Black communities; it's also connected to so much poverty, so much hopelessness, so much depression that is fueled by more bad food." At the same time, food is a bridge over such societal problems that connects rural Black youth in the NBCFGFR to sustainable Black food futures where they

Miss Katrina with North Bolivar County Good Food Revolution members during "practice" at the organization's headquarters, Mound Bayou, Mississippi, 2020. (Photo by David Hanson)

reshape and transform their own relationships with food and the spaces where they consume food.[88]

For example, "practice" begins with the youth preparing a meal together with ingredients grown on the farm and then sitting around the table in the dining room of the NBCGFR's headquarters. This large table represents a terrain by which food is physically and metaphorically placed at the center. The youth gather around the table not only to share in eating the food they prepared but also to think through how their everyday lives shape their relationships with food. For many of them, food is consumed on the go, rarely in a space where they can slow down and experience a meal. In fact, the ability to slow down and eat a meal at a table allows them, as one of the youth told me, to move beyond feelings of being "trapped" by the prevalence of convenient foods at gas stations in their community and fast-food restaurants like Burger King, McDonald's, Popeyes, and Taco Bell. These places "are all in one spot—it's like you're crowded and trapped; you can't go nowhere."[89] In many respects, the table at the NBCGFR headquarters is a reprieve from everyday eating practices shaped by such convenience and fast food. While most times the youth prepare a meal together, in other instances the youth just meet to talk around the table about life through the lens of food.

Katrina calls the process of providing a space for the youth to either cook a meal together or just sit around a table and talk about food as "back-to-the-table." The process of "back-to-the-table" transforms the kitchen table into the domain where youth use food to make sense of the present en route to the future, and positively impacts the youth in important ways. First, the idea of "back-to-the-table," also allows the youth to prepare and test out new healthier meals. Katrina explains that letting the youth taste the food they prepare is critical. "You can't just talk about eating better. You can't talk about living better. Talking is over. That does not work. . . . You have to show and tell."[90] Therefore, when the youth go out into the community to promote healthier lifestyles, they are speaking from experience. When they prepare meals at market locations, they are sure of what they are trying to do in their community and the community recognizes the importance of what they are doing. Because of this, many community members have connected healthier lifestyles to the work of the NBCGFR.

Second, the "back-to-the-table" process is also important in that it allows the youth to think about food beyond the act of farming or working at the market. As such, food is removed from a context that, in many ways, decenters the youth as humans who have their own relationships with food beyond the farm and the mobile market. A sole focus on food through the lens of production and marketing for the community creates a silence around personal relationships with food. Recognizing this, Katrina organizes the leadership efforts to get at the heart of these issues so the youth can look at food through the lens of self. This process humanizes food relations beyond the production, consumption, distribution, and preparation of food.

Third, this transformative method of "back-to-the-table" has forced the youth to have critical conversations about their relationships with food, especially the fact that for most of them this relationship has been shaped by family histories of diet-related illnesses. These same issues also inspire them to want to eat better as a model for their families. "High blood pressure runs in our family, heart failure—the list goes on and on," Tanielle told me in an interview. "So, that changed the way I was eating. I was like, I can't live like that. . . . So I'm actually trying to get them on board. It's kind of slow but they're coming along. . . . We take turns in the kitchen and so I'll try to have something healthy. Sometimes they'll eat it, sometimes they won't but, I'm trying."[91] Similarly, Tyra's relationship with food is shaped by her family's struggle with obesity. "Just about my whole family is obese. . . . Everybody is about over 200 pounds in my family. I think it's maybe our food consumption [that] is making us this big, but that was one thing that drew me to [the NBCGFR] because I see that healthy food changes things. . . . It's changed our bodies, our mindset," Tyra told me.[92] For her, food is a "life-or-death" situation in that "you choose what you want to eat, you choose what you want to eat to save your life."[93] By joining the project over three years ago and learning how healthy food can change her life, Tyra has been able to influence her family. For instance, due to Tyra's involvement in the project, her entire family has begun to support the market and attempt to eat healthier foods.

When I asked Tyra what healthy food means to her, she stated that healthy food "makes your body feel good. If it's healthy, it shouldn't make your body ache like bad foods. So something that makes your stomach smile."[94] In this line of thinking about healthy food that makes your "stomach smile," Trayla told me that her own personal relationship with food was shaped by digestive issues she had from a heavy consumption of fast food as a child. Before joining the project, Trayla explained to me that she had been eating "carelessly" with a diet that consisted of mostly McDonald's and Wendy's. Due to this diet of heavily processed fast food, Trayla suffered from a reoccurring stomach virus as a child into her early teenage years. "Every other year, I was already preparing myself to have a stomach virus because I was just going out and eating," she told me in an interview. Trayla also experienced food poisoning a few times from eating fast food, which she states was more painful than the stomach virus. But after joining the NBCGFR, and subtle changes in her diet and eating more at home with the help of her mom, Trayla states that she hasn't experienced the virus or food poisoning in over two years and feels much better. She attributes these changes in her and her immediate family's relationship with food to the youth leadership development activities designed by Katrina. Trayla explains:

> See, when we talk to Katrina, she talks about food justice and food as being medicine. . . . When I get home, I tell my mama. She tries new things; she tried new vegetables. She might do salads one night. And she might do something else. We have changed in eating healthy more at home from this program. We tried various grass-fed beef. . . . That's how it's changing my life. The more I eat healthy, the more I stay away from the doctors and hospitals and buying medicine and paying for medicine. Or the more that I eat healthy, I don't feel bad.

> I feel good, I feel like energy, I have energy. . . . I have more get up and go when I eat healthy. I could say, no, I don't feel like going to go do this because I have eaten chicken at McDonald's and Popeyes. Well, now I can just, oh, I ate a salad today; I feel like I could go run to the mountain and back.[95]

The experiences of Tanielle, Tyra, and Trayla undoubtedly capture how youth in the NBCGFR now understand how food can be a root cause of health problems, but it can also be used to give and sustain life. For other youth like Larry Mims II, learning about nutritious food through leadership development has given them a new outlook on life. Larry explained to me in an interview that he describes the consistent ability to eat healthy food "as achieving something in life . . . because if you don't eat healthy food, it's going to put a literal toll on your body. I've known that for years, because I've really gained a lot of weight over the years. I weighed 260. I weigh in the 240s now, because I've started exercising, started eating healthy, because it's really important."[96]

In many ways, the youth are discovering the difference between what Katrina describes as "eating to live" versus "living to eat." As she explains, "It's a difference between eating to live and living to eat. There's a big difference. . . . So when someone is living to eat, everything is based around food. When I eat to live, I'm actually hungry; my body needs nourishment; I need to fulfill that nourishment that my body needs to keep me going. So I'm not just sitting down to just binge on so much comfort food; I'm eating the things that fuel my body to keep me going." Fueling the body with the right foods helps the youth feel safe and understand the importance of caring for themselves and helps build internal satisfaction and confidence that can then translate into success in other areas of their project including the farm, market, and community outreach. In many respects, "living to eat" is about survival and "eating to live" is about thriving.[97]

Indeed, thriving is an important part of what Katrina sees as the "bigger picture" for the youth. The bigger picture is to empower the youth to develop better relationships with food, recognizing that it is not about instant gratification. Katrina asserts that developing a better relationship with food is "a lifestyle change, but it has to be little bits at a time . . . little solutions to problems."[98] In some ways, as Judy told me, the bigger picture is to inspire and support the youth in "rewriting their own stories through food."[99] The fact that the youth are changing their own lives has had an impact on their families and their communities. But the ultimate goal of such changes is to create a generational shift where no one else in their community will be hungry or suffer from diet-related illnesses due to an inadequate local food environment.

In Katrina's eyes, this generational shift must start with the youth believing that they can do it. Many of the youth, like Tyra, wish that they had learned about healthy food and eating practices as a child. "I wish I knew earlier what I could do to do better for myself and my family, but I thank everyone, Judy especially, for getting me in this program, because I know I can help myself now, like, it's never too late to change how you eat," Tyra emotionally explained to me.[100] This change that she has observed in her life, like many of her other peers, demonstrates how the youth are building their capacity to thrive and taking ownership of their futures.

Without a doubt, Katrina's framework of a "game plan and a strategy" has inspired the youth in the NBCGFR to generate a model of care for self and community with food at the center. This model empowers the youth to care for themselves, which includes taking ownership and control of their lives, as they take care of their community. Although Katrina is not really into sports, she told me, "I can relate to being a cornerman in a boxing ring or being a coach that shows up to practice and goes over the plays and teaches them how to execute plays . . . so then they can believe that they can do it. They can articulate it better, do better in an interview, do things that are better for them." Indeed, "practice" is a core component of the model of care for self and community that the youth rely on and Katrina's presence at "practice" has made a tremendous impact on the youth. But Katrina is just not showing up to "execute plays"; she is also showing up because she knows that the youth are the future of the community.[101] Therefore, it's imperative that they learn to take care of themselves and see that process as central to their food justice work. While the NBCGFR agripreneurship and farm projects require the youth to expend a lot of energy for their community, laboring at the market and working on the land, the youth leadership development arm of the NBCGFR centers and invests in the youth themselves. Reminding them that they are not just passive participants in the rebuilding of their local food system. Recognizing that their lives and personal relationships with food matter, the youth can lay the foundation for shaping Black food futures in the Delta and beyond.

Conclusion

This chapter examined how the unfinished work of the civil rights struggle for emancipatory food power, launched by the NBCFC to end food insecurity in the Delta, continues over fifty years later through the Black youth-led food justice work of the NBCGFR. It began with the powerful words of Black food activist Shakirah Simley: "In a very real sense, the future of food is people. . . . This future was also written long ago. . . . And it is young black people who will lead the conversation on changing our food and farming systems."[102] This statement refers to a future, a place yet seen but written in the past. This future is a moment when young Black people chart the path to Black food futures. In many respects, Simley's words speak to the ways in which the food story of the Mississippi civil rights movement provides some nutrients to the soil in which the production of Black food futures will emerge. The seeds for the soil and tools needed to harvest such futures are in the hands of young Black people in the NBCGFR that connects them to the past and enables them to visualize a different world beyond what they see. A world where their communities have the power to create and shape the ways in which nutritious food is accessed, produced, consumed, and distributed.

This chapter illustrated how the NBCGFR is guided by the belief that food is a pathway to emancipation from the conditions and circumstances that perpetuate food apartheid. The NBCGFR members also see their work as a critical space for them to find purpose amid current realities of racialized, poverty-induced food insecurity that could otherwise evoke feelings of intense hopelessness. For instance, NBCGFR member Quantrell told me in an interview that since joining the group,

> I feel better about my community. Now that I have this, I feel like I'm doing something. I feel like I'm . . . I feel like I've got a reason to actually get up and come out here early in the morning, even when I don't want to, and plant all this stuff, and do all that. I feel like that's the reason to do it, because *I want to see* my community do better. *I want to see* my community eat better. *I want to see* more healthy people in my community. . . . That's the biggest part to me, because I had family members that passed away, always eating a lot of fast food, and close friends, and stuff like that. So that's really the most important part to me, helping people get better and eat healthier so they won't have to pass away from that.[103]

As I listened to Quantrell, all I could keep thinking about was the cadence and conviction of his voice every time he said, "I want to see." I thought about the ways in which folks like Judy Belue, Black farmer-mentor Artman Jackson, or "Miss Katrina" gave Quantrell and others in the NBCGFR the "lens" to see beyond the tremendous toll that nonexistent access to fresh produce and other foods has taken on their families and communities and imagine food justice possibilities.

Throughout this chapter, we have seen how the creative organizing strategies of framing, of mobilizing indigenous resources, and of understanding how positionality are intertwined in the NBCGFR's agripreneurship, farming, and leadership development activities. These activities collectively sharpen the lens by which the youth in the NBCGFR use to build their local food justice movement in the Delta. Through agripreneurship, the youth are given the resources and business acumen to understand the economics of sustainable food production that provides a foundation for community-embedded market mechanisms. Farming activities allow the youth to learn and attain indigenous knowledge from a generation of Black farmers who are aging and who are hoping to get a return on this social investment that changes the food realities and lives of generations not yet born. Youth leadership development efforts position food as the foundation of a personalized strategic blueprint that challenges the youth to move past a passive position and look within themselves for the capacity to yield social change in and outside their community. Together, the three activities of the NBCGFR characterize how Black youth in the Delta are continuing the food story of the Mississippi civil rights movement.

But questions surrounding how long this ongoing food story will continue, at least through the NBCGFR, linger. The NBCGFR situates youth as the entry point by which Black communities can enter the contemporary struggle for food justice, which is critically important. Yet, how long will the youth in the NBCGFR use food justice as a space to build emancipatory food power, and what will life look like when Black food futures are materialized? While food power politics look different today as the agricultural and local foodscape of the Delta has changed over time, what has remained static is the fact that most rural Black people in the region still do not control when, where, and how they access food. Such persistent food conditions speak to issues of power and how youth will be able to address them. As a youth-led food justice movement, how will the NBCGFR contend with the static nature of this foodscape? How will the NBCGFR keep making progress as youth members get older or consider leaving the region for better opportunities and social amenities? This problem is not unique to the NBCGFR, as Sekou Franklin writes that "the transient nature of student and youth formations almost guarantees that these organizations will be short-lived, unless they recruit new members, develop new leaders, or regenerate resources."[104]

For the past four years, the NBCGFR has been able to successfully recruit youth through local stakeholders in Delta Fresh. Some of them have been inspired to pursue higher education in agriculture. Yet, each new class of youth recruits presents another learning curve that must be addressed in order to push the NBCGFR forward.

At the same time, each new class of youth in the NBCGFR requires mentorship from an older Black farming population that is getting older and slowly declining. Who will be the next generation of Black farmers and local food advocates who will invest in youth in groups like the NBCGFR? How will knowledge be passed down that will translate into meaningful action? While financial resources can be replaced by securing additional funds to support the work, people and the knowledge they possess cannot. These hard questions about the future expose challenges, not only to the work of the NBCFGR but also to the future of Black youth–led food justice movements across the nation. Such questions about the future were not fully taken up by the NBCGFR's predecessors in the NBCFC. During the Mississippi civil rights movement, the NBCFC navigated extreme conditions that amplified the dire, ever-present food and precarious economic situation among Black sharecroppers in the Delta. Due to their proximity to such overt inequality, the NBCFC's main goal was to create a mechanism to generate emancipatory food power to address the immediate food and economic needs of their communities. Less focus was put on building the next generation of activists that would continue their important work.

Building on Black agrarian traditions of growing food, this history teaches us that the NBCFC tilled the soil needed to address immediate food and economic needs en route to Black food futures where Black people will not be forced to navigate food and economic insecurity. The responsibility of the NBCGFR is to further prepare this soil for the production of Black food futures by gleaning lessons from the past and configuring a Black youth–led food justice movement space that accounts for the revolving door of youth activists that could threaten the vision of the group. This movement space is a practice area for the youth in the NBCGFR to rehearse and realize the past dreams of emancipatory food power. Simultaneously, the practice area allows the youth to revise past dreams that failed to yield Black food futures—thus providing lessons. Such lessons link the past with real experiences that have the potential to manifest into meaningful new actions. They also give the youth an expansive set of seeds and tools that will produce Black food futures that will not only change the Delta but will also be a roadmap for others in the long pursuit of emancipatory food power.

Conclusion

I began this book with the words of Black Chef Omar Tate: "Food is a weapon that has been used against us, but food is also a shield." Tate's words, which echo the words of activist Fannie Lou Hamer and others before her, offer us a different pathway to think about the relationship between Black people and food, calling explicit attention to the multiple uses of food to enforce and resist inequality in Black life.[1] "Food is a weapon that has been used against us" tells a story of food power that illuminates how food is transformed into a site of inequality designed to harm Black people. "But food is also a shield" points to a story of emancipatory food power that authorizes Black people to use food as a site of social, political, and economic change that can protect them from food as a form of inequality. For some, the first story of oppression has been rehearsed too often and does not offer a blueprint for how to overcome such oppression. For others, the second story helps us more today by showing how Black people created food mechanisms to free themselves, even if temporarily, from oppression. But the contours of both stories, when read together, unveil a collage of food stories about food power politics in Black life that has been dormant. In the context of the civil rights movement, these food stories are part of what prominent activists Bob Moses and Charlie Cobb described as an "important dimension of the movement [that] has been almost completely lost in the imagery of hand-clapping, song-filled rallies for protest demonstrations that have come to define portrayals of 1960s civil rights meetings: dynamic individual leaders using their powerful voices to inspire listening crowds."[2]

Throughout this book, I argued that the food story of the Mississippi civil rights movement is one of those stories. By focusing on food, I addressed questions that challenge us to rethink the magnitude of struggles that characterize the civil rights movement, while also centering the people who did the often-undervalued work of navigating food power politics in the Delta. Without question, the food story of the Mississippi civil rights movement represents a small slice of the comprehensive narrative of the movement that is composed of thousands of local stories that stretch beyond events and demonstrations in the arenas of voting rights, education, and public accommodations. This book grapples with the food question of the Mississippi civil rights movement, which is a perspective that we have yet to fully explore in studies of the movement. The food question presents an opportunity to expand the civil rights story by introducing new actors, struggles, initiatives, projects, and programs that can help us understand how everyday struggles to access food in Black life not only were central to the political strategy of the movement but also paved the way for new articulations of civil rights activism. These new articulations of civil rights activism were based on a political-economic analysis of what it meant for Black people in the rural South to be a self-determined people in the face of a food environment structured by white supremacy. After all, the food weaponized against Black people cemented white power over Black lives and the crucial need for immediate social, political, and economic change in Black communities in the Mississippi civil rights movement.

In a broader sense, this food story also cultivates an analytical and interpretative lens by which we can begin to unearth and explore other food stories of the movement and the broader Black freedom struggle from slavery through today. The theoretical framework—food power politics—at the heart of this book gives us a critical tool to excavate history of Black life that reframes how we study the relationship between food and Black people. Food is not just something that Black people eat in the context of their cultural experiences or to simply obtain nourishment for life, as scholars in critical food studies have made clear.[3] Food is a site of fundamental questions of racism, resistance, Black freedom, white supremacy, inequality, and justice. The food story of the Mississippi civil rights movement offers us a landscape on which to explore these questions that point us to this book's major throughline: power.

Power pervades every aspect of the food story of the Mississippi civil rights movement. The nucleus of power relations in this story is the plantation that comes in and out of the spotlight. By situating food at the center of narratives of the movement, *Food Power Politics* redirects our attention to the plantation as a set of intersecting yet conflicting power structures that shape life in and outside of the geographic and social lines that demarcate plantation grounds. Such structures are often assumed and rarely interrogated in the shadows of movement histories, contributing to an underdeveloped analysis of how power is defined and constructed in particular contexts that shaped movement politics. The ideas that breathe life into power structures spill over into everyday Black life and trickle down to the ways in which Black people access food. What happens when power infiltrates the relationship between Black people and food? To be sure, power always surrounds this relationship, but what happens when Black people have to explicitly think about power in the context of their food realities? One answer to these questions, as this book demonstrates, is that Black people begin to actively negotiate what it means to be Black and access food in a racist and unequal society. Many Black food justice activists agree with Malik Yakini, Black activist-farmer and executive director of the Detroit Black Community Food Security Network (DBCFSN), that there must be a fundamental shift in power so that Black people can define their food realities as they continue to struggle for total freedom.[4] In order for us to understand this fundamental shift in power, I argue that we need an explicit analysis of power. In some instances, Black people in social movement spaces say they want "power," but what does this really convey? Is it that Black people want the same power that oppresses them? Or are they fighting for a different kind of power?

Indeed, *Food Power Politics* raises more questions than it answers. But it provides some insights that can help us understand these questions that are not necessarily new in that power has always been a central actor in Black struggle. In the civil rights and Black power eras, there was a rubric of power that suggested that equality meant having the same power as white people. But white power, at least in the context of the food story of the Mississippi civil rights movement, was predicated on a violent, racialized social hierarchy that sustained the idea that Black people were inferior. Black sharecroppers worked with activists to obtain power that did not operate within this hierarchy. In fact, they wanted the power to control their entire lives, which undoubtedly included the ability to establish their own relationships in the production, consumption, and distribution of food.

The tensions between these conflicting notions of power, as analyzed and reiterated throughout the food story of the Mississippi civil rights movement, reveal that "one of the most intimate ways in which [Black people] experience violence and assert [their] resistance is through [their] food," borrowing the words of Dara Cooper, activist and former executive director of the National Black Food and Justice Alliance (NBFJA).[5] As *Food Power Politics* has taught us, violence looks like dismantling a federal food program to force Black people into submission, inciting the 1962–63 Greenwood Food Blockade. Violence looks like white grocers organizing a campaign to manipulate the Federal Food Stamp Program to increase the vulnerability of Black people to the machinations of interactions between white political and economic actors. Resistance looks like leveraging resources to create a localized food program, "Food for Freedom," supported by a massive national network and food pipeline. Resistance looks like creating a local Black food economy through the North Bolivar County Farm Cooperative (NBCFC) that reconfigured the terms by which Black people accessed food and protested high rates of unemployment. Resistance looks like continuing the food work of the Mississippi civil rights movement by creating the North Bolivar County Good Food Revolution (NBCGFR) as a platform for Black youth to claim their rightful place as the next generation of food justice activists and thinkers who want to change their community using food.

These instantiations of power through violence and resistance in the food story of the Mississippi civil rights movement reveal the dynamic nature of power in the context of food that is instructive today. The Greenwood Food Blockade and the food stamps campaign initiated by white grocers expose the earlier inadequacies of federal food programs that could haunt Black communities today. For example, while the Federal Food Stamp Program—known today as the US Department of Agriculture's (USDA) Supplemental Nutrition Assistance Program (SNAP)—has evolved tremendously since the 1960s, the food story of the Mississippi civil rights movement illustrates what happens when federal food programs, in the hands of the wrong people, can leave Black people hungrier and in need of food. What this program ultimately reinforces is that Black people do not have the power to control their food realities and if the federal government decreases funding or local agencies decide to revise the requirements to access SNAP, Black people and others who are dependent on this aid have to reconfigure their lives to accommodate these decisions. Such everyday decisions show us how Black food realities in particular are shaped by local, state, and national political systems. At the same time, the food story of the Mississippi civil rights movement suggests a solution to the political instability of federal food programs and even the lack of access to nutrient-rich foods in Black communities. This story shows that Black people, as well as other marginalized populations, can build food justice movements to construct mechanisms that could lead toward reliable access and consumption of nutritious food. In the civil rights movement, food justice was realized through struggles for emancipatory food power that arose in response to the Greenwood Food Blockade and was clarified in the development of the NBCFC that set the stage for the emergent food justice work of Black youth in the NBCGFR.

Food Power Politics uses the food story of the Mississippi civil rights movement to provide a glimpse into the past of how Black communities struggled to generate food-based solutions to promote freedom as they simultaneously navigated a bundle of explosive food-centered tactics used against them. Sociologist Rinaldo Walcott theorizes these moments as "glimpses of Black freedom, those moments of the something more that exist inside of the dire conditions of our present Black unfreedom."[6] Such glimpses in this book provide a new language like the concept and theory of food power politics that could be useful to scholars and activists concerned with analyzing the role of power in the relationship between Black people and food. For scholars, this theory is another lens by which we can analyze the taken-for-granted or largely invisible connections between inadequate access to food, structural inequalities, and social movements. This analysis will refine how we study food as a site of power and also as a tool of liberation in struggles for power, especially in the context of international politics. As mentioned in the introduction of this book, the concept of food power is understood in struggles between two nations. This book translates this into everyday life, which provides another way to link international food struggles to everyday instances of food activism, which could connect often isolated struggles for food sovereignty across the world.

At the same time, *Food Power Politics* could be useful to the general public. Museum curators seeking to discover fresh insights into the civil rights movement could use this book to build a more complete story of the movement for public consumption. Every year, thousands of students, community members, and other stakeholders visit museums in the South to learn about the history of the civil rights movement. In fact, for some, their first encounter with this history is through museum exhibits. This book could be used, as historian Kathryn Nasstrom writes, to "cultivate more stories" about the movement, "especially different stories from those people, places, and perspectives we have not yet heard from" that would enhance the portfolio of museums.[7] Museum curators take on the responsibility of creating collaborative spaces to learn various aspects of civil rights movement history. Food could provide a new entry point to helping the public learn about the movement but also what the movement teaches them about the role of food as a form of oppression and resistance in social struggle and Black life.

Rather than separating the story of oppression from resistance, *Food Power Politics* enables us to understand what Black activists are fighting for *and* against in the contemporary moment of food justice and how it connects to the past. This book locates the contemporary moment within the history of the civil rights movement and, by extension, the ongoing Black freedom struggle, which contributes to the arsenal of tactics and theories that activists, advocates, farmers, and communities could use to sharpen their analysis of the dynamics of power that show up in different ways in different contexts. Such dynamics demonstrate how the often-overlooked violence of white supremacy extends into the everyday food realities of Black people, especially as it relates to the political nuances of food policies created to help those who live in poverty. A 2020 report by the Duke University World Food Policy Center found that narratives of white supremacy "function to center whiteness across the food system, effectively reinforcing systemic racial inequality."[8] This analysis is crucial to the knowledge base of activists seeking to understand the structures that work against the realization of Black food futures. While *Food Power Politics* operates within the context of the Delta and Mississippi as a space to amplify this analysis, activists outside the state and beyond the South can think about how the history of power in their region—Who has it? Where does it emanate from? And how can we work against it while developing our understandings of power?—shapes and informs their food realities and solutions. These questions create a forum that enables Black people to dream and imagine what life would be like if they could take full control of their lives through access to food and land, which has always been a vital component of Black "freedom dreams," as historian Robin D. G. Kelley has argued.[9]

This point is crucial in that the word "control" in this context pushes us to think critically about what "access" to food and land mean in terms of power and Black freedom. To be sure, for those who dream about Black freedom, access to food is about not just availability but also the ability to shape the terms by which food is accessed. Looking back at chapter 4, this line of thinking demonstrates the possibilities of emancipatory food power given the myriad of struggles that Black people are forced to navigate today, especially young Black people who are navigating a new world of reemerging social unrest and a new version of white supremacy within the context of the COVID-19 pandemic of which Black communities have been forced to bear the brunt. Ongoing reports of statistics surrounding the pandemic do not adequately depict the vivid impact of this global health crisis on Black and other marginalized communities and how it is intensified by gentrification, climate change, and global market fluctuations. Young Black people in some of these communities are using food justice and food sovereignty to take on the pandemic as they clear the way toward sustainable Black food futures. They are supported by previous generations of activists and community members who want to ensure that young Black people have the necessary tools to not only fill a void in their communities but also create a path for future generations of youth concerned about community well-being. For example, as this book is going to the press, the Black youth in the NBCGFR are working to think through what food access looks like in this current context. But they are not working in isolation. They are working alongside other food justice groups led by young Black people like AfroGreen'D in Fort Worth, Texas; Sankofa Farms in Durham, North Carolina; and the DB-CFSN Food Warriors program in Detroit, Michigan, to name a few. These groups are continuing the food work of their predecessors in the food story of the Mississippi civil rights movement.

Food Power Politics raises one final question: How can we build and sustain emancipatory food power amid the seemingly irreversible and all-consuming presence of inequality? This question does not have a one-size-fits-all answer. It requires us all—activists, scholars, community leaders, everyday people—to consider our own power in remedying the awful reality of food insecurity. In many ways, this reality has become ubiquitous. But food insecurity is not just a statistic or a condition in which people find themselves based on a set of circumstances. It is a very intimate oppression that permeates every aspect of life. Indeed, to undermine it is a daunting task. This book reveals that Black communities—throughout time and space—have a roadmap that brings us closer to shaping a food-secure world at every turn. Historically, there have been disappointments and detours along the way, but Black communities have always found alternate routes. Remembering the routes through Black food stories in places like the Delta will be essential as we actively envision what tomorrow will look and feel like for our food-insecure communities as we journey toward reshaping our worlds through emancipatory food power.

Acknowledgments

This may be the hardest section to write in my entire book. I am sitting at my desk in my office in the Department of African American Studies at the University of Illinois at Urbana-Champaign, thinking about how I want to acknowledge every person who contributed to the creation of this book. I am sure that I will miss someone. Just know that it was not my intention to leave anyone out.

I first want to thank God for the opportunity to live out my dreams as part of His plan for my life. Indeed, being a professor is my dream job and the road to get here was something out of a movie for sure. However, God's plan is always best. I am grateful to be here in this moment of my life.

I am forever grateful, thankful, and indebted to my immediate family for their unwavering love, prayers, and support throughout this entire journey. To my mommy, Cheryl, I love you so much. I am more than confident that you have a direct line to God, and I thank you for being my mother—always praying for me and reminding me to keep and seek God first in all that I say or do. To my daddy, Bobby Sr., I am pretty sure that chapter 2 of this book could not have been written without you. Thank you for your love and the many hours of conversations about this project. Thank you for always being just one phone call away. I hope chapter 2 meets your standards. To my sister, Sherry, thank you for being the loving, protective big sister and editor that you are. You were my first example of academic excellence, and I still want to be like you when I grow up. To my niece, Kyleigh, and nephew, Josiah, I want you both to know that Uncle B. J. loves you. You both bring so much joy into my life, and I look forward to watching you grow up and achieve all your dreams.

This book emerged from Charles Payne's seminal text *I've Got the Light of Freedom* and ideas generated in my doctoral dissertation at Cornell University, supported by my dissertation committee, who I call the Dream Team: Scott Peters, Lori Leonard, and Noliwe Rooks. Just a few weeks before I defended my dissertation in May 2018, I had the opportunity to meet and have lunch with Charles Payne along with other graduate students during his visit to Cornell to give a talk. While his research had since evolved beyond civil rights studies, I was still interested in asking him about his work in Greenwood. During our conversation, I asked him about archival sources, the interviews he conducted, and his fieldwork in Greenwood. I even had the opportunity to tell him about my dissertation project that recovered a food story of the Mississippi civil rights movement and how it was born out of his work. I also brought my copy of his book for him to sign. As we were wrapping up lunch, I asked him to sign my book, and he wrote on the first page of the book, "Bobby, thanks for telling the next part of the story." I do my very best to do that in this book, and I hope that he and many others will be proud.

Without the support of my dissertation committee, I would not have been able to complete this work. I am grateful for all their support and for reading through the earlier versions of the chapters in this book. It means a lot to have them in my corner. Scott, thank you for chairing my dissertation committee and supporting me during a critical time in my graduate studies. I also want to thank you for introducing me to Payne's book in your community organizing class in 2016. Thank you for pushing me to confidently think beyond Payne's book and make connections to issues today. To Lori, thanks for seeing something in me when I took your qualitative methods course in the spring of 2015, introducing me to Michel-Rolph Trouillot's *Silencing the Past* and challenging me to think beyond my research ideas at the time. You have been a mentor and friend, and I hope you see your impact on me throughout this book. To Noliwe, thank you for believing in me and always being a text away. I want to also thank you for simply forwarding me the email in March 2017—right after my A-exam—about the Medgar and Myrlie Evers Research Scholars program at the Mississippi Department of Archives and History (MDAH) in Jackson, Mississippi. That fellowship, and my time in Jackson, changed my life and the trajectory of my dissertation and this book. I also want to thank Barry Maxwell for introducing me to the late Clyde Woods's game-changing book, *Development Arrested*, while I was a graduate teaching assistant in his Introduction to American Studies course at Cornell. Clyde Woods taught me about the Delta and provided me with a language and cadence when talking about rural Black life in the Delta and how it collides with power structures throughout Mississippi and the nation.

Speaking of Mississippi, I could not have completed this research without the Medgar and Myrlie Evers Research Scholarship that allowed me to live in Mississippi during the summer of 2017 and conduct critical research at MDAH. Thank you Reena Evers-Everette, Corrine Anderson, Jeanne Middleton-Hairston and the Medgar and Myrlie Evers Institute. I remember the many early mornings traveling down Highway 51 to the Winter Archives and History Building, excited and worried about having enough time to unravel the many puzzles in the archives. I am thankful that I didn't have to do it alone thanks to the generosity of the entire Archival, Reading, and Media room staff at MDAH, including Archie Skiffer, Laura Heller, Joyce Lawson, and Clinton Bagley. Our many conversations generated many of the ideas in this book. Special thanks to Stephanie Davidson and Stacy Ware for treating me like a member of their family while living in Jackson during the summer of 2017. Stephanie, thank you for the consistent check-ins and dinners. Stacy, thank you for the fun times in the city and opening up your home to me. I also want to thank John Spann and Michael Morris. John, thank you for always being supportive of my work and always opening up your home to me during my visits to Jackson and the Delta. I hope that you recognize the impact you have had on this project. Mike, I still remember you traveling with me to the Delta to meet with Senator David Jordan and activist Theodore "Weight" Johnson. Our trip to the Delta provided me with firsthand knowledge of the Greenwood struggle from local people in Greenwood. I will never forget driving up I-55 along the eastern corridor of the Delta and talking about life, archives, the movement, and southern rap music. I remember attending church with Senator David Jordan, and afterward, he took us to meet Weight Johnson, and then Johnson took us to meet Mr. O. C. Gibson and Gibson's granddaughter LaVorgis M. Sturkey. I will never forget that experience. I also want to thank Mrs. Hattie B. Jordan and Mr. J. D. Tiggs at the Fannie Lou Hamer Museum in Ruleville, Mississippi, and Mrs. Hilda Casin at the Black History Gallery in McComb, Mississippi.

Interestingly, while I was in Jackson in 2017, I attended a monthlong series of events hosted by the Fannie Lou Hamer Institute at the COFO center at Jackson State University, in which many civil rights activists and scholars met up and revisited the movement to prepare for the commemoration of Mrs. Hamer's 100th birthday. I also had the opportunity to attend the opening of the Mississippi Civil Rights Museum in December 2017 and the adjoining commemoration lectures. At such events, I had the opportunity to cross paths with movement folks like Charlie Cobb, Mary King, Frank Figgers, Rev. Ed King, Rev. Wendell Paris Sr., and a host of other unsung heroes of the movement. I also met scholars such as historians Clayborne Carson, John Dittmer, and Emilye Crosby, who have written extensively about the Student Nonviolent Coordinating Committee (SNCC) and the Mississippi movement.

Two sponsoring entities offered me two years of critical leave time: the American Council of Learned Societies (2021–22) and the National Endowment for the Humanities (2022–23). Their financial and academic support made a difference, and this book is a direct product of my time on leave. Any views, findings, conclusions, or recommendations expressed in this book do not necessarily reflect those of the National Endowment for the Humanities, the American Council of Learned Societies, or any other funding entities that supported this work. I appreciate my home institution, the University of Illinois at Urbana-Champaign, for providing me the resources and support to apply for these prestigious fellowships—special thanks to Maria Gillombardo, Cynthia Oliver, Shelley Weinberg, Carol Symes, Gabriel Solis, and the entire RAPD office. I am especially grateful to Ronald W. Bailey, former head of the Department of African American Studies, who generously afforded me leave time to produce this book. I also want to thank him for his mentorship and guidance during my long days of writing in my office.

Additional financial support to carry out the research for this book came from the Medgar and Myrlie Evers Institute in partnership with the Mississippi Department of Archives and History and W. K. Kellogg Foundation, the University of Illinois at Urbana-Champaign's Chancellor's Postdoctoral Fellowship, National Endowment for the Humanities, Study the South Research Fellowship in the Center for the Study of Southern Culture at the University of Mississippi, and Special Collections and University Archives at the University of Illinois at Chicago. As it relates to the Study the South Research Fellowship at the University of Mississippi, I want to thank James G. Thomas Jr. at the Center for the Study of Southern Culture and Leigh McWhite, Jennifer Ford, and the entire staff in the Department of Archives & Special Collections at the J. D. Williams Library for all their assistance.

A special word of thanks goes to Lucas Church at the University of North Carolina (UNC) Press. I am forever thankful for Joseph Ewoodzie Jr. introducing me to Lucas in 2018 at the American Sociological Association (ASA) annual meeting in Philadelphia. From the moment I pitched the book to Lucas in the exhibit hall in Philadelphia, he saw potential in me as a young scholar and the importance of my research. His guidance, patience, and consistent support were unwavering as an editor throughout the development of this book. Thank you to all the UNC Press staff who assisted Lucas in working with me on this book. Thank you to the two anonymous manuscript and proposal reviewers selected by UNC Press. I greatly appreciate the time and care they took in providing such attentive, constructive, generative, and supportive feedback. Their comments and critical engagement with my work undoubtedly strengthened this book. I also want to thank Leah Jordan for her time, compassion, and energy in helping me work through the final months of revising this book. While she often says that she did very little in the process, I want to say that Leah pushed me to be a better, more confident writer and was always available for a quick question or writing session. I hope that she sees her impact in the text. Thomas J. Ward Jr., thank you for sharing your extensive notes and working bibliography on L. C. Dorsey and the North Bolivar County Farm Cooperative (NBCFC) that you used to write *Out in the Rural*. I am grateful for your generosity and willingness to share those materials with me. The materials were beneficial to the development of chapter 3 of this book. I also want to thank the staff at the Wisconsin Historical Society Archives for their assistance in locating documents on the NBCFC used in chapter 3.

At the University of Illinois at Urbana-Champaign, I have benefited from colleagues within and beyond the Department of African American Studies. I thank Desirée McMillion, Merle Bowen, Erik McDuffie, Irvin Hunt, Karen Flynn, Krystal Small, William Conwill, Esther Ngumbi, John Meyers, Leonard McKinnis, Pia Hunter, Megan Dailey, Theopolies Moton, Yuridia Ramírez, and Nathan Castillo for their interest in my work. Special thanks to Faye Harrison for inviting me to discuss my research with our colleagues and graduate students enrolled in the department's Research Seminar in the fall of 2019. I want to thank my mentors during my time as an undergraduate at Prairie View A&M University—Alfred Parks, Wash A. Jones, Miron Billingsley, and Kimberly Gay. Thank you all for always being just one phone call away and consistently reminded me to "stay the course." I am truly standing on your shoulders.

During my time at Cornell University, I was blessed to have a community of people who encouraged me, including Enongo Lumumba-Kasongo, Chavez Carter, Dexter Thomas, Wendy Henderson, Martha Smith, Arlene Richardson, Ruby Brown, Pastor Nathaniel Wright, Calvary Baptist Church family and prayer group, Megan Mingo, Tess Pendergrast, Keith Fraley, Marla Love, Kelsie Roach, Earl Roach, Ray Hage, DJ Ferman-Leon, Yoselinda Mendoza, Devin and Erin McCauley, Jeff Liebert, Nicole LaFave, Russell Rickford, and Adrienne Clay. I want to thank Riché Richardson for graciously sharing her materials on the process of publishing a first book in the academy. Those materials were invaluable throughout the writing of this book. I still remember our conversation in her office before I left Cornell for Illinois—her advice continues to guide me. A special thank you goes to Sherry Zhang for being my writing-accountability partner and holding me accountable throughout the years (each hashtag counts). We started writing together in 2017 and developed a close friendship while writing our dissertations in Mann Library that has continued although we are both faculty at different universities. To the Mann Library staff, especially Mel, Selena, Erica, and Camille, thanks for the candy and friendly support throughout my last year of intensive dissertation writing in graduate school.

The final chapter of this book would not exist without the support of a number of folks in the Delta. They didn't make me feel like an "outsider" coming into town to do research and then leave. They opened their homes, churches, and community centers to me. First, I want to thank Leslie Hossfeld for introducing me to Judy Belue, former executive director of the Delta Fresh Foods Initiative. Judy took a chance on me as a young researcher and connected me with members of the North Bolivar Good Food Revolution (NBCGFR), including Trayla Britton, Quantrell Holmes, Tonitria Hunt, Larry Mims II, Tyra Slaughter, and Tanielle Woods. I owe so much to the youth for taking the time to talk with me and trust me with their stories. Talking with them changed my life, and I hope that readers are inspired by their words. Judy also connected me with a network of Black farmers in the Delta including Chris Johnson, Larry Haywood, Robbie Pollard, and Artman Jackson. Larry Haywood passed away in May 2021, and I still remember sitting in his driveway talking about his life and vision for the Delta. Judy passed away unexpectedly in March 2022, and I am grateful to have known her. The passion she had for the youth and the future of the Delta food system will live on through the work she did in the region.

Because of Judy, I met Katrina Sanders, who was willing to talk to me about her life in the Delta and her work with the youth. Katrina's words bring life to chapter 4, and I am happy to call her my friend. I also want to thank Katrina for introducing me to Black farmer Jerry Evans, who was willing to help me during my time in the Delta and to drive me around the area to meet other Black farmers. I also want to thank Cora Jackson for responding to my last-minute email while I was in the Delta for fieldwork and inviting me to visit Delta Hands for Hope in Shaw and interview her. Because of this connection, I was able to meet and talk with L. Nicole Stringfellow, Kierra T. Jones, and Chiquikta Fountain. Their insights provided the context needed to make sense of my experiences in the Delta.

A special word of thanks goes to civil rights activist and photographer Doris Derby and her assistant, Maude Bruce, whom I had the pleasure of working with to secure images for chapter 3 and the cover of this book. I spent many long nights meeting virtually with Doris Derby—due to the pandemic—discussing my book and working through her private collection and archive of pictures from the Mississippi civil rights movement, including the work of L. C. Dorsey and the NBCFC. She curated the pictures used and called me frequently for updates on the book. Doris Derby passed away unexpectedly in March 2022, and I am saddened that she won't be able to see her amazing work published in this book. I want to thank Elizabeth Loch at the Carter G. Woodson Regional Library and Crystal Henry at Redux/*New York Times* for their help in securing images for chapter 1. I want to thank David Hanson for allowing me to use one of his images in chapter 4. As it relates to the production process of this book, I want to sincerely thank Kristen Bettcher at Westchester Publishing Services who was the production editor, Jessica Ryan for her critical proofreading services, and Eric Anderson and Arc Indexing Inc. for their crucial work on the index.

I am grateful to my extended family and close friends for loving me and encouraging me in their own way throughout this journey: Letitia Anderson (Brianna), Roshawn Anderson (Rakhia), Bill and Lucy Anderson, Blount family, Anderson family, Cheryl Jones and family, Francis Loftis, Nelicia Loftis, Charleasia King, Alonté Johnson,

Teresa Mathews Smith and family, Carrell Johnson, Jamila Simon, Charlie Lester, Rafael Aponte (Nandi), John Briscoe, Devon Worth, Andre (Smiley) Collins, Kenyana Blount, Alana Bryant, Royce Brooks, the Great Commission Baptist Church family, and so many more—who have cheered me on from near and far.

A special word of thanks to my close family members who passed away before seeing this book come to life: my grandmothers Willie Mae Anderson and Eva Mae Jackson; my great-grandfather William Oscar (My Daddy) Blount Sr.; Aunt Helen Anderson Washington; Uncle Roy Lee Jackson; and Uncle William (Peter Rabbit) Jackson Sr.

I'll end my acknowledgments here. With a final word about my immediate family. This book is dedicated to them: my mommy (Cheryl), daddy (Bobby Sr.), sister (Sherry), niece (Kyleigh), and nephew (Josiah). Your love and support mean the world to me. You have been with me every step of the way and I thank God for blessing me to continue on this path with you all by my side. Y'all are my fan club. Y'all are my home. Love you deeply.

Bobby J. Smith II
March 2023

Notes

Introduction

1. Douglass, *Narrative*; Jacobs, *Incidents*.

2. Roane, "Plotting the Black Commons."

3. Smith, "Greenwood Food Blockade"; Smith, "Food and the Mississippi Civil Rights Movement."

4. "Operation Breadbasket: Inspection Team," box 149, folder 3, Rev. Addie Wyatt and Rev. Claude Wyatt Papers, Chicago Public Library, Carter G. Woodson Regional Library, Vivian G. Harsh Research Collection of Afro-American History and Literature; Deppe, *Operation Breadbasket*.

5. Potorti, "'Feeding the Revolution'"; Bloom and Martin, *Black against Empire*; Hilliard, *Black Panther Party*.

6. Harris, *High on the Hog*; McCutcheon, "Returning Home"; Opie, *Southern Food and Civil Rights*.

7. Mintz, *Sweetness and Power*; Hearn, *Theorizing Power*; Lukes, *Power*; Foucault, "Subject and Power"; Wolf, "Distinguished Lecture"; Mills, *Power Elite*; Flannery and Mincyte, "Food as Power."

8. Barnett and Duvall, "Power in International Politics"; Scott, *Weapons of the Weak*.

9. Paarlberg, "Failure of Food Power"; Wallensteen, "Scarce Goods as Political Weapons"; Gross and Feldman, "'We Didn't Want'"; McDonald, *Food Power*.

10. hooks, *Talking Back*, 175–76.

11. Hearn, *Theorizing Power*, 6–7; Avelino, "Theories of Power."

12. Smith, "Building Emancipatory Food Power."

13. Avelino, "Theories of Power," 429.

14. Ture and Hamilton, *Black Power*.

15. Penniman, *Farming While Black*; Reese and Cooper, "Making Spaces Something like Freedom"; Smith, "Fannie Lou Hamer's Pioneering Food Activism"; Edge, *Potlikker Papers*, 58–66; White, "Pig and a Garden"; McCutcheon, "Fannie Lou Hamer's Freedom Farms"; Smith, "Building Emancipatory Food Power."

16. Cobb, *Most Southern Place on Earth*.

17. Height, *Open Wide the Freedom Gates*, 188.

18. Woods, *Development Arrested*.

19. Hartman, *Lose Your Mother*, 6; Foster, *I Don't Like the Blues*.

20. Wright Austin, *Transformation of Plantation Politics*, 27–29.

21. Asch, *Senator and the Sharecropper*.

22. Cooley, *To Live and Dine in Dixie*; Opie, *Southern Food and Civil Rights*; Wallach, *Every Nation Has Its Dish*.

23. Baker, "Bigger than a Hamburger"; Smith, "Food and the Mississippi Civil Rights Movement."

24. Lawson and Payne, *Debating the Civil Rights Movement*; Crosby, *Civil Rights History*; Morris, *Origins of the Civil Rights Movement*; Payne, *I've Got the Light*; Dittmer, *Local People*; Carson, *In Struggle*; Zinn, *SNCC*; Hamlin, *Crossroads at Clarksdale*; Andrews, *Freedom Is a Constant Struggle*; Ownby, *Civil Rights Movement in Mississippi*; McGuire and Dittmer, *Freedom Rights*; Lawson, "Freedom Then, Freedom Now"; Hall, "Long Civil Rights Movement"; Theoharis, "Black Freedom Studies"; Cha-Jua and Lang, "'Long Movement' as Vampire."

25. Theoharis, "Black Freedom Studies"; Bond, "Vietnam, Black Power"; Hogan, "Grassroots Organizing."

26. Woods, *Development Arrested*.

27. Grim, "Justice for Black Farmers Act."

28. Payne, *I've Got the Light*.

29. Allen and Sachs, "Women and Food Chains"; Daniels, "Invisible Work"; Payne, *I've Got the Light*.

30. Harris, *High on the Hog*, 205–6.

31. Marvin Rich, "Civil Rights Progress Out of the Spotlight," *The Reporter*, March 7, 1968, box 9, folder 25, Race Relations Collection, Archives & Special Collections, J. D. Williams Library, University of Mississippi, Oxford, 1.

32. Smith, "Food Justice"; Agyeman and McEntee, "Moving the Field"; Alkon and Agyeman, *Cultivating Food Justice*; Mares and Alkon, "Mapping the Food Movement"; Caruso, "Searching for Food (Justice)": Hislop, "Reaping Equity."

33. White, *Freedom Farmers*; Reese, *Black Food Geographies*, Sbicca, *Food Justice Now!*; Broad, *More Than Just Food*; Povitz, *Stirrings*.

34. McEntee, "Realizing Rural Food Justice," 241.

35. Payne, *I've Got the Light*, 410–11.

36. Trouillot, *Silencing the Past*.

37. Trouillot, *Silencing the Past*, 55.

38. Levine, "Discipline and Pleasure," 322.

39. Payne, *I've Got the Light*.

40. Zinn, SNCC; Carson, *In Struggle*; Dittmer, *Local People*.

41. O. C. Gibson interviewed by author; Charles Evers interviewed by author; J. D. Tiggs interviewed by author; Rev. Ed King interviewed by author; Senator David Jordan interviewed by author; Theodore Johnson interviewed by author.

42. Hamlin, "Vera Mae Pigee (1925–)," 291.

43. National Black Food and Justice Alliance, "NBFJA Platform."

44. Tonitria Hunt interviewed by author; Trayla Britton interviewed by author; Quantrell Holmes interviewed by author; Tyra Slaughter interviewed by author; Tanielle Woods interviewed by author; Larry Mims II interviewed by author.

45. Katrina Sanders interviewed by author; Cora Jackson interviewed by author; Kierra T. Jones interviewed by author; L. Nicole Stringfellow interviewed by author; Herman Johnson Sr. interviewed by author.

Chapter One

1. "Leflore County Won't Have Commodity Program," *Greenwood Commonwealth*, November 9, 1962, box 18044 (microform), Mississippi Department of Archives and History, Jackson.

2. Sam Block, State of Mississippi, County of Leflore, Sworn Deposition, July 12, 1964, Council of Federated Organizations Records, box 1, folder 12, Mississippi Department of Archives and History, Jackson.

3. Payne, *I've Got the Light*.

4. "Leflore County Won't Have Commodity Program," *Greenwood Commonwealth*, November 9, 1962, box 18044 (microform), Mississippi Department of Archives and History, Jackson.

5. Lovett, *Civil Rights Movement in Tennessee*.

6. Charles Cobb and Charles McLaurin, November 19, 1962, SNCC Report on the condition of Negro farmers in Ruleville, Mississippi, Student Nonviolent Coordinating Committee papers, 1959–72 (microform), reel 38, 119, Mississippi, Greenville Sit-In, June 29, 1963–February 6, 1966, n.d., University of Illinois at Urbana-Champaign Library, Urbana.

7. Payne, *I've Got the Light*, 158; Lawson, "Freedom Then, Freedom Now"; Hall, "Long Civil Rights Movement"; Theoharis, "Black Freedom Studies."

8. Dittmer, *Local People*.

9. de Jong, "Staying in Place."

10. Vance, *Human Factors in Cotton Culture*, 296–97.

11. Cobb, *Most Southern Place on Earth*.

12. Ochiltree, "'Just and Self-Respecting System'?"

13. Ferris, *Edible South*, 100.

14. Jordan, *David L. Jordan*.

15. Evers and Peters, *For Us, the Living*.

16. Cooley, "Freedom's Farms."

17. McMillen, *Citizens' Council*.

18. de Jong, "Staying in Place," 387.

19. Zinn, *SNCC*.

20. Howerton and Trauger, "'Oh Honey, Don't You Know?,'" 741.

21. Payne, *I've Got the Light*.

22. Dittmer, *Local People*, 118.

23. Chapman, "Historical Study."

24. Dorsey quoted in Powledge, *Free at Last?*, 193–94.

25. Galtung, "Violence, Peace, and Peace Research."

26. "Leflore County Won't Have Commodity Program," *Greenwood Commonwealth*, November 9, 1962, box 18044 (microform), Mississippi Department of Archives and History, Jackson.

27. Henry and Curry, *Aaron Henry*, 132.

28. McAdam, "Recruitment to High-Risk Activism," 67.

29. "In Ruleville, Miss.: Surplus Food Denied to Registrants," December 19, 1962. In Carson, *Student Voice 1960–1965*, 62.

30. Payne, *I've Got the Light*.

31. Guy Carawan, "The Story of Greenwood, Mississippi," 1965 (New York: Folkways Records), Civil Rights Movement Archive, www.crmvet.org/crmpics/albums/65_greenwood_liner.pdf.

32. Bob Moses to Martha Prescod, December 11, 1962, Civil Rights Movement Archive, www.crmvet.org/lets/6212_moses-prescod-letter.pdf.

33. Charles Cobb and Charles McLaurin, November 19, 1962, SNCC Report on the condition of Negro farmers in Ruleville, Mississippi, Student Nonviolent Coordinating Committee papers, 1959–72 (microform), reel 38, 119, Mississippi, Greenville Sit-In, June 29, 1963–February 6, 1966, n.d., University of Illinois at Urbana-Champaign Library, Urbana.

34. Henry and Curry, *Aaron Henry*, 132.

35. Charles McDew and William Mahoney, March 12, 1963, Food for Freedom Program Recruitment Letter, Student Nonviolent Coordinating Committee papers, 1959–72 (microform), reel 49, 157, Programs, Food for Freedom, March 12–July 16, 1963, n.d., University of Illinois at Urbana-Champaign Library, Urbana.

36. Numerous letters sent out by Bill Mahoney regarding the Food for Freedom Program are located in the Student Nonviolent Coordinating Committee papers, 1959–72 (microform), reel 49, 157. Programs, Food for Freedom, March 12–July 16, 1963, n.d., University of Illinois at Urbana-Champaign Library, Urbana.

37. William Mahoney to Reverend Nickerson, April 19, 1963, Student Nonviolent Coordinating Committee papers, 1959–72 (microform), reel 49, 157, Programs, Food for Freedom, March 12–July 16, 1963, n.d., University of Illinois at Urbana-Champaign Library, Urbana.

38. Charles McDew and William Mahoney to Honorable Congressman John Lindsay, March 12, 1963, Student Nonviolent Coordinating Committee papers, 1959–72 (microform), reel 49, 157, Programs, Food for Freedom, March 12–July 16, 1963, n.d., University of Illinois at Urbana-Champaign Library, Urbana.

39. Charles McDew and William Mahoney to Honorable Congressman John Lindsay, March 12, 1963.

40. Martin Luther King Jr. quoted in "By Cong. Diggs, Dr. King, etc."

41. SNCC Statement: Michigan Student Held on 15,000 Bond by Mississippi Police: Shipment of Food and Clothing Withheld from Needy, January 2, 1963, Student Nonviolent Coordinating Committee papers, 1959–72 (microform), reel 38, 136, Mississippi, Leflore County, January 2, 1963–July 25, 1964, n.d., University of Illinois at Urbana-Champaign Library, Urbana; "Free 2 Students"; "Homefront 'CARE' Program Launched for Mississippi."

42. "Food for Freedom Committee."

43. Edward R. Dudley, April 5, 1963, By the President of the Borough of Manhattan: A Proclamation, Food for Freedom Week, reel 49, 157, Programs, Food for Freedom, March 12–July 16, 1963, n.d., University of Illinois at Urbana-Champaign Library, Urbana.

44. Dudley, April 5, 1963, By the President of the Borough of Manhattan.

45. Still, "Economic Pressure."

46. Hamlin, *Crossroads at Clarksdale*, 65.

47. Hamlin, *Crossroads at Clarksdale*, 12; Dittmer, *Local People*, 148; Naples, "Activist Mothering"; Daniels, "Invisible Work."

48. Naples, "Activist Mothering," 448.

49. Williams-Forson, *Building Houses*, 7.

50. Hamlin, *Crossroads at Clarksdale*, 60.

51. Hamlin, *Crossroads at Clarksdale*, 105; Dittmer, *Local People*, 148.

52. Morrison, *Aaron Henry of Mississippi*, 66.

53. Henry and Curry, *Aaron Henry*, 133.

54. Lee, *For Freedom's Sake*, 62.

55. Payne, *I've Got the Light*; Sam Block, State of Mississippi, County of Leflore, Sworn Deposition, July 12, 1964, Council of Federated Organizations Records, box 1, folder 12, Mississippi Department of Archives and History, Jackson.

56. Block, State of Mississippi, County of Leflore, Sworn Deposition, July 12, 1964; Swarns and Eveleigh, "In Covering Civil Rights"; Freddie Greene Biddle interviewed by Emilye Crosby, December 10, 2015, Civil Rights History Project, Southern Oral History Program, Smithsonian National Museum of African American History and Culture and the Library of Congress, www.loc.gov/item/2016655420/.

57. Moses, Kamii, Swap, and Howard, "Algebra Project," 424–26.

58. Still, "Economic Pressure against 5,000 Families."

59. Give Food for Freedom in Mississippi! (poster), n.d., Student Nonviolent Coordinating Committee papers, 1959–72 (microform), reel 49, 157, Programs, Food for Freedom, March 12–July 16, 1963, n.d., University of Illinois at Urbana-Champaign Library, Urbana.

60. Henry and Curry, *Aaron Henry*, 136.

61. Payne, *I've Got the Light*, 158–59.

62. "C-R Committee Backs County on Free Food," *Greenwood Commonwealth*, February 7, 1963, box 18046 (microform), Mississippi Department of Archives and History, Jackson.

63. "Dick Gregory Food Invasion Turns Out to Be Laffing Stock," *Jackson Advocate*, February 23, 1963, Mississippi State Sovereignty Commission Records Online Collection, SCR ID 10-52-0-30-1-1-1, Mississippi Department of Archives and History, Jackson, https://da.mdah.ms.gov/sovcom/result.php?image=images/png/cd09/067270.png&otherstuff=10|52|0|30|1|1|1|66402|; William Peart, "Ross Says 'Race Agitators' Could Halt Food Program," *Jackson Daily News*, February 14, 1963, Mississippi State Sovereignty Commission Records Online Collection, SCR ID 10-52-0-29-1-1-1, Mississippi Department of Archives and History, Jackson, https://da.mdah.ms.gov/sovcom/result.php?image=images/png/cd09/067252.png&otherstuff=10|52|0|29|1|1|1|66384|.

64. Peart, "Ross Says."

65. Thatcher Walt, "Negro Here Hits 'Food Publicity,'" *Greenwood Commonwealth*, February 9, 1963, box 18046 (microform), Mississippi Department of Archives and History, Jackson.

66. "Dick Gregory Negro Comic Invades State with Foods," *Jackson Advocate*, February 16, 1963, box 30578, (microform), Mississippi Department of Archives and History, Jackson.

67. "Dick Gregory Food Invasion Turns Out to Be Laffing Stock."

68. Bob Moses to Northern Supporters, February 27, 1963, Civil Rights Movement Archive, www.crmvet.org/lets/moses63.htm.

69. Constancia Romilly, (n.d.), SNCC Report on Leflore County, Student Nonviolent Coordinating Committee papers, 1959–72 (microform), reel 38, 136, Mississippi, Leflore County, January 2, 1963–July 25, 1964, n.d., University of Illinois at Urbana-Champaign Library, Urbana; "SNCC Internal Newsletter," March 22, 1963, Civil Rights Movement Archive, https://www.crmvet.org/docs/6303_sncc_newsletter.pdf.

70. Bob Moses to Northern Supporters, February 27, 1963.

71. "SNCC Internal Newsletter," March 22, 1963.

72. Romilly, n.d., SNCC Report on Leflore County.

73. "Diggs Demands"; "NAACP Asks Probe, Food."

74. Leflore County Board of Supervisors, March 20, 1963, Statement, Series 3, Subseries 4, box 25, folder 25–53, James O. Eastland Collection, Archives & Special Collections, J. D. Williams Library, University of Mississippi, Oxford.

75. Leflore County Board of Supervisors, March 20, 1963, Statement.

76. Leflore County Board of Supervisors, March 20, 1963, Statement.

77. Thatcher Walt, "Pressured Supervisors Vote for Commodities," *Greenwood Commonwealth*, March 20, 1963, Series 3, Subseries 4, box 25, folder 25–53, James O. Eastland Collection, Archives & Special Collections, J. D. Williams Library, University of Mississippi, Oxford.

78. "SNCC Internal Newsletter," March 22, 1963.

79. Walt, 1963, "Pressured Supervisors Vote for Commodities"; "First Food Shipment Here; County Is Hiring Workers," *Greenwood Commonwealth*, March 22, 1963, Series 3, Subseries 4, box 25, folder 25–53, James O. Eastland Collection, Archives & Special Collections, J. D. Williams Library, University of Mississippi, Oxford.

80. "SNCC Internal Newsletter," March 22, 1963.

81. Foreman quoted in "Miss. Bows to Pressure: 22,000 to Eat Again as U.S. Intervenes County Officials Given Ultimatum," *Afro-American (1893–1988)*, March 30, 1963, www.proquest.com.proxy2.library.illinois.edu/historical-newspapers/miss-bows-pressure/docview/532262156/se-2?accountid=14553.

82. SNCC Fourth Annual Conference "On Food and Jobs" Program, Civil Rights Movement Archive, 1963, www.crmvet.org/docs/631129_sncc_food_conf.pdf.

83. "Press Release: Leadership Training Conference of the Student Nonviolence Coordinating Committee," n.d., Civil Rights Movement Archive, www.crmvet.org/docs/631129_sncc_conf.pdf.

84. "Over 300 Attend SNCC Conference: D.C. Gathering Deals with 'Food and Jobs,'" December 9, 1963. In Carson, *Student Voice*, 88.

85. SNCC Fourth Annual Conference "On Food and Jobs" Program.

86. Why a Conference on Jobs and Food? (n.d.), Student Nonviolent Coordinating Committee papers, 1959–72 (microform), reel 54, 71, Fourth Annual Leadership Conference, October 26, 1963–March 12, 1964, n.d., University of Illinois at Urbana-Champaign Library, Urbana.

87. SNCC Fourth Annual Conference "On Food and Jobs" Program.

88. See Fay Bennett, "The Condition of Farm Workers in 1963: Report to the Board of Directors of National Sharecropper Fund," Civil Rights Movement Archive, n.d., www.crmvet.org/docs/nsf_farm_workers-63.pdf. In this report, Bennett explains the "Agricultural Dilemma" discussed at the conference.

89. Daniel, *Dispossession*.

Chapter Two

1. Morris Lewis Jr. memo to Retail Customers, November 15, 1962, Series 3, Subseries 7, box 11, folder 11–73, James O. Eastland Collection, Archives & Special Collections, J. D. Williams Library, University of Mississippi, Oxford.

2. Morris Lewis Jr. to Erle Johnston Jr., September 4, 1963, Mississippi State Sovereignty Commission Records Online Collection, SCR ID 6-70-0-84-1-1-1, Mississippi Department of Archives and History, Jackson, https://da.mdah.ms.gov/sovcom/result.php?image=images/png/cd07/051214.png&otherstuff=6%7C70%7C0%7C84%7C1%7C1%7C1%7C50490%7C#; Erle Johnston Jr. to Morris Lewis Jr., September 5, 1963, Mississippi State Sovereignty Commission Records Online Collection, SCR ID 6-70-0-85-1-1-1, Mississippi Department of Archives and History, Jackson, https://da.mdah.ms.gov/sovcom/result.php?image=images/png/cd07/051215.png&otherstuff=6%7C70%7C0%7C85%7C1%7C1%7C1%7C50491%7C#; John H. Hough Jr. to Erle Johnston Jr., September 5, 1963, Mississippi State Sovereignty Commission Records Online Collection, SCR ID 6-70-0-78-1-1-1-6-70-0-78-3-1-1, Mississippi Department of Archives and History, Jackson, https://da.mdah.ms.gov/sovcom/result.php?image=images/png/cd07/051204.png&otherstuff=6|70|0|78|1|1|1|50480|; B. Pittman, "Citizens Council Paid $5000 per Month by State," *Jackson Daily News*, December 30, 1960, December, Citizens Council, 1959–60, Subject Files, Mississippi Department of Archives and History, Jackson.

3. Moye, *Let the People Decide*, 112.

4. Rand, "Food Stamp Plan," 14.

5. Coppock, "Food Stamp Plan," 134.

6. MacDonald, "Food Stamps," 643.

7. Rand, "Food Stamp Plan," 14–15.

8. Coppock, "Food Stamp Plan," 133–34.

9. MacDonald, "Food Stamps," 644–46; Institute of Medicine and National Research Council, *Supplemental Nutrition Assistance Program*, 29–31.

10. Johnson, "Remarks upon Signing the Food Stamp Act."

11. Hamer, "Testimony," 96.

12. McKittrick, "On Plantations," 952.

13. McKittrick, "On Plantations," 948.

14. Alex Waites and Rollie Eubanks, *Mississippi: Poverty, Despair—A Way of Life*, July 13, 1967, Group IV, Series A, Administrative File, Annual Conventions, folder: Mississippi, 1967, NAACP Papers, Part 01: Supplement, 1966–70, Library of Congress, Washington, DC, https://hv.proquest.com/pdfs/009052/009052_005_0292/009052_005_0292_From_1_to_21.pdf.

15. Dittmer, *Local People*, 385–86.

16. "Statement of Mrs. L. C. Dorsey," in US Congress, Senate, Select Committee on Nutrition and Human Needs, *Hearings*, 927.

17. Rooks, *Cutting School*, 2.

18. McKittrick, "On Plantations," 952.

19. Lewis, *Wholesaler-Retailer*, 8–9; Berman, *House of David*, 63–64.

20. Wynter, "Novel and History," 100.

21. Woods, *Development Arrested*, 4–5.

22. Lewis, *Wholesaler-Retailer*, 9.

23. Lewis, *Wholesaler-Retailer*, 9. In some sources, Edmond F. Noel's first name is spelled "Edmund."

24. Vardaman quoted in White, "Anti-racial Agitation," 49.

25. Nash, "Edmund Favor Noel," 8.

26. James, "Transformation of the Southern Racial State," 192, 205.

27. Lewis, *Wholesaler-Retailer*, 10.

28. Lewis, *Wholesaler-Retailer*, 11–13.

29. Vance, *Human Factors in Cotton Culture*, 175–79.

30. Bull, "General Merchant," 37–38.

31. Ochiltree, "'Just and Self-Respecting System'?"; Lewis, *Wholesaler-Retailer*, 12.

32. Davis, Gardner, and Gardner, *Deep South*, 348.

33. Davis, Gardner, and Gardner, *Deep South*, 348.

34. Evers and Peters, *For Us, the Living*, 84.

35. Crenshaw, "Race, Reform, and Retrenchment," 1377.

36. Lewis, *Wholesaler-Retailer*, 13–14.

37. Vance, *Human Factors in Cotton Culture*, 296–98.

38. Lewis, *Wholesaler-Retailer*, 13–14.

39. Cash and Lewis, *Delta Council*.

40. Lewis, *Wholesaler-Retailer*, 14–15.

41. Berman, *House of David*.

42. Berman, *House of David*, 73.

43. Berman, *House of David*, 77.

44. Lewis, *Wholesaler-Retailer*, 15.

45. Morris Lewis Jr. memo to Retail Customers, November 15, 1962, Series 3, Subseries 7, box 11, folder 11–73, James O. Eastland Collection, Archives & Special Collections, J. D. Williams Library, University of Mississippi, Oxford.

46. Hamer, "To Tell It," 89.

47. Morris Lewis Jr. memo to Retail Customers, November 15, 1962.

48. Morris Lewis Jr. memo to Retail Customers, November 15, 1962, 1.

49. Morris Lewis Jr. memo to Retail Customers, November 15, 1962, 1–3.

50. Morris Lewis Jr. memo to Retail Customers, November 15, 1962, 2.

51. "Indianolan Hits Food Dole Plan," *Delta Democrat-Times*, November 19, 1962, box 22693 (microform), Mississippi Department of Archives and History, Jackson.

52. "Threat to Enterprise Seen in Growing Commodity Plan," *Enterprise-Tocsin*, November 22, 1962, box 22079 (microform), Mississippi Department of Archives and History, Jackson.

53. Morris Lewis Jr. to Honorable James O. Eastland, November 27, 1962, Series 3, Subseries 7, box 11, folder 11–73, James O. Eastland Collection, Archives & Special Collections, J. D. Williams Library, University of Mississippi, Oxford; Annis, *Big Jim Eastland*.

54. James O. Eastland to Mr. Morris Lewis Jr., December 6, 1962, Series 3, Subseries 7, box 11, folder 11–73, James O. Eastland Collection, Archives & Special Collections, J. D. Williams Library, University of Mississippi, Oxford.

55. Mike Wallace interview with Senator James Eastland of Mississippi, July 28, 1957, Series 2, Subseries 12, box 1, folder 1–13, James O. Eastland Collection, Archives & Special Collections, J. D. Williams Library, University of Mississippi, Oxford.

56. Moye, *Let the People Decide*.

57. "Material for Bolivar County Farm Bureau Speech, February 7, 1966," February 7,1966, Series 2, Subseries 6, box 4, folder 4–10, James O. Eastland Collection, Archives & Special Collections, J. D. Williams Library, University of Mississippi, Oxford; Woods, *Development Arrested*, 198.

58. Moye, *Let the People Decide*, 19.

59. James O. Eastland to Mrs. Otto Ward, March 28, 1966, Series 3, Subseries 4, box 53, folder 53–25, James O. Eastland Collection, Archives & Special Collections, J. D. Williams Library, University of Mississippi, Oxford.

60. Testimony of Congressman Jamie L. Whitten, D. of Miss., Before the Rules Committee, US House of Representatives, January 29, 1964, Series 15, box 1, folder: 1964, Jamie L. Whitten Collection, Archives & Special Collections, J. D. Williams Library, University of Mississippi, Oxford; Press Release, March 6, 1964, Series 11, box 3, folder: 1964, Jamie L. Whitten Collection, Archives & Special Collections, J. D. Williams Library, University of Mississippi, Oxford.

61. Press Release, March 6, 1964, Series 11, box 3, folder: 1964, Jamie L. Whitten Collection, Archives & Special Collections, J. D. Williams Library, University of Mississippi, Oxford.

62. "Conversation with James Eastland," March 18, 1964, Digital Recording, Secret White House Tapes, Lyndon B. Johnson Presidency, Citation Number: 2554, Miller Center, University of Virginia, Charlottesville, https://millercenter.org/the-presidency/secret-white-house-tapes/conversation-james-eastland-march-19-1964.

63. "Conversation with James Eastland," March 18, 1964.

64. *Congressional Record*, 88th Cong., 2d Sess., April 8, 1964, vol. 110, pt. 6: 7308.

65. *Congressional Record*, 88th Cong., 2d Sess., June 30, 1964, vol. 110, pt. 12: 15430.

66. *Congressional Record*, 88th Cong., 2d Sess., June 30, 1964, vol. 110, pt. 12: 15430.

67. *Congressional Record*, 88th Cong., 2d Sess., June 30, 1964, vol. 110, pt. 12: 15431.

68. Lewis, *Wholesaler-Retailer*, 18; Alex Waites and Rollie Eubanks, July 13, 1967, "Mississippi: Poverty, Despair—A Way of Life," Group IV, Series A, Administrative File, Annual Conventions, folder: Mississippi, 1967, NAACP Papers, Part 01: Supplement, 1966–70, Library of Congress, Washington, D.C., https://hv.proquest.com/pdfs/009052/009052_005_0292/009052_005_0292_From_1_to_21.pdf, 2.

69. "Morris Lewis Jr."

70. "What You Should Know about Food Stamps," January 1967, box 1, folder 14, Fannie Lou Hamer Collection, Archives & Special Collections, J. D. Williams Library, University of Mississippi, Oxford.

71. "What You Should Know about Food Stamps," January 1967, box 1, folder 14, Fannie Lou Hamer Collection, Archives & Special Collections, J. D. Williams Library, University of Mississippi, Oxford.

72. Curtis C. Whittington to Senator James O. Eastland, April 1, 1964, Series 3, Subseries 1, box 165, folder 165–39, James O. Eastland Collection, Archives & Special Collections, J. D. Williams Library, University of Mississippi, Oxford.

73. V. T. Brett to Senator James Eastland, March 26, 1966, Series 3, Subseries 4, box 53, folder 53–25, James O. Eastland Collection, Archives & Special Collections, J. D. Williams Library, University of Mississippi, Oxford.

74. C. M. Dorrough Sr. to Senator James O. Eastland, May 12, 1966, Series 3, Subseries 4, box 52, folder 52–94, James O. Eastland Collection, Archives & Special Collections, J. D. Williams Library, University of Mississippi, Oxford.

75. C. M. Dorrough Sr. to Senator James O. Eastland, May 12, 1966.

76. Transcripts for the 1966 four-part series Super—Supermarkets (The Problem) on food stamps of the morning Mid-South Network Radio WONA (Winona) can be found in Series 3, Subseries 1, box 165, folder 165–41, James O. Eastland Collection, Archives & Special Collections, J. D. Williams Library, University of Mississippi, Oxford.

77. Mid-South Network Radio WONA (Winona), Super—Supermarkets (The Problem): Food Stamp Series—Report No. 1, March 30, 1966.

78. Senator James O. Eastland to Bob Chisholm, April 5, 1966, Series 3, Subseries 1, box 165, folder 165–41, James O. Eastland Collection, Archives & Special Collections, J. D. Williams Library, University of Mississippi, Oxford.

79. Cooley, "Freedom's Farms."

80. Cooley, "Freedom's Farms," 209.

81. Newman, *Divine Agitators*, 163.

82. "What You Should Know about Food Stamps," January 1967, box 1, folder 14, Fannie Lou Hamer Collection, Archives & Special Collections, J. D. Williams Library, University of Mississippi, Oxford.

83. Waites and Eubanks, "Mississippi."

84. Waites and Eubanks, "Mississippi," 7.

85. Waites and Eubanks, "Mississippi," 7.

86. Waites and Eubanks, "Mississippi," 4–5.

87. Senate Subcommittee on Employment, Manpower, and Poverty of the Committee on Labor and Public Welfare, *Examination of the War on Poverty*; A. B. Albritton, "Senators to Probe State Poverty War," *Clarion-Ledger*, April 9, 1967, Robert F. Kennedy, Subject Files, Mississippi Department of Archives and History, Jackson.

88. A. B. Albritton, "Senators to Probe State Poverty War."

89. "Statement of the Community Leaders Panel: Fannie Lou Hamer," Senate Subcommittee on Employment, Manpower, and Poverty of the Committee on Labor and Public Welfare, *Examination of the War on Poverty*, 582. In the transcript of this panel, Fannie Lou Hamer's last name is misspelled as "Hammer."

90. Cobb, "'Somebody Done Nailed Us,'" 918.

91. Cooley, "Freedom's Farms," 208.

92. "Statement of the Community Leaders Panel: Unita Blackwell," Senate Subcommittee on Employment, Manpower, and Poverty of the Committee on Labor and Public Welfare, *Examination of the War on Poverty*, 585.

93. "Statement of the Community Leaders Panel: Unita Blackwell," 592–93.

94. "Statement of the Community Leaders Panel: Unita Blackwell," 585; Kornbluh, "Food as a Civil Right."

95. "Statement of Miss Marian Wright," Senate Subcommittee on Employment, Manpower, and Poverty of the Committee on Labor and Public Welfare, Examination of the War on Poverty, 652. In the transcript of this statement, Marian Wright's first name is misspelled as "Marion."

96. "Statement of the Community Leaders Panel: Unita Blackwell," 585.

97. Combahee River Collective, "Black Feminist Statement," 275.

98. Reese and Cooper, "Making Spaces Something like Freedom," 452.

Chapter Three

1. "Statement of Mrs. L. C. Dorsey, Director, North Bolivar County Farm Cooperative, Bolivar County, Miss.," Senate Select Committee on Nutrition and Human Needs, *Hearings Part 4—Housing and Sanitation*, 927–28.

2. "Statement of Mrs. L. C. Dorsey," 928.

3. Kelley, *Freedom Dreams*, ix.

4. Woods, *Development Arrested*, 217.

5. King, "Martin Luther King Jr. Saw Three Evils."

6. Robnett, *How Long?*, 20.

7. West, *Race Matters*, 15.

8. Charles McDew and William Mahoney, Food for Freedom Program Recruitment Letter, March 12, 1963, Student Nonviolent Coordinating Committee papers, 1959–72 (microform) reel 49, 157, Programs, Food for Freedom, March 12–July 16, 1963, n.d.), University of Illinois at Urbana-Champaign Library, Urbana.

9. Smith II, Kaiser, and Gómez, "Identifying Factors."

10. "The Founding of Mound Bayou," 10, *Mound Bayou Voice*, July 1971, T/021, box 4, folder 35, James W. Loewen Collection, 1858–1979, bulk 1967–78, Mississippi Department of Archives and History, Jackson.

11. "The Early Years," 14, *Mound Bayou Voice*, July 1971, T/021, box 4, folder 35, James W. Loewen Collection, 1858–1979, bulk 1967–78, Mississippi Department of Archives and History, Jackson.

12. Washington, "Town Owned by Negroes," 9127.

13. "Early Years," 14.

14. "Portrait of a Black Town: Mound Bayou—Past, Present, & Future," 1, *Mound Bayou Voice*, July 1971, T/021, box 4, folder 35, James W. Loewen Collection, 1858–1979, bulk 1967–78, Mississippi Department of Archives and History, Jackson.

15. Robinson, "Community Part," 2068.

16. "Statement of Mrs. L. C. Dorsey," 927.

17. Grim, "Impact," 183.

18. Grim, "Impact," 170.

19. Cobb, "'Somebody Done Nailed Us'," 918.

20. "Prepared Statement of L. C. Dorsey, Director, North Bolivar County Farm Cooperative, Bolivar County, Miss.," Senate Select Committee on Nutrition and Human Needs, *Hearings Part 4—Housing and Sanitation*, 930.

21. Beale, "Rural-Urban Migration of Blacks," 303.

22. Student Nonviolent Coordinating Committee, n.d., Cotton Workers Form Labor Union, Student Nonviolent Coordinating Committee papers, 1959–72 (microform), reel 14, 3, Press Releases, March 1962–July 15, 1968, n.d., University of Illinois at Urbana-Champaign Library, Urbana.

23. Poor People's Conference, January 31, 1966, Statement Issued from the Greenville Air Force base, box 13a, folder: FDP—Newsletters, Mississippi Council on Human Relations Records, 1960–80, Mississippi Department of Archives and History, Jackson.

24. Alex Waites and Rollie Eubanks, July 13, 1967, "Mississippi: Poverty, Despair—A Way of Life," Group IV, Series A, Administrative File, Annual Conventions, folder: Mississippi, 1967, NAACP Papers, Part 01: Supplement, 1966–70, Library of Congress, Washington, DC, https://hv.proquest.com/pdfs/009052/009052_005_0292/009052_005_0292_From_1_to_21.pdf, 1.

25. Ward, *Out in the Rural*, 2–10.

26. Ward, *Out in the Rural*.

27. Ward, *Out in the Rural*, 23.

28. H. Jack Geiger, The Tufts-Delta Health Center: A Progress Report, October 1968, box 36, folder: Tufts, Mississippi Council on Human Relations Records, 1960–80, Mississippi Department of Archives and History, Jackson, 1.

29. "Statement of Dr. Jack Geiger," Senate Select Committee on Nutrition and Human Needs, *Hearings Part 4—Housing and Sanitation*, 904–5.

30. "The Agricultural Co-Operative as a Possible Means of Providing Food for Needy Persons," n.d., box 1, folder 1, North Bolivar County Farm Cooperative Records, 1967–69, Wisconsin Historical Society Archives, Madison.

31. "Agricultural Co-Operative as a Possible Means"; "Statement of Mrs. L. C. Dorsey," 929.

32. Kenneth L. Dean, "Report on Poverty," April 24, 1967, box 36, folder: Poverty Statistics, Mississippi Council on Human Relations Records, 1960–80, Mississippi Department of Archives and History, Jackson, 4.

33. Jack Geiger interviewed by Robert Korstad and Neil Boothby, April 22, 1992, https://livinghistory.sanford.duke.edu/interviews/jack-geiger/?search=geiger.

34. Hossfeld, Kerr, and Belue, "Good Food Revolution," 57.

35. Smith, *Sick and Tired*.

36. Jack Geiger interviewed by Robert Korstad and Neil Boothby, April 22, 1992.

37. John Hatch interviewed by Robert Korstad and Neil Boothby, April 23, 1992.

38. L. C. Dorsey interviewed by Robert Korstad and Neil Boothby, April 22, 1992, https://livinghistory.sanford.duke.edu/interviews/l-c-dorsey/.

39. Dorsey, "Harder Times Than These," 28–31; "L. C. Dorsey Funeral Program," L. C. Dorsey, Subject Files, Mississippi Department of Archives and History, Jackson.

40. "L. C. Dorsey Funeral Program"; Todd Moye, "An Interview with L. C. Dorsey," January 13, 1995, AU 677 (transcript), Mississippi Department of Archives and History, Jackson.

41. Dorsey, "Harder Times Than These," 28.

42. L. C. Dorsey interviewed by Robert Korstad and Neil Boothby, April 22, 1992.

43. Ward, *Out in the Rural*.

44. L. C. Dorsey interviewed by Robert Korstad and Neil Boothby, April 22, 1992.

45. L. C. Dorsey interviewed by Robert Korstad and Neil Boothby, April 22, 1992.

46. "L. C. Dorsey Funeral Program"; Ward, *Out in the Rural*.

47. "Personal Data," n.d., box 1, folder: Dorsey, L. C., Eric Smith Papers, 1965–74, Wisconsin Historical Society Archives, Madison; "Statement of Mrs. L. C. Dorsey," 926; "L. C. Dorsey Funeral Program."

48. Ward, *Out in the Rural*.

49. Dorsey, "Harder Times Than These," 30.

50. L. C. Dorsey interviewed by Robert Korstad and Neil Boothby, April 22, 1992.

51. Black, *People and Plows against Hunger*, 6.

52. L. C. Dorsey, "North Bolivar County Farm Cooperative, A.A.L. 1969 Progress Report," Select Committee on Nutrition and Human Needs, *Hearings Part 4—Housing and Sanitation*, 933.

53. L. C. Dorsey interviewed by Owen Brooks, Audio Recordings—Mississippi Oral History Interviews, Civil Rights Movement Archive, 2006, www.crmvet.org/audio/msoh/2006_dorsey_lc.mp3.

54. Jakubek and Wood, "Emancipatory Empiricism"; White, *Freedom Farmers*; Reese, *Black Food Geographies*; Quisumbing King, Wood, Gilbert, and Sinkewicz, "Black Agrarianism"; Smith, "Black Agrarianism"; Densu, "Theoretical and Historical Perspectives."

55. "General Meeting around the Co-Op Idea," n.d., box 1, folder: Bolivar Co-Op, Eric Smith Papers, 1965–74, Wisconsin Historical Society Archives, Madison; L. C. Dorsey interview, n.d., *Jack Geiger Collection on Delta Health Center*, Southern Historical Collection, Louis Round Wilson Library, University of North Carolina at Chapel Hill, https://dcr.lib.unc.edu/record/8b34436d-6727-4d99-8a19-aa8d79aaf8a6.

56. L. C. Dorsey interview, n.d., *Jack Geiger Collection on Delta Health Center*.

57. John Hatch, "Historical Sketch and Progress Report on the North Bolivar County Farm Cooperative AAL," January 8, 1969, box 1, folder 1, North Bolivar County Farm Cooperative Records, 1967–69, Wisconsin Historical Society Archives, Madison; Black, *People and Plows against Hunger*, 26.

58. Dorsey, "North Bolivar County Farm Cooperative, A.A.L. 1969 Progress Report," 933–38.

59. L. C. Dorsey interview, n.d., *Jack Geiger Collection on Delta Health Center*, Southern Historical Collection, Louis Round Wilson Library, University of North Carolina at Chapel Hill, https://dcr.lib.unc.edu/record/8b34436d-6727-4d99-8a19-aa8d79aaf8a6.

60. Ward, *Out in the Rural*, 126.

61. Ward, *Out in the Rural*, 120.

62. Black, *People and Plows against Hunger*, 7.

63. L. C. Dorsey interview, n.d., *Jack Geiger Collection on Delta Health Center*; Robinson, Community Part," 2067–69.

64. "Cooperative Organizational Structure," n.d., box 1, folder 1, North Bolivar County Farm Cooperative Records, 1967–69, Wisconsin Historical Society Archives, Madison.

65. Hatch, "Historical Sketch and Progress Report," 3.

66. Hatch, "Historical Sketch and Progress Report," 7.

67. Kerssen and Brent, "Grounding the U.S. Food Movement"; Fannie Lou Hamer, Typescript of speech "If the Name of the Game Is Survive, Survive, September 27, 1971" by Fannie Lou Hamer, T/012, box 1, folder 3, Fannie Lou Townsend Hamer Collection, Mississippi Department of Archives and History, Jackson.

68. Ward, *Out in the Rural*, 116.

69. Ward, *Out in the Rural*, 120; Hatch, "John Hatch on Community Organizing in the Mississippi Delta, 1965."

70. "Articles of Association of North Bolivar County Farm Cooperative (A.L.L.)," n.d., box 1, folder 1, North Bolivar County Farm Cooperative Records, 1967–69, Wisconsin Historical Society Archives, Madison, 1–2.

71. Hatch, "Historical Sketch and Progress Report," 3–4; "ByLaws of North Bolivar County Farm Cooperative (A.L.L.)," n.d., box 1, folder 1, North Bolivar County Farm Cooperative Records, 1967–69, Wisconsin Historical Society Archives, Madison, 3.

72. Finney and McGranahan, "Community Support and Goal Displacement," 13.

73. Black, *People and Plows against Hunger*, 60.

74. Dorsey, "North Bolivar County Farm Cooperative, A.A.L. 1969 Progress Report," 937.

75. Dorsey, "North Bolivar County Farm Cooperative, A.A.L. 1969 Progress Report," 937; Ward, *Out in the Rural*, 115; Black, *People and Plows against Hunger*, 60.

76. Dorsey, "North Bolivar County Farm Cooperative, A.A.L. 1969 Progress Report," 933–38; Ward, *Out in the Rural*, 115; "How the Co-Op Works," n.d., box 1, folder 1, North Bolivar County Farm Cooperative Records, 1967–69, Wisconsin Historical Society Archives, Madison.

77. Robinson, "Community Part," 2068.

78. Robinson, "Community Part," 2068; Hatch, "Historical Sketch and Progress Report," 3–4; Black, *People and Plows against Hunger*, 33–34.

79. Rutherford Associates, "Food Processing in the Mississippi Delta," October 1, 1970, box 1, folder 4, Charles Howard Baer Papers, 1963–72, Wisconsin Historical Society Archives, Madison.

80. L. C. Dorsey interviewed by Robert Korstad and Neil Boothby, April 22, 1992; "Establishing a Retail Farm Supply Store at a Low Income Farm Cooperative," Spring 1974, Madison Measure for Measure Records, 1965–77, box 1, folder 19, Wisconsin Historical Society Archives, Madison.

81. "Establishing a Retail Farm Supply Store at a Low Income Farm Cooperative," 4; Black, *People and Plows against Hunger*; Ward, *Out in the Rural*, 131.

82. "Technological Considerations," n.d., box 1, folder 1, North Bolivar County Farm Cooperative Records, 1967–69, Wisconsin Historical Society Archives, Madison; Dorsey, "North Bolivar County Farm Cooperative, A.A.L. 1969 Progress Report," 937.

83. "How the Co-Op Works," 5.

84. Hatch, "Historical Sketch and Progress Report," 4.

85. "How the Co-Op Works," 5; Roy E. Brown, "TDHCT Food and Nutrition Cooperative Project," January 20, 1968, box 1, folder 1, North Bolivar County Farm Cooperative Records, 1967–69, Wisconsin Historical Society Archives, Madison.

86. Brown, "TDHCT Food and Nutrition Cooperative Project."

87. "General Meeting around the Co-Op Idea."

88. Ward, *Out in the Rural,* 115.

89. Hatch, "Historical Sketch and Progress Report," 4.

90. "Northern Bolivar County Co-Op Farm," n.d., box 1, folder: Book, Eric Smith Papers, 1965–74, Wisconsin Historical Society Archives, Madison, 3.

91. "Small Co-Ops Given Grants by Ford Fund"; Black, *People and Plows against Hunger.*

92. "Statement of Mrs. L. C. Dorsey," 928.

93. Dorsey, "North Bolivar County Farm Cooperative, A.A.L. 1969 Progress Report," 934–38.

94. L. C. Dorsey to North Bolivar County Farm Co-Op Members, November 12, 1968, box 1, folder 1, North Bolivar County Farm Cooperative Records, 1967–69, Wisconsin Historical Society Archives, Madison, 2; "Prepared Statement of L. C. Dorsey," 931; "N. B. C. Farm Co-Op Meeting August 2, 1968," August 2, 1968, box 1, folder 2, North Bolivar County Farm Cooperative Records, 1967–69, Wisconsin Historical Society Archives, Madison, 1.

95. L. C. Dorsey interviewed by Robert Korstad and Neil Boothby, April 22, 1992.

96. L. C. Dorsey to North Bolivar County Farm Co-Op Members, November 12, 1968, 2.

97. Mrs. Young Interview, n.d., *Jack Geiger Collection on Delta Health Center,* Southern Historical Collection, Louis Round Wilson Library, University of North Carolina at Chapel Hill, https://dcr.lib.unc.edu/record/uuid:8d918272-4c1a-48d6-a1c9-9ea990cb0436.

98. L. C. Dorsey to North Bolivar County Farm Co-Op Members, November 12, 1968, 2.

99. L. C. Dorsey interviewed by Robert Korstad and Neil Boothby, April 22, 1992; James O. Taylor and L. C. Dorsey, "People in the Co-Op," n.d., box 1, folder 1, North Bolivar County Farm Cooperative Records, 1967–69, Wisconsin Historical Society Archives, Madison; "Agricultural Co-Operative as a Possible Means"; "N. B. C. Farm Co-Op Meeting August 2, 1968."

100. "Winstonville Area North Bolivar Farm Co-Op Organization," n.d., box 1, folder 1, North Bolivar County Farm Cooperative Records, 1967–69, Wisconsin Historical Society Archives, Madison.

101. Dorsey, "North Bolivar County Farm Cooperative, A.A.L. 1969 Progress Report," 935.

102. L. C. Dorsey interviewed by Robert Korstad and Neil Boothby, April 22, 1992.

103. L. C. Dorsey interviewed by Robert Korstad and Neil Boothby, April 22, 1992; Dorsey, "North Bolivar County Farm Cooperative, A.A.L. 1969 Progress Report," 934.

104. L. C. Dorsey interviewed by Robert Korstad and Neil Boothby, April 22, 1992.

105. Dorsey, "North Bolivar County Farm Cooperative, A.A.L. 1969 Progress Report," 935.

106. Dorsey, "North Bolivar County Farm Cooperative, A.A.L. 1969 Progress Report," 934; Smith II, Kaiser, and Gómez, "Identifying Factors."

107. Dailey, Conroy, and Shelley-Tolbert, "Using Agricultural Education," 11.

108. Dorsey, "North Bolivar County Farm Cooperative, A.A.L. 1969 Progress Report," 935.

109. "Prepared Statement of L. C. Dorsey," 932.

110. Dorsey, "North Bolivar County Farm Cooperative, A.A.L. 1969 Progress Report," 937–38.

111. Dorsey, "North Bolivar County Farm Cooperative, A.A.L. 1969 Progress Report," 935.

112. Dorsey, "North Bolivar County Farm Cooperative, A.A.L. 1969 Progress Report," 934.

113. Dorsey, "North Bolivar County Farm Cooperative, A.A.L. 1969 Progress Report," 935.

114. Hickmott, "Black Land, Black Capital," 505.

115. Bublitz, Peracchio, Andreasen, Kees, Kidwell, Miller, Motley, Peter, Rajagopal, Scott, and Vallen, "Quest for Eating Right," 3.

116. Dorsey, "North Bolivar County Farm Cooperative, A.A.L. 1969 Progress Report," 936.

117. Allen and Sachs, "Women and Food Chains," 3.

118. "Statement of Mrs. L. C. Dorsey," 928.

119. Dorsey, "North Bolivar County Farm Cooperative, A.A.L. 1969 Progress Report," 936.

120. "Mound Bayou Today," *Mound Bayou Voice*, July 1971, T/021, box 4, folder 35, James W. Loewen Collection, 1858–1979, bulk 1967–78, Mississippi Department of Archives and History, Jackson, MS, 34; "C. Preston Holmes."

121. Bublitz, Peracchio, Andreasen, Kees, Kidwell, Miller, Motley, Peter, Rajagopal, Scott, and Vallen, "Quest for Eating Right," 3.

122. Mrs. Young Interview, n.d., *Jack Geiger Collection on Delta Health Center*, Southern Historical Collection, Louis Round Wilson Library, University of North Carolina at Chapel Hill, https://dcr.lib.unc.edu/record/uuid:8d918272-4c1a-48d6-a1c9-9ea990cb0436.

123. Herman Johnson Sr. interviewed by the author.

124. Herman Johnson Sr. interviewed by the author; Dorsey, "North Bolivar County Farm Cooperative, A.A.L. 1969 Progress Report," 935.

125. "Prepared Statement of L. C. Dorsey," 931; Dorsey, "North Bolivar County Farm Cooperative, A.A.L. 1969 Progress Report," 934.

126. James O. Taylor and L. C. Dorsey, "People in the Co-Op," n.d., box 1, folder 1, North Bolivar County Farm Cooperative Records, 1967–69, Wisconsin Historical Society Archives, Madison.

127. Dorsey, "North Bolivar County Farm Cooperative, A.A.L. 1969 Progress Report," 935.

128. Rutherford Associates, "Food Processing in the Mississippi Delta."
129. Rutherford Associates, "Food Processing in the Mississippi Delta," 9.
130. Knight, "For Us by Us (FUBU)."
131. Hatch, "Historical Sketch and Progress Report," 6.
132. "Establishing a Retail Farm Supply Store," 7.
133. "Establishing a Retail Farm Supply Store," 7.
134. Ward, *Out in the Rural*, 133.
135. Dorsey quoted in Ward, *Out in the Rural*, 133.
136. Black, *People and Plows against Hunger*.
137. Crowe, Martin, and Brown, "Mound Bayou Mississippi Story."
138. "Technology Transfer Center," n.d., Outreach Centers, Alcorn State University Extension Program, Alcorn State, MS, www.alcorn.edu/academics/schools-and-departments/school-of-agriculture-and-applied-sciences/land-grant-programs/extension-and-outreach/outreach-centers/technology-transfer-center; Black, *People and Plows against Hunger*, 85.
139. John Coleman, personal communication, July 2020.
140. L. C. Dorsey, Jack Geiger, and John Hatch interviewed by Robert Korstad and Neil Boothby, April 23, 1992, https://livinghistory.sanford.duke.edu/interviews/l-c-dorsey-jack-geiger-and-john-hutch/.

Chapter Four

1. Hossfeld, Kerr, and Belue, "Good Food Revolution."
2. Meikle, "Globalization."
3. US Department of Agriculture, *2017 Census of Agriculture Mississippi 2nd Congressional District Profile*.
4. US Department of Agriculture, *2017 Census of Agriculture Mississippi State Profile*. Statistics were calculated using data from the county profiles of Bolivar, Sunflower, Washington, Tallahatchie, and Yazoo in US Department of Agriculture, National Agricultural Statistics Service, *2017 Census of Agriculture*.
5. US Department of Agriculture, *2017 Census of Agriculture Bolivar County Mississippi Profile*.
6. MacKendrick, "Foodscape," 16.
7. Hossfeld, Kerr, and Belue, "Good Food Revolution," 4–5.
8. Cora Jackson quoted in Eller, *Fighting Hunger*.
9. Kunnerth, "Delta Paradox."
10. Feeding America, *2019 Map the Meal Gap*; Coleman-Jensen, Rabbitt, Gregory, and Singh, *Household Food Security*, 8.
11. Dalaker, *10-20-30 Provision*, 14.
12. Mississippi State Department of Health, Office of Health Data and Research, *2018 Bolivar County Health Profile*.
13. Coleman-Jensen, Rabbitt, Gregory, and Singh, *Household Food Security*, 19; US Department of Agriculture, *2019 State Fact Sheets: Mississippi*.
14. These statistics were calculated using data from Dalaker, *10-20-30 Provision*.
15. Dalaker, *10-20-30 Provision*.

16. Presser, "Black American Amputation Epidemic."

17. Penniman, *Farming While Black*, 4.

18. US Department of Agriculture, National Agricultural Statistics Service, *2017 Census of Agriculture Mississippi State Profile*; Meter and Goldenberg, *Overview*.

19. Ginwright, *Black Youth Rising*, 147.

20. Andrews, "Social Movements and Policy Implementation," 75; Franklin, *After the Rebellion*, 28.

21. Franklin, *After the Rebellion*; Franklin, *Young Crusaders*; Broad, *More Than Just Food*; Steel, "Youth and Food Justice."

22. Franklin, *After the Rebellion*, 29.

23. Franklin, *After the Rebellion*, 28.

24. Franklin, *After the Rebellion*, 42; For a broader understanding of framing in social movement theory, see Goffman, *Frame Analysis*, and Benford and Snow, "Framing Processes and Social Movements." Here, the use of indigenous resources is aligned with the indigenous perspective outlined in Morris, *Origins of the Civil Rights Movement*, 282–286.

25. Franklin, *After the Rebellion*, 43–45.

26. Moore, Belue, and Smith, "Social Justice for Lunch," 2–3.

27. Moore, Belue, and Smith, "Social Justice for Lunch," 2–3.

28. Founding member quoted in Allen, "Bolivar Students."

29. Brown, "Delta Fresh Foods Awarded Grant."

30. Hossfeld, Kerr, and Belue, "Good Food Revolution," 4–5.

31. Delta Fresh Foods Initiative, "Message from the Board."

32. Tyra Slaughter quoted in Evans, *Building the Future*.

33. Hossfeld, Kerr, and Belue, "Good Food Revolution."

34. LeBroderick Woods quoted in Watts, "Farmers Markets."

35. Tonitria Hunt interviewed by author.

36. Trayla Britton interviewed by author.

37. Quantrell Holmes interviewed by author.

38. Tanya Fields quoted in Malone, "What We Talk About."

39. Hossfeld, Kerr, and Belue, "Good Food Revolution"; Arrington, "Community Surveyed."

40. Tanielle Woods interviewed by author.

41. Brown, "Delta Fresh Foods Awarded Grant"; Hossfeld, Kerr, and Belue, "Good Food Revolution."

42. Cistrunk, Oliver, Kerr, Trinh, Kobia, Hossfeld, Johnson, and Jones, "Ecological Approach."

43. Hossfeld, Kerr, and Belue, "Good Food Revolution."

44. Hossfeld, Kerr, and Belue, "Good Food Revolution."

45. Tyra Slaughter interviewed by author.

46. Tanielle Woods interviewed by author.

47. Hossfeld, Kerr, and Belue, "Good Food Revolution."

48. Hossfeld, Kerr, and Belue, "Good Food Revolution," 7.

49. Tanielle Woods quoted in Watts, "Farmers Markets."

50. Reese, *Black Food Geographies*, 45.

51. Hossfeld, Kerr, and Belue, "Good Food Revolution"; Delta Fresh Foods Initiative, "Current Project."

52. Watts, "Farmers Markets"; Hossfeld, Kerr, and Belue, "Good Food Revolution"; Delta Fresh Foods Initiative, "Current Project."

53. Wilson, "Capital's Need," 261.

54. Reese, "In the Food Justice World," 33–37.

55. Rani, *Study Material*, 15.

56. Bornstein, *How to Change the World*, 1.

57. Tanielle Woods quoted in Watts, "Farmers Markets."

58. Patron quoted in Watts, "Farmers Markets."

59. Hossfeld, Kerr, and Belue, "Good Food Revolution."

60. Hanson and Pochee-Smith, *Delta Fresh FINAL 2k*.

61. Du Bois, "Talented Tenth," 54.

62. Brown, "Moving Beyond Charity," 9.

63. Lawrence-Jacobson, "Intergenerational Community Action," 138.

64. Lyson, "Civic Agriculture," 94.

65. LeBroderick Woods quoted in Watts, "Farmers Markets."

66. Trayla Britton interviewed by author.

67. Tyra Slaughter interviewed by author.

68. Reese, *Black Food Geographies*, 138.

69. Delta Fresh Foods Initiative, "Current Project."

70. Hossfeld, Kerr, and Belue, "Good Food Revolution."

71. Tyra Slaughter interviewed by author.

72. Chris Johnson, personal communication, July 8, 2020.

73. Larry Mims II interviewed by author.

74. Larry Haywood quoted in Evans, *Building the Future*.

75. Larry Haywood interviewed by David Hanson, personal communication, August 30, 2021.

76. Jackson quoted in Evans, *Building the Future*.

77. Robbie Pollard, personal communication, July 9, 2020.

78. Judy Belue, personal communication, July 8, 2020.

79. Tonitria Hunt interviewed by author.

80. Reggie quoted in Evans, *Building the Future*.

81. Quantrell Holmes interviewed by author.

82. Tyra Slaughter interviewed by author.

83. Tanielle Woods interviewed by author.

84. Trayla Britton interviewed by author.

85. Judy Belue, personal communication, February 10, 2021.

86. Ginwright, *Black Youth Rising*, 57.

87. Katrina Sanders interviewed by author.

88. Katrina Sanders interviewed by author.

89. Trayla Britton interviewed by author.

90. Katrina Sanders interviewed by author.

91. Tanielle Woods interviewed by author.

92. Tyra Slaughter interviewed by author.

93. Hanson and Pochee-Smith, *Delta Fresh FINAL 2k*.
94. Tyra Slaughter interviewed by author.
95. Trayla Britton interviewed by author.
96. Larry Mims II interviewed by author.
97. Katrina Sanders interviewed by author.
98. Katrina Sanders interviewed by author.
99. Judy Belue, personal communication, May 14, 2020.
100. Tyra Slaughter interviewed by author.
101. Katrina Sanders interviewed by author.
102. Simley, "More Abundant Share."
103. Quantrell Holmes interview with author (emphasis added).
104. Franklin, *After the Rebellion*, 93–94.

Conclusion

1. Tate, "Black Culinary and Food Traditions"; Height, *Open Wide the Freedom Gates*, 188.
2. Moses and Cobb, *Radical Equations*, 81.
3. Williams-Forson and Wilkerson, "Intersectionality and Food Studies"; Nestle and McIntosh, "Writing the Food Studies Movement"; Belasco, Bentley, Biltekoff, Williams-Forson, and de la Peña, "Frontiers of Food Studies"; Ewoodzie, *Getting Something to Eat*; Williams-Forson, *Eating While Black*.
4. Yakini, "What Ferguson Means," 1.
5. Cooper, "Black Food as Resistance," 146.
6. Walcott, *Long Emancipation*, 2.
7. Nasstrom, "Between Memory and History," 363.
8. Conrad, *Research Brief*, 1.
9. Kelley, *Freedom Dreams*.

Bibliography

Primary Sources

Manuscript and Archive Collections

ANN ARBOR, MICHIGAN

ProQuest Historical Newspapers: Black Newspapers
  https://about.proquest.com/en/products-services/histnews-bn/
ProQuest History Vault: NAACP Papers
  https://proquest.libguides.com/historyvault/NAACP

CHAPEL HILL, NORTH CAROLINA

Louis Round Wilson Special Collections Library, University of North Carolina
  Southern Historical Collection
    Jack Geiger Collection on the Delta Health Center (05699)

CHARLOTTESVILLE, VIRGINIA

The Presidential Recordings Program, Miller Center, University of Virginia
  Secret White House Tapes, Lyndon B. Johnson Presidency
    https://millercenter.org/the-presidency/secret-white-house-tapes

CHICAGO, ILLINOIS

Chicago Public Library
  Carter G. Woodson Regional Library
    Vivian G. Harsh Research Collection of Afro-American History and Literature
      Chicago SNCC History Project Archives, 1960–2011, box 3
      Rev. Addie Wyatt and Rev. Claude Wyatt Papers, box 149

DURHAM, NORTH CAROLINA

Sanford School of Public Health Policy, Duke University
  DeWitt Wallace Center for Media & Democracy
    Rutherford Living History, livinghistory.sanford.duke.edu

GAMBIER, OHIO

Kenyon College
  North by South: The African American Great Migration, http://northbysouth.kenyon.edu

JACKSON, MISSISSIPPI

Mississippi Department of Archives and History
  Citizens Council, 1959–60, Subject Files
  Council of Federated Organizations Records, box 1

Delta Democrat-Times, microform, box 22693
Enterprise-Tocsin, microform, box 22079
Fannie Lou Townsend Hamer Collection, T/012/box 1
Greenwood Commonwealth, microform, boxes 18044, 18046
Jackson Advocate, microform, box 30578
James W. Loewen Collection, 1858–1979, bulk 1967–78, T/021/box 4
L. C. Dorsey, Subject Files
Mississippi Council on Human Relations Records, 1960–80, boxes 13a, 36
Mississippi State Sovereignty Commission Records Online Collection
https://da.mdah.ms.gov/sovcom/
Oral History Audio and Transcripts
Robert F. Kennedy, Subject Files

MADISON, WISCONSIN
Wisconsin Historical Society Archives
Charles Howard Baer Papers, 1963–72, box 1
Eric Smith Papers, 1965–74, box 1
Madison Measure for Measure Records, 1965–77, box 1
North Bolivar County Farm Cooperative Records, 1967–69, box 1

OXFORD, MISSISSIPPI
University of Mississippi
J. D. Williams Library
Department of Archives and Special Collections
Fannie Lou Hamer Collection, box 1
James O. Eastland Collection, boxes 1, 4, 11, 25, 52, 53, 165
Jamie L. Whitten Collection, box 3
Race Relations Collection, box 9

SAN FRANCISCO, CALIFORNIA
Civil Rights Movement Archive, Veterans of the Southern Freedom Movement (1951–68), crmvet.org

SANTA BARBARA, CALIFORNIA
University of California
The American Presidency Project, www.presidency.ucsb.edu

URBANA, ILLINOIS
University of Illinois at Urbana-Champaign Library
Student Nonviolent Coordinating Committee Papers, 1959–72, microform, reels 38, 49, 54.

WASHINGTON, DC
Smithsonian National Museum of African American History and Culture and the Library of Congress
Civil Rights History Project, Southern Oral History Program, www.loc.gov/collections/civil-rights-history-project/about-this-collection

Interviews by Author

Trayla Britton, Mound Bayou, MS, July 6, 2020.
Charles Evers, Jackson, MS, June 14, 2017.
O. C. Gibson, Greenwood, MS, June 18, 2017.
Quantrell Holmes, Mound Bayou, MS, July 7, 2020.
Tonitria Hunt, Mound Bayou, MS, July 2, 2020.
Cora Jackson, Shaw, MS, June 26, 2020.
Herman Johnson Sr., Mound Bayou, MS, August 20, 2021.
Theodore Johnson, Greenwood, MS, June 18, 2017.
Kierra T. Jones, Mound Bayou, June 30, 2020.
Senator David L. Jordan, Jackson, MS, June 9, 2017.
Rev. Ed King, Jackson, MS, August 21, 2017.
Larry Mims II, Mound Bayou, MS, June 30, 2020.
Katrina Sanders, Cleveland, MS, July 6, 2020.
Tyra Slaughter, Mound Bayou, MS, July 7, 2020.
L. Nicole Stringfellow, Shaw, MS, July 2, 2020.
J. D. Tiggs, Ruleville, MS, June 10, 2017.
Tanielle Woods, Mound Bayou, MS, June 30, 2020.

Magazines and Newspapers

Afro-American
The Atlantic
Bolivar Commercial
Chicago Daily Defender
Clarion-Ledger
Delta Democrat-Times
Food & Wine
Grace & Glory
Greenwood Commonwealth
HuffPost
Jackson Advocate
Jackson Daily News
Jet
Los Angeles Sentinel
Mississippi Public Broadcasting News
Mound Bayou Voice
New Journal and Guide
New York Times
Orlando Sentinel
ProPublica
Rewire News Group
Southern Exposure
The Southern Patriot
The Student Voice
Supermarket News
The World's Work

Secondary Sources

Agyeman, Julian, and Jesse McEntee. "Moving the Field of Food Justice Forward through the Lens of Urban Political Ecology." *Geography Compass* 8, no. 3 (2014): 211–20.

Alkon, Alison, and Julian Agyeman. *Cultivating Food Justice: Race, Class, and Sustainability*. Cambridge, MA: MIT Press, 2011.

Allen, Leah. "Bolivar Students Share Delta Farm Knowledge." *Bolivar Commercial*, August 6, 2018.

Allen, Patricia, and Carolyn Sachs. "Women and Food Chains: The Gendered Politics of Food." *International Journal of Sociology of Agriculture and Food* 15, no. 1 (2007): 1–23.

Andrews, Kenneth T. *Freedom Is a Constant Struggle: The Mississippi Civil Rights Movement and Its Legacy*. Chicago: University of Chicago Press, 2004.

Andrews, Kenneth T. "Social Movements and Policy Implementation: The Mississippi Civil Rights Movement and the War on Poverty, 1965 to 1971." *American Sociological Review* 66, no. 1 (2001): 71–95.

Annis, J. Lee, Jr. *Big Jim Eastland: The Godfather of Mississippi*. Jackson: University Press of Mississippi, 2016.

Arrington, Tevin. "Community Surveyed on Availability of Produce." *Bolivar Commercial*, October 2, 2017.

Asch, Chris Myers. *The Senator and the Sharecropper: The Freedom Struggles of James O. Eastland and Fannie Lou Hamer*. Chapel Hill: University of North Carolina Press, 2008.

Avelino, Flor. "Theories of Power and Social Change: Power Contestations and Their Implications for Research on Social Change and Innovation." *Journal of Political Power* 14, no. 3 (2021): 425–48.

Baker, Ella. "Bigger than a Hamburger." *Southern Patriot*, May 18, 1960. www.crmvet.org/docs/sncc2.htm.

Barnett, Michael, and Raymond Duvall. "Power in International Politics." *International Organization* 59, no. 1 (2005): 39–75.

Beale, Calvin L. "Rural-Urban Migration of Blacks: Past and Future." *American Journal of Agricultural Economics* 53, no. 2 (1971): 302–7.

Belasco, Warren, Amy Bentley, Charlotte Biltekoff, Psyche Williams-Forson, and Carolyn de la Peña. "The Frontiers of Food Studies." *Food, Culture, & Society* 14, no. 3 (2011): 301–14.

Benford, Robert D., and David A. Snow. "Framing Processes and Social Movements: An Overview and Assessment." *Annual Review of Sociology* 26 (2000): 611–39.

Berman, Robert L. *A House of David in the Land of Jesus*. New Orleans: Pelican Publishing, 2007.

Black, Herbert. *People and Plows against Hunger: Self-help Experiment in a Rural Community*. Boston: Marlborough House, 1975.

Bloom, Joshua, and Waldo E. Martin. *Black against Empire: The History and Politics of the Black Panther Party*. Oakland: University of California Press, 2016.

Bond, Julian. "Vietnam, Black Power, and the Assassination of Martin Luther King." In *Julian Bond's Time to Teach: A History of the Southern Civil Rights Movement*, edited by Pamela Horowitz and Jeanne Theoharis, 294–315. Boston: Beacon, 2021.

Bornstein, David. *How to Change the World: Social Entrepreneurs and the Power of New Ideas*. New York: Penguin Books, 2004.

Broad, Garrett M. *More Than Just Food: Food Justice and Community Change*. Oakland: University of California Press, 2016.

Brown, Heber, III. "Moving beyond Charity: How Rev. Vernon Johns Can Help Churches Do Food Ministry Better." *Grace and Glory* 13, no. 11 (July 2020): 8–9. https://issuu.com/gracenglorymagazine/docs/july2020gracenglory/8?fbclid=IwAR09WlMLF37JMJfPINfaNVRgqwuemKQXb4Plk7QhogdTVWYhatNJUVj7Lok.

Brown, Jarquita. "Delta Fresh Foods Awarded Grant." *Bolivar Commercial*, July 27, 2017.

Bublitz, Melissa G., Laura A. Peracchio, Alan R. Andreasen, Jeremy Kees, Blair Kidwell, Elizabeth Gelfand Miller, Carol M. Motley, Paula C. Peter,

Priyali Rajagopal, Maura L. Scott, and Beth Vallen. "The Quest for Eating Right: Advancing Food Well-Being." *Journal of Research for Consumers* 19 (2011): 1–12.

Bull, Jacqueline P. "The General Merchant in the Economic History of the New South." *Journal of Southern History* 18, no. 1 (1952): 37–59.

"By Cong. Diggs, Dr. King, etc.: Action Launched to Aid Starving Miss. Citizens." *New Journal and Guide (1916–2003)*, February 23, 1963. www.proquest.com.proxy2.library.illinois.edu/historical-newspapers/cong-diggs-dr-king-etc/docview/568709185/se-2?accountid=14553.

"C. Preston Holmes." N.d. Fly Away—The Great Migration: The Movement of African Americans from the Mississippi Delta to Chicago, Kenyon College, Gambier, Ohio. http://northbysouth.kenyon.edu/1999/family/webpage2.htm.

Carson, Clayborne. *In Struggle: SNCC and the Black Awakening of the 1960s*. Cambridge, MA: Harvard University Press, 1995.

———. *The Student Voice, 1960–1965: Periodical of the Student Nonviolent Coordinating Committee*. Westport, CT: Meckler, 1990.

Caruso, Christine. "Searching for Food (Justice): Understanding Access in an Under-served Food Environment in New York City." *Journal of Critical Thought and Praxis* 3, no. 1 (2014): 1–18.

Cash, William, and R. Daryl Lewis. *The Delta Council: Fifty Years of Service to the Mississippi Delta*. Stoneville: Delta Council, 1986.

Cha-Jua, Sundiata Keita, and Clarence Lang. "The 'Long Movement' as Vampire: Temporal and Spatial Fallacies in Recent Black Freedom Studies." *Journal of African American History* 92, no. 2 (2007): 265–88.

Chapman, Oscar James. "A Historical Study of Negro Land-Grant Colleges in Relationship with Their Social, Economic, Political, and Educational Backgrounds and a Program for Their Improvement." PhD diss., Ohio State University, 1940.

Cistrunk, Kenya M., Brittney Oliver, Laura Jean Kerr, Maria Trinh, Caroline Kobia, Leslie Hossfeld, Kecia R. Johnson, and Claudette Jones. "An Ecological Approach to Understanding Program Management Practices for Food Pantries in Rural Communities." *Journal of Community Engagement and Scholarship* 12, no. 1 (2019): 68–77.

Cobb, James C. *The Most Southern Place on Earth: The Mississippi Delta and the Roots of Regional Identity*. New York: Oxford University Press, 1992.

———. "'Somebody Done Nailed Us on the Cross': Federal Farm and Welfare Policy and the Civil Rights Movement in the Mississippi Delta." *Journal of American History* 77, no. 3 (1990): 912–36.

Coleman-Jensen, Alisha, Matthew P. Rabbitt, Christian A. Gregory, and Anita Singh. *Household Food Security in the United States in 2019*. ERR-275, US Department of Agriculture, Economic Research Service, 2020. www.ers.usda.gov/webdocs/publications/99282/err-275.pdf?v=7598.5.

Combahee River Collective. "A Black Feminist Statement." *Women's Studies Quarterly* 42, no. 3/4 (2014): 271–80.

Conrad, Alison. *Research Brief: Identifying and Countering White Supremacy Culture in Food Systems*. World Food Policy Center, Sanford School of Public Health Policy. Durham, NC: Duke University, September 2020. https://wfpc.sanford.duke.edu/sites/wfpc.sanford.duke.edu/files/Whiteness-Food-Movements-Research-Brief-WFPC-October-2020.pdf.

Cooley, Angela Jill. "Freedom's Farms: Activism and Sustenance in Rural Mississippi." In *Dethroning the Deceitful Pork Chop: Rethinking African American Foodways from Slavery to Obama*, edited by Jennifer Jensen Wallach, 199–214. Fayetteville: University of Arkansas Press, 2015.

———. *To Live and Dine in Dixie: The Evolution of Urban Food Culture in the Jim Crow South*. Athens: University of Georgia Press, 2015.

Cooper, Dara. "Black Food as Resistance: Land, Justice, and Black Liberation." In *Black Food: Stories, Art and Recipes from across the African Diaspora*, edited by Bryant Terry, 144–46. Berkeley: Ten Speed Press, 2021.

Coppock, Joseph D. "The Food Stamp Plan Moving Surplus Commodities with Special Purpose Money." *Transactions of the American Philosophical Society* 37, no. 2 (1947): 131–200.

Crenshaw, Kimberlé. "Race, Reform, and Retrenchment: Transformation and Legitimation in Antidiscrimination Law." *Harvard Law Review* 101, no. 7 (1988): 1331–87.

Crosby, Emilye. *Civil Rights History from the Ground Up: Local Struggles, a National Movement*. Athens: University of Georgia Press, 2011.

Crowe, Milburn, John Martin, and Luther Brown. "The Mound Bayou Mississippi Story." Delta Center for Culture and Learning, Delta State University, Cleveland, MS, n.d.

Dailey, Amber, Carol A. Conroy, and Cynthia A. Shelley-Tolbert. "Using Agricultural Education as the Context to Teach Life Skills." *Journal of Agricultural Education* 42, no. 1 (2001): 11–20.

Dalaker, Joseph. *The 10-20-30 Provision: Defining Persistent Poverty Counties*. CRS Report No. R45100. Washington, DC: Congressional Research Service, 2021. https://crsreports.congress.gov/product/pdf/R/R45100.

Daniel, Pete. *Dispossession: Discrimination against African American Farmers in the Age of Civil Rights*. Chapel Hill: University of North Carolina Press, 2013.

Daniels, Arlene Kaplan. "Invisible Work." *Social Problems* 34, no. 5 (1987): 403–15.

Davis, Allison, Burleigh B. Gardner, and Mary R. Gardner. *Deep South: A Social Anthropological Study of Caste and Class*. Chicago: University of Chicago Press, 1941.

de Jong, Greta. "Staying in Place: Black Migration, the Civil Rights Movement, and the War on Poverty in the Rural South." *Journal of African American History* 90, no. 4 (2005): 387–409.

Delta Fresh Foods Initiative. "Current Project: North Bolivar County Good Food Revolution." N.d. www.deltafreshfoods.org/practice-areas.html.

———. "A Message from the Board." N.d. www.deltafreshfoods.org/attorneys.html.

Densu, Kwasi. "Theoretical and Historical Perspectives on Agroecology and African American Farmers: Toward a Culturally Relevant Sustainable Agriculture." In *Land and Power: Sustainable Agriculture and African Americans*, edited by Jeffrey L. Jordan, Edward Pennick, Walter A. Hill, and Robert Zabawa, 93–107. Waldorf, MD: Sustainable Agriculture Research and Education Outreach, 2009.
Deppe, Martin L. *Operation Breadbasket: An Untold Story of Civil Rights in Chicago, 1966–1971*. Athens: University of Georgia Press, 2017.
"Diggs Demands U.S. Act in Miss. Food Denial." *Chicago Daily Defender (Daily Edition) (1960–1973)*, February 18, 1963. www.proquest.com.proxy2.library.illinois.edu/historical-newspapers/diggs-demands-u-s-act-miss-food-denial/docview/493961048/se-2?accountid=14553.
Dittmer, John. *Local People: The Struggle for Civil Rights in Mississippi*. Urbana: University of Illinois Press, 1994.
Dorsey, L. C. "Harder Times Than These." *Southern Exposure* 10, no. 1 (1982): 28–31.
Douglass, Frederick. *Narrative of the Life of Frederick Douglass, an American Slave*. New Haven, CT: Yale University Press, 2016.
Du Bois, W. E. B. "The Talented Tenth." In *The Negro Problem: A Series of Articles by Representative American Negroes of Today*, 31–75. New York: James Pott, 1903.
Edge, John T. *The Potlikker Papers: A Food History of the Modern South*. New York: Penguin Books, 2017.
Eller, Emrys, producer. *Fighting Hunger in the Mississippi Delta*. The Hechinger Report, August 7, 2017. www.youtube.com/watch?v=ENOQyjIfawU.
Evans, Arthur, director. *Building the Future: North Bolivar Good Food Revolution*. August 29, 2019. *Rosedale Freedom Project*. https://vimeo.com/356743521/9c8d7c3d35.
Evers, Myrlie, and William Peters. *For Us, the Living*. Garden City, NY: Doubleday, 1967.
Ewoodzie, Joseph C., Jr. *Getting Something to Eat in Jackson: Race, Class, and Food in the American South*. Princeton, NJ: Princeton University Press, 2021.
Feeding America. *2019 Map the Meal Gap, Food Insecurity in Mississippi District 2*. https://map.feedingamerica.org/district/2019/overall/mississippi/district/2/.
Ferris, Marcie Cohen. *The Edible South: The Power of Food and the Making of an American Region*. Chapel Hill: University of North Carolina Press, 2014.
Finney, Henry C., and David McGranahan. "Community Support and Goal Displacement in a Poor Peoples' Cooperative Farm: A Case Study of Organizational Adaptation to Environmental Uncertainty." Discussion Papers, Institute for Research on Poverty: University of Wisconsin-Madison, 1972.
Flannery, Ezekiel, and Diana Mincyte. "Food as Power." *Cultural Studies ↔ Critical Methodologies* 10, no. 6 (2010): 423–27.
"Food for Freedom Committee to Help Persecuted Negroes." *Los Angeles Sentinel (1934–2005)*, September 12, 1963. www.proquest.com.proxy2.library.illinois.edu/historical-newspapers/food-freedom-committee-help-persecuted-negroes/docview/564653788/se-2?accountid=14553.

Foster, B. Brian. *I Don't Like the Blues: Race, Place, and the Backbeat of Black Life*. Chapel Hill: University of North Carolina Press, 2020.

Foucault, Michel. "The Subject and Power." In *Art after Modernism: Rethinking Representation*, edited by Brian Wallis, 417–32. Boston/New York: David R. Godine/New Museum of Contemporary Art, 1984.

Franklin, Sekou M. *After the Rebellion: Black Youth, Social Movement Activism, and the Post–Civil Rights Generation*. New York: New York University Press, 2014.

Franklin, V. P. *The Young Crusaders: The Untold Story of the Children and Teenagers Who Galvanized the Civil Rights Movement*. Boston: Beacon, 2021.

"Free 2 Students Who Took Food to Miss. Needy." *Chicago Daily Defender (Daily Edition) (1960–1973)*, January 28, 1963. www.proquest.com.proxy2.library.illinois.edu/historical-newspapers/free-2-students-who-took-food-miss-needy/docview/493949101/se-2?accountid=14553.

Galtung, Johan. "Violence, Peace, and Peace Research." *Journal of Peace Research* 6, no. 3 (1969): 167–91.

Ginwright, Shawn A. *Black Youth Rising: Activism and Radical Healing in Urban America*. New York: Teachers College Press, 2010.

Goffman, Erving. *Frame Analysis: An Essay on the Organization of Experience*. New York: Harper & Row, 1974.

Grim, Valerie. "The Impact of Mechanized Farming on Black Farm Families in the Rural South: A Study of Farm Life in the Brooks Farm Community, 1940–1970." *Agricultural History* 68, no. 2 (1994): 169–84.

———. "The Justice for Black Farmers Act: Historical Perspectives." Presidential Plenary Session at the 2021 Agricultural History Society Meeting, June 1, 2021.

Gross, Aeyal, and Tamar Feldman. "'We Didn't Want to Hear the Word "Calories"': Rethinking Food Security, Food Power, and Food Sovereignty—Lessons from the Gaza Closure." *Berkeley Journal of International Law* 33, no. 2 (2015): 379–441.

Hall, Jacquelyn Dowd. "The Long Civil Rights Movement and the Political Uses of the Past." *Journal of American History* 91, no. 4 (2005): 1233–63.

Hamer, Fannie Lou. "Testimony before the Democratic Reform Committee, Jackson, Mississippi, May 22, 1969." In *The Speeches of Fannie Lou Hamer: To Tell It Like It Is*, edited by Maegan Parker Brooks and Davis W. Houck, 95–97. Jackson: University Press of Mississippi, 2011.

———. "To Tell It Like It Is." In *The Speeches of Fannie Lou Hamer: To Tell It Like It Is*, edited by Maegan Parker Brooks and Davis W. Houck, 86–93. Jackson: University Press of Mississippi, 2011.

Hamlin, Françoise N. *Crossroads at Clarksdale: The Black Freedom Struggle in the Mississippi Delta after World War II*. Chapel Hill: University of North Carolina Press, 2012.

———. "Vera Mae Pigee (1925–): Mothering the Movement." In *Mississippi Women: Their Histories, Their Lives*, edited by Martha H. Swain, Elizabeth Anne Payne, and Marjorie Julian Spruill, 281–98. Athens: University of Georgia Press, 2003.

Hanson, David, and Brooke Pochee-Smith. *Delta Fresh FINAL 2k*. April 20, 2020. Brooke Pochee-Smith. www.youtube.com/watch?v=jwuKp4JhdSs.

Harris, Jessica B. *High on the Hog: A Culinary Journey from Africa to America*. New York: Bloomsbury Publishing, 2011.
Hartman, Saidiya. *Lose Your Mother: A Journey along the Atlantic Slave Route*. New York: Farrar, Straus and Giroux, 2008.
Hatch, John. "John Hatch on Community Organizing in the Mississippi Delta, 1965." *American Journal of Public Health* 104, no. 11 (2014): 2066–67.
Hearn, Jonathan. *Theorizing Power*. New York: Palgrave Macmillan, 2012.
Height, Dorothy. *Open Wide the Freedom Gates: A Memoir*. New York: PublicAffairs, 2003.
Henry, Aaron, and Constance Curry. *Aaron Henry: The Fire Ever Burning*. Jackson: University Press of Mississippi, 2000.
Hickmott, Alec Fazackerley. "Black Land, Black Capital: Rural Development in the Shadows of the Sunbelt South, 1969–1976." *Journal of African American History* 101, no. 4 (2016): 504–34.
Hilliard, David. *The Black Panther Party: Service to the People Programs*. Albuquerque: University of New Mexico Press, 2008.
Hislop, Rasheed Salaam. "Reaping Equity: A Survey of Food Justice Organizations in the U.S.A." Master's thesis, University of California, Davis, 2014.
Hogan, Wesley C. "Grassroots Organizing in Mississippi That Changed National Politics." In *The Civil Rights Movement in Mississippi*, edited by Ted Ownby, 3–34. Jackson: University Press of Mississippi, 2013.
"Homefront 'CARE' Program Launched for Mississippi." *Afro-American* (1893–1988), January 5, 1963. www.proquest.com.proxy2.library.illinois.edu/historical-newspapers/homefrontcareprogram-launched-mississippi/docview/532132708/se-2?accountid=14553.
hooks, bell. *Talking Back: Thinking Feminist, Thinking Black*. Boston: South End Press, 1989.
Hossfeld, Leslie, Laura Jean Kerr, and Judy Belue. "The Good Food Revolution: Building Community Resiliency in the Mississippi Delta." *Social Sciences* 8, no. 2 (2019): 1–10.
Howerton, Gloria, and Amy Trauger. "'Oh Honey, Don't You Know?' The Social Construction of Food Access in a Food Desert." *ACME: An International Journal for Critical Geographies* 16, no. 4 (2017): 740–60.
Institute of Medicine and National Research Council. *Supplemental Nutrition Assistance Program: Examining the Evidence to Define Benefit Adequacy*. Washington, DC: National Academies Press, 2013.
Jacobs, Harriet. *Incidents in the Life of a Slave Girl*. New York: Oxford University Press, 1988.
Jakubek, Joseph, and Spencer D. Wood. "Emancipatory Empiricism: The Rural Sociology of W.E.B. Du Bois." *Sociology of Race and Ethnicity* 4, no. 1 (2018): 14–34.
James, David R. "The Transformation of the Southern Racial State: Class and Race Determinants of Local-State Structures." *American Sociological Review* 53, no. 2 (1988): 191–208.
Johnson, Lyndon B. "Remarks upon Signing the Food Stamp Act." August 31, 1964. The American Presidency Project, University of California, Santa Barbara. www.presidency.ucsb.edu/documents/remarks-upon-signing-the-food-stamp-act.

Jordan, David L. *David L. Jordan: From the Mississippi Cotton Fields to the State Senate, A Memoir*. Jackson: University Press of Mississippi, 2014.

Kelley, Robin D. G. *Freedom Dreams: The Black Radical Imagination*. Boston: Beacon, 2002.

Kerssen, Tanya M., and Zoe W. Brent. "Grounding the U.S. Food Movement: Bringing Land into Food Justice." In *The New Food Activism: Opposition, Cooperation, and Collective Action*, edited by Alison Alkon and Julie Guthman, 284–315. Oakland: University of California Press, 2017.

King, Martin Luther, Jr. "Martin Luther King Jr. Saw Three Evils in the World." *Atlantic*, January 29, 2021. www.theatlantic.com/magazine/archive/2018/02/martin-luther-king-hungry-club-forum/552533/.

Knight, Melanie. "For Us by Us (FUBU): The Politicized Space of Black Women's Entrepreneurship in Canada." *Southern Journal of Canadian Studies* 5, no. 1 (2012): 160–81.

Kornbluh, Felicia. "Food as a Civil Right: Hunger, Work, and Welfare in the South after the Civil Rights Act." *Labor Studies in Working Class History of the Americas* 12, no. 1–2 (2015): 135–58.

Kunnerth, Jeff. "Delta Paradox: The Richest Land, The Poorest People." *Orlando Sentinel*, September 10, 1989. www.orlandosentinel.com/news/os-xpm-1989-09-10-8909103446-story.html.

Lawrence-Jacobson, Abigail R. "Intergenerational Community Action and Youth Empowerment." *Journal of Intergenerational Relationships* 4, no. 1 (2006): 137–47.

Lawson, Steven F. "Freedom Then, Freedom Now: The Historiography of the Civil Rights Movement." *American Historical Review* 96, no. 2 (1991): 456–71.

Lawson, Steven F., and Charles Payne. *Debating the Civil Rights Movement, 1945–1968*. 2nd ed. Lanham, MD: Rowman & Littlefield, 2006.

Lee, Chana Kai. *For Freedom's Sake: The Life of Fannie Lou Hamer*. Urbana: University of Illinois Press, 1999.

Levine, Philippa. "Discipline and Pleasure: Response." *Victorian Studies* 46, no. 2 (2004): 319–25.

Lewis, Morris, Jr. *Wholesaler-Retailer: The Story of the Lewis Grocer Company and Sunflower Food Stores, Newcomen Publication Number: 1021*. New York: Newcomen Society in North America, 1975.

Lovett, Bobby L. *The Civil Rights Movement in Tennessee: A Narrative History*. Knoxville: University of Tennessee Press, 2005.

Lukes, Steven. *Power: A Radical View*. 2nd ed. New York: Palgrave Macmillan, 2005.

Lyson, Thomas A. "Civic Agriculture and Community Problem Solving." *Culture & Agriculture* 27, no. 2 (2005): 92–98.

MacDonald, Maurice. "Food Stamps: An Analytical History." *Social Science Review* 51, no. 4 (1977): 642–58.

MacKendrick, Norah. "Foodscape." *Contexts* 13, no. 3 (2014): 16–18.

Malone, Regina. "What We Talk about When We Talk about Black Unwed Mothers: A Q&A with Tanya Fields of the BLK Projek." *Rewire News Group*, November 26, 2013. https://rewirenewsgroup.com/article/2013/11/26/what-we-talk-about-when-we-talk-about-black-unwed-mothers-a-qa-with-tanya-fields-of-the-blk-projek/.

Mares, Teresa, and Alison Alkon. "Mapping the Food Movement: Addressing Inequality and Neoliberalism." *Environment and Society: Advances in Research* 2, no. 1 (2011): 68–86.
McAdam, Doug. "Recruitment to High-Risk Activism: The Case of Freedom Summer." *American Journal of Sociology* 92, no. 1 (1986): 64–90.
McCutcheon, Priscilla. "Fannie Lou Hamer's Freedom Farms and Black Agrarian Geographies." *Antipode* 51, no. 1 (2019): 207–24.
———. "'Returning Home to Our Rightful Place': The Nation of Islam and Muhammad Farms." *Geoforum* 49 (2013): 61–70.
McDonald, Bryan L. *Food Power: The Rise and Fall of the Postwar American Food System*. New York: Oxford University Press, 2017.
McEntee, Jesse C. "Realizing Rural Food Justice: Divergent Locals in the Northeastern United States." In *Cultivating Food Justice: Race, Class, and Sustainability*, edited by Alison Alkon and Julian Agyeman, 239–59. Cambridge, MA: MIT Press, 2011.
McGuire, Danielle L. "Introduction." In *Freedom Rights: New Perspectives on the Civil Rights Movement*, edited by Danielle L. McGuire and John Dittmer, 1–8. Lexington: University Press of Kentucky, 2011.
McGuire, Danielle L., and John Dittmer. *Freedom Rights: New Perspectives on the Civil Rights Movement*. Lexington: University Press of Kentucky, 2011.
McKittrick, Katherine. "On Plantations, Prisons, and a Black Sense of Place." *Social & Cultural Geography* 12, no. 8 (2011): 947–63.
McMillen, Neil R. *The Citizens' Council: Organized Resistance to the Second Reconstruction, 1954–64*. Urbana: University of Illinois Press, 1971.
Meikle, Paulette Ann. "Globalization and Its Effects on Agriculture and Agribusiness in the Mississippi Delta: A Historical Overview and Prospects for the Future." *Journal of Rural Social Sciences* 31, no. 2 (2016): 130–54.
Meter, Ken, and Megan Phillips Goldenberg. *An Overview of the Mississippi Farm and Food Economy*. Minneapolis: Crossroads Resource Center, 2014. www.crcworks.org/msfood.pdf.
Mills, C. Wright. *The Power Elite*. New York: Oxford University Press, 1956.
Mintz, Sidney W. *Sweetness and Power: The Place of Sugar in Modern History*. New York: Penguin Books, 1985.
Mississippi State Department of Health. Office of Health Data and Research. *2018 Bolivar County Health Profile*. 2018. https://msdh.ms.gov/msdhsite/files/profiles/Bolivar.pdf.
Moore, Deborah, Judy Belue, and Brooke Smith. "Social Justice for Lunch: Delta Fresh Foods Initiative at the National Farm to Cafeteria Conference." *Food Justice Voices*. New York: Why Hunger, 2015. https://whyhunger.org/wp-content/uploads/2015/05/Food_Justice_Voices_Social_Justice_for_Lunch_DFFI_WhyHunger%20.pdf.
Morris, Aldon D. *The Origins of the Civil Rights Movement: Black Communities Organizing for Change*. New York: Free Press, 1984.
"Morris Lewis Jr." *Supermarket News*, February 7, 1994. https://www.supermarketnews.com/archive/morris-lewis-jr.

Morrison, Minion K. C. *Aaron Henry of Mississippi: Inside Agitator*. Fayetteville: University of Arkansas Press, 2015.

Moses, Robert P., and Charles E. Cobb Jr. *Radical Equations: Math Literacy and Civil Rights*. Boston: Beacon, 2001.

Moses, Robert P., Mieko Kamii, Susan McAllister Swap, and Jeffrey Howard. "The Algebra Project: Organizing in the Spirit of Ella." *Harvard Educational Review* 59, no. 4 (1989): 423–43.

Moye, J. Todd. *Let the People Decide: Black Freedom and White Resistance Movements in Sunflower County, Mississippi, 1945–1986*. Chapel Hill: University of North Carolina Press, 2004.

"NAACP Asks Probe, Food: Sen. Ellender 'Justifies' Terror in Mississippi." *New Journal and Guide (1916–2003)*, March 16, 1963. www.proquest.com.proxy2.library.illinois.edu/historical-newspapers/naacp-asks-probe-food/docview/568793484/se-2?accountid=14553.

Naples, Nancy A. "Activist Mothering: Cross-generational Continuity in the Community Work of Women from Low-income Urban Neighborhoods." *Gender & Society* 6, no. 3 (1992): 441–63.

Nash, Jere. "Edmund Favor Noel (1908–1912) and the Rise of James K. Vardaman and Theodore G. Bilbo." *Journal of Mississippi History* 81, nos. 1 and 2 (2019): 3–21.

Nasstrom, Kathryn L. "Between Memory and History: Autobiographies of the Civil Rights Movement and the Writing of Civil Rights History." *Journal of Southern History* 74, no. 2 (2008): 325–64.

National Black Food and Justice Alliance. "NBFJA Platform." N.d. www.blackfoodjustice.org/about-us-1.

Nestle, Marion, and W. Alex McIntosh. "Writing the Food Studies Movement." *Food, Culture, & Society* 13, no. 2 (2010): 159–79.

Newman, Mark. *Divine Agitators: The Delta Ministry and Civil Rights in Mississippi*. Athens: University of Georgia Press, 2004.

Ochiltree, Ian D. "'A Just and Self-Respecting System'?: Black Independence, Sharecropping, and Paternalistic Relations in the American South and South Africa." *Agricultural History* 72, no. 2 (1998): 352–80.

Opie, Frederick Douglass. *Southern Food and Civil Rights: Feeding the Revolution*. Charleston, SC: American Palate, 2017.

Ownby, Ted. *The Civil Rights Movement in Mississippi*. Jackson: University Press of Mississippi, 2013.

Paarlberg, Robert L. "The Failure of Food Power." *Policy Studies Journal* 6, no. 4 (1978): 537–42.

Payne, Charles. *I've Got the Light of Freedom: The Organizing Tradition and the Mississippi Freedom Struggle*. Berkeley: University of California Press, 2007.

Penniman, Leah. *Farming While Black: Soul Fire Farm's Practical Guide to Liberation on the Land*. White River Junction, VT: Chelsea Green Publishing, 2018.

Potorti, Mary. "'Feeding the Revolution': The Black Panther Party, Hunger, and Community Survival." *Journal of African American Studies* 21 (2017): 85–110.

Povitz, Lana Dee. *Stirrings: How Activist New Yorkers Ignited a Movement for Food Justice*. Chapel Hill: University of North Carolina Press, 2019.

Powledge, Fred. *Free at Last?: The Civil Rights Movement and the People Who Made It*. Boston: Little, Brown, 1991.
Presser, Lizzie. "The Black American Amputation Epidemic." *ProPublica*, May 19, 2020. https://features.propublica.org/diabetes-amputations/black-american-amputation-epidemic/.
Quisumbing King, Katrina, Spencer D. Wood, Jess Gilbert, and Marilyn Sinkewicz. "Black Agrarianism: The Significance of African American Landownership in the Rural South." *Rural Sociology* 83, no. 3 (2018): 677–99.
Rand, Harold S. "The Food Stamp Plan Raises an Issue." *National Municipal Review* 29, no. 1 (1940): 14–17.
Rani, Voliveru Sudha. *Study Material, AEXT 391: Entrepreneurship Development*. Department of Agricultural Extension, Rajaendranagar: Acharya N-G Ranga Agricultural University, n.d.
Reese, Ashanté M. *Black Food Geographies: Race, Self-Reliance, and Food Access in Washington, DC*. Chapel Hill: University of North Carolina Press, 2019.
———. "In the Food Justice World but Not of It: Everyday Black Food Entrepreneurship." In *Black Food Matters: Racial Justice in the Wake of Food Justice*, edited by Hanna Garth and Ashanté M. Reese, 29–52. Minneapolis: University of Minnesota Press, 2020.
Reese, Ashanté M., and Dara Cooper. "Making Spaces Something like Freedom: Black Feminist Praxis in the Re/Imagining of a Just Food System." *ACME: An International Journal for Critical Geographies* 20, no. 4 (2021): 450–59.
Roane, J. T. "Plotting the Black Commons." *Souls* 20, no. 3 (2018): 239–66.
Robinson Pearl B. "The Community Part in Health Center Program." *American Journal of Public Health* 104, no. 11 (2014): 2067–69.
Robnett, Belinda. *How Long? How Long?: African American Women in the Struggle for Civil Rights*. New York: Oxford University Press, 1997.
Rooks, Noliwe M. *Cutting School: The Segrenomics of American Education*. New York: New Press, 2017.
Sbicca, Joshua. *Food Justice Now! Deepening the Roots of Social Struggle*. Minneapolis: University of Minnesota Press, 2018.
Scott, James C. *Weapons of the Weak: Everyday Forms of Peasant Resistance*. New Haven, CT: Yale University Press, 1985.
Simley, Shakirah. "A More Abundant Share—The Future of Food Is Black." *HuffPost*, February 6, 2017. www.huffpost.com/entry/future-of-food-is-black_b_5895f081e4b0c1284f263d69.
"Small Co-Ops Given Grants by Ford Fund." *Afro-American* (1893–1988), July 12, 1969. www.proquest.com.proxy2.library.illinois.edu/historical-newspapers/small-co-ops-given-grants-ford-fund/docview/532251900/se-2?accountid=14553.
Smith, Bobby J., II. "Building Emancipatory Food Power: Freedom Farms, Rocky Acres, and the Struggle for Food Justice." *Journal of Agriculture, Food Systems, and Community Development* 8, no. 4 (2019): 33–43.
———. "Food and the Mississippi Civil Rights Movement: Re-Reading the 1962–1963 Greenwood Food Blockade." *Food, Culture, & Society* 23, no. 3 (2020): 382–98.

———. "Food Justice, Intersectional Agriculture, and the Triple Food Movement." *Agriculture and Human Values* 36, no. 4 (2019): 825–35.

———. "The Greenwood Food Blockade: The White Citizens Council, SNCC, and the Politics of Food Access." *Gravy* 66 (Winter 2017): 60–65. www.southernfoodways.org/the-greenwood-food-blockade/.

Smith, Bobby J., II, Harry Kaiser, and Miguel Gómez. "Identifying Factors Influencing a Hospital's Decision to Adopt a Farm-to-Hospital Program." *Agricultural and Resource Economics Review* 42, no. 3 (2013): 508–17.

Smith, Kimberly. "Black Agrarianism and the Foundations of Black Environmental Thought." *Environmental Ethics* 26, no. 3 (2004): 267–86.

Smith, Nia-Raquelle. "Fannie Lou Hamer's Pioneering Food Activism Is a Model for Today." *Food & Wine*, September 15, 2020. www.foodandwine.com/news/fannie-lou-hamer-food-activism-pioneer.

Smith, Susan L. *Sick and Tired of Being Sick and Tired: Black Women's Health Activism in America, 1890–1950*. Philadelphia: University of Pennsylvania Press, 1995.

"SNCC Internal Newsletter." March 22, 1963. www.crmvet.org/docs/6303_sncc_newsletter.pdf.

Steel, Anim. "Youth and Food Justice: Lessons from the Civil Rights Movement." *Food First Backgrounder* 16, no. 3 (Fall 2010): 1–3.

Still, Larry. "Economic Pressure against 5,000 Families Affects 22,000 People." *Jet*, February 21, 1963. https://books.google.com/books?id=9rsDAAAAMBAJ&printsec=frontcover&source=gbs_ge_summary_r&cad=0#v=onepage&q&f=false.

Swarns, Rachel L., and Darcy Eveleigh. "In Covering Civil Rights, Reporter Enhanced His Words with Film." *New York Times*, February 4, 2017. www.nytimes.com/2017/02/04/us/unpublished-black-history-claude-sitton-civil-rights.html.

Tate, Omar. "Black Culinary and Food Traditions," Afternoon Keynote Panel at the 2019 Black Urban Growers Conference, New York City, NY, October 26, 2019.

Theoharis, Jeanne. "Black Freedom Studies: Re-imagining and Redefining the Fundamentals." *History Compass* 2, no. 2 (2006): 348–67.

Trouillot, Michel-Rolph. *Silencing the Past: Power and the Production of History*. Boston: Beacon, 1995.

Ture, Kwame, and Charles V. Hamilton. *Black Power: The Politics of Liberation*. New York: Vintage Books, 1992.

US Census Bureau. *2019 Quick Facts Bolivar County, Mississippi*. 2019. www.census.gov/quickfacts/fact/table/bolivarcountymississippi/PST045219.

US Congress. House. *Congressional Record*, 88th Cong., 2nd sess., April 8, 1964, vol. 110, pt. 6—bound ed. Washington, DC: US Government Printing Office, 1964.

US Congress. Senate. *Congressional Record*, 88th Cong., 2nd sess., June 30, 1964, vol. 110, pt. 12—bound edition. Washington, DC: US Government Printing Office, 1964.

US Congress. Senate. Select Committee on Nutrition and Human Needs. *Hearings before the Select Committee on Nutrition and Human Needs, Part 4—Housing and*

Sanitation, 91st Cong., 2nd sess., 1970. Washington, DC: US Government Printing Office, 1970.

US Congress. Senate. Subcommittee on Employment, Manpower, and Poverty of the Committee on Labor and Public Welfare. *Examination of the War on Poverty: Hearings before the Subcommittee on Employment, Manpower, and Poverty of the Committee on Labor and Public Welfare, Part 2*, 90th Cong., 1st sess., 1967. Washington, DC: US Government Printing Office, 1967.

US Department of Agriculture. Economic Research Service. *2019 State Fact Sheets: Mississippi*, 2019. https://data.ers.usda.gov/reports.aspx?StateFIPS=28&StateName=Mississippi&ID=17854.

US Department of Agriculture. National Agricultural Statistics Service. *2017 Census of Agriculture Bolivar County Mississippi Profile*, 2017. www.nass.usda.gov/Publications/AgCensus/2017/Online_Resources/County_Profiles/Mississippi/cp28011.pdf.

US Department of Agriculture. National Agricultural Statistics Service. *2017 Census of Agriculture Mississippi 2nd Congressional District Profile*, 2017. www.nass.usda.gov/Publications/AgCensus/2017/Online_Resources/Congressional_District_Profiles/cd2802.pdf.

US Department of Agriculture. National Agricultural Statistics Service. *2017 Census of Agriculture Mississippi State Profile*, 2017. www.nass.usda.gov/Publications/AgCensus/2017/Online_Resources/County_Profiles/Mississippi/cp99028.pdf.

US Department of Agriculture. National Agricultural Statistics Service. *2017 Census of Agriculture Sunflower County Mississippi Profile*, 2017. www.nass.usda.gov/Publications/AgCensus/2017/Online_Resources/County_Profiles/Mississippi/cp28133.pdf.

US Department of Agriculture. National Agricultural Statistics Service. *2017 Census of Agriculture Tallahatchie County Mississippi Profile*, 2017. www.nass.usda.gov/Publications/AgCensus/2017/Online_Resources/County_Profiles/Mississippi/cp28135.pdf.

US Department of Agriculture. National Agricultural Statistics Service. *2017 Census of Agriculture Washington County Mississippi Profile*, 2017. www.nass.usda.gov/Publications/AgCensus/2017/Online_Resources/County_Profiles/Mississippi/cp28151.pdf.

US Department of Agriculture. National Agricultural Statistics Service. *2017 Census of Agriculture Yazoo County Mississippi Profile*, 2017. www.nass.usda.gov/Publications/AgCensus/2017/Online_Resources/County_Profiles/Mississippi/cp28163.pdf.

Vance, Rupert B. *Human Factors in Cotton Culture: A Study in the Social Geography of the American South*. Chapel Hill: University of North Carolina Press, 1929.

Walcott, Rinaldo. *The Long Emancipation: Moving toward Black Freedom*. Durham, NC: Duke University Press, 2021.

Wallach, Jennifer Jensen. *Every Nation Has Its Dish: Black Bodies and Black Food in Twentieth-Century America*. Chapel Hill: University of North Carolina Press, 2019.

Wallensteen, Peter. "Scarce Goods as Political Weapons: The Case of Food." *Journal of Peace Research* 13, no. 4 (1976): 277–98.
Ward, Thomas J., Jr. *Out in the Rural: A Mississippi Health Center and Its War on Poverty*. New York: Oxford University Press, 2017.
Washington, Booker T. "A Town Owned by Negroes: Mound Bayou, Miss., An Example of Thrift and Self-Government." *The World's Work, Volume XIV* (May 1907): 9125–34.
Watts, Alexandra. "Farmers Markets Bring Together Communities in Mississippi Delta." *Mississippi Public Broadcasting News*, September 17, 2019. www.mpbonline.org/blogs/news/farmers-markets-bring-together-communities-in-mississippi-delta/.
West, Cornel. *Race Matters*. Boston: Beacon, 1993.
White, Eugene E. "Anti-Racial Agitation as a Campaign Device: James K. Vardaman in the Mississippi Gubernatorial Campaign of 1903." *Southern Speech Journal* 10, no. 3 (1945): 49–56.
White, Monica M. *Freedom Farmers: Agricultural Resistance and the Black Freedom Movement*. Chapel Hill: University of North Carolina Press, 2018.
———. "'A Pig and a Garden': Fannie Lou Hamer and the Freedom Farms Cooperative." *Food and Foodways* 25, no. 1 (2017): 20–39.
Williams-Forson, Psyche A. *Building Houses Out of Chicken Legs: Black Women, Food, and Power*. Chapel Hill: University of North Carolina Press, 2006.
———. *Eating While Black: Food Shaming and Race in America*. Chapel Hill: University of North Carolina Press, 2022.
Williams-Forson, Psyche, and Abby Wilkerson. "Intersectionality and Food Studies." *Food, Culture, & Society* 14, no. 1 (2011): 7–28.
Wilson, Bobby M. "Capital's Need to Sell and Black Economic Development." *Urban Geography* 33, no. 7 (2012): 961–78.
Wolf, Eric R. "Distinguished Lecture: Facing Power—Old Insights, New Questions." *American Anthropologist* 92, no. 3 (1990): 586–96.
Woods, Clyde. *Development Arrested: The Blues and Plantation Power in the Mississippi Delta*. New York: Verso, 1998.
Wright Austin, Sharon D. *The Transformation of Plantation Politics: Black Politics, Concentrated Poverty, and Social Capital in the Mississippi Delta*. Albany: State University of New York Press, 2006.
Wynter, Sylvia. "Novel and History, Plot and Plantation." *Savacou*, no. 5 (1971): 95–102.
Yakini, Malik. "What Ferguson Means for the Food Justice Movement: Issue 1." *Food Justice Voices*. New York: Why Hunger, 2015. https://whyhunger.org/wp-content/uploads/2015/10/Food_Justice_Voices_Ferguson_ISSUE_1_Malik_Yankini.pdf.
Zinn, Howard. *SNCC: The New Abolitionists*. Boston: Beacon, 1964.

Index

Note: page numbers in italics refer to illustrations

Printed in the USA
CPSIA information can be obtained
at www.ICGtesting.com
LVHW042239280923
759681LV00002B/13

9 781469 675060